INDIAN PHILOSOPHY

INDIAN PHILOSOPHY

AN INTRODUCTION

M. Ram Murty

broadview press

Library and Archives Canada Cataloguing in Publication
Murty, M. Ram (Maruti Ram)
Indian philosophy : an introduction / M. Ram Murty.

Includes bibliographical references and index.
ISBN 978-1-55481-035-2

1. Indian philosophy. I. Title.

B5131.M87 2012 181'.4 C2012-907049-1

Broadview Press is an independent, international publishing house, incorporated in 1985.

We welcome comments and suggestions regarding any aspect of our publications — please feel free to contact us at the addresses below or at broadview@broadviewpress.com.

North America
PO Box 1243, Peterborough, Ontario, Canada K9J 7H5
2215 Kenmore Ave., Buffalo, New York, USA 14207
Tel: (705) 743-8990; Fax: (705) 743-8353
email: customerservice@broadviewpress.com

UK, Europe, Central Asia, Middle East, Africa, India, and Southeast Asia
Eurospan Group, 3 Henrietta St., London WC2E 8LU, United Kingdom
Tel: 44 (0) 1767 604972; Fax: 44 (0) 1767 601640
email: eurospan@turpin-distribution.com

Australia and New Zealand
NewSouth Books
c/o TL Distribution
15-23 Helles Avenue, Moorebank, NSW, Australia 2170
Tel: (02) 8778 9999; Fax: (02) 8778 9944
email: orders@tldistribution.com.au

www.broadviewpress.com

Edited by Robert M. Martin

Designed by Chris Rowat Design, Daiva Villa

Broadview Press acknowledges the financial support of the Government of Canada through the Canada Book Fund for our publishing activities.

PRINTED IN CANADA

To my teachers, with gratitude and humility

However high a bird may soar, there are regions higher still.
—Sri Ramakrishna

Who are you, reader, reading my poems a hundred years hence?
I cannot send you one single flower from this wealth of spring,
One single streak of gold from yonder clouds.
Open your doors and look abroad.
From your blossoming garden gather fragrant memories
Of the vanished flowers of a hundred years before.
In the joy of your heart may you feel the living joy that sang
One spring morning, sending its glad voice across a hundred years.
—Rabindranath Tagore

CONTENTS

ACKNOWLEDGEMENTS

I would like to thank Professor Kumar Murty of the University of Toronto and Swami Tyagananda of the Vedānta Society of Boston for reading through earlier drafts of this book and giving me helpful comments. I also thank Professor Vikraman Balaji for comments on the last chapter. I am grateful to Professors David Bakhurst and Christine Overall of the Department of Philosophy of Queen's University who first encouraged me to begin this project. I also thank Mary Smith and her study group that found this book to be a valuable resource in their study of Indian philosophy. Thanks also to Jennifer Read who helped with the typing, Agnes Herzberg for proofreading, and Broadview Press for publishing the work. I especially thank Robert Martin for his meticulous copy-editing. I am also grateful to the referees for their comments on earlier versions of this book. In addition, I thank Judith Earnshaw and Anne Hodgetts for their careful proofreading, and Daiva Villa for typesetting and design.

PREFACE

This book is based on an introductory course given at Queen's University during various semesters from 2004 to 2012. It was intended to be a survey course and its primary aim was to initiate the student to the main topics of study. This is not an easy task. On the one hand, the early writings of Indian philosophy are in Sanskrit and it is difficult to find faithful translations that the student may consult. On the other hand, the wide spectrum of philosophical thought with its own peculiar vernacular makes it a challenge to communicate intelligibly the abstruse and diverse concepts to the English speaking student who (we may assume) has no knowledge either of Sanskrit or Indian philosophy. In this book, I have tried to meet this challenge and it is meant as an introduction to what is clearly a vast topic with an ancient past. In this endeavour, I aimed at conveying the spirit and excitement of such a study. If the book excites the student to pursue further studies in this direction, I will feel amply rewarded.

The course was directed at senior undergraduate students and beginning graduate students. Choosing a text for the course was difficult. In the end, I opted for the classical work by Sarvepalli Radhakrishnan and Charles Moore entitled *A Sourcebook in Indian Philosophy* published by Princeton University Press. This book has its merit, the most notable being that it gathers together in one place the relevant epochs, gives copious references, and has more material than can be covered in any single term introductory course. At the same time, the size of the book makes it somewhat unsuitable for an introductory course. Moreover, the translations of the Upanishads and the Bhagavadgīta are taken from two of Radhakrishnan's earlier works where the full Sanskrit text and translations are given. When certain passages are esoteric, this necessitates going to the original source and verifying the translations to gain a wider understanding. Even in an introductory course, such attention should be given to the accuracy of translations to be faithful to the original works. Thus, I found it necessary to augment the course with lecture notes. These lecture notes can be read independently of the Radhakrishnan and Moore tome. In fact, the final size of these notes makes them ideal for use in an introductory course at the undergraduate level. In this context, I have included two appendices that list some possible essay topics for the interested student. This is to guide the student to engage in further research. Since students come from diverse backgrounds and have varying abilities in writing, a short piece entitled "How to Write an Essay" is included as an appendix. The index contains a listing of many of the Sanskrit terms used in the text and these terms appear in italics for ease of reference. Topics that are treated at some length appear with a boldface page entry in the index.

This introduction has another value. If one surveys the literature on this topic, it is found that many of the treatments are mingled with mythology, mysticism, anthropology, and religion. The pure philosophy is nowhere to be found except perhaps in some encyclopedic accounts of Radhakrishnan. This book takes up the fundamental questions of philosophy and delineates in a brief survey what centuries of Indian philosophical thought have to say about these questions. I must admit that there is an emphasis on the neo-vedantic perspective in that I have followed, for the most part, interpretations of Shankara, and later Vivekananda, Sri Aurobindo and Sarvepalli Radhakrishnan. For instance, I have selected the interpretive framework of Shankara and Radhakrishnan in my discussion of the Upanishads and the Bhagavadgīta. The reader can find other viewpoints in the five-volume treatise of Dasgupta listed in the Works Cited section. There, students will find supplementary texts that will help in their study. For the student who wants to go deeper into Indian philosophy, I would suggest the work of Dasgupta and the two-volume tome of Radhakrishnan for further reading.

M. Ram Murty
Kingston, Ontario

INTRODUCTION

WHY STUDY INDIAN PHILOSOPHY?

It is clear that when we meet the world and experience it, not all of it makes sense. Hence it is natural to inquire into the meaning of things. Such an inquiry can be traced to several ancient civilizations. When we look at Indian philosophy, particularly the thought embodied in the ancient writings of the Upanishads, we can only marvel at the boldness of this questioning in that remote and early period of human history. The dating of these writings is not clear. It is believed that a long period of time must have elapsed before these thoughts, passed down in the oral tradition, were written down. There is some evidence that some of the hymns of the Rg Veda were part of the culture as long ago as 1500 BCE. Many of these may have been written down a few centuries before the time of Buddha, around 500 BCE. If we separate out the stray mythological components and verses pertaining to some social customs of the time, we find in these writings the true spirit of philosophy, an intense zeal to understand and to gain knowledge.

If knowledge is infinite then it seems humanly impossible to acquire all knowledge. In the Mundaka Upanishad, it is asked, "What is that by knowing which everything is known?" (*Kasmin nu bhagavo vijnāte sarvam idam vijnātam bhavati iti*) (Mundaka Up. 1.1.3).[1]

In Chāndogya Upanishad (6.1.4), we meet with a slightly more precise reformulation of the question. "Just as the knowledge of one slab of clay

1 Unless otherwise noted, all Sanskrit texts and their translations with respect to the Upanishads are taken from Radhakrishnan's *The Principal Upanishads*. Footnote references to other works will be shortened versions; full publication information can be found in the Works Cited section at the end of this book.

gives us knowledge of all clay, what is that, by knowing which everything else becomes known."

Here we see something very fundamental. The individual who asks this question implies that we can understand through the method of analogy or through general principles. The implication is that there must be a subtle method of going from the particular to the general. Second, the person seems to think it may be possible to enter into the heart of knowledge, to arrive at the essence of knowledge. Third, and perhaps most importantly, this individual implies, by asking a question, that we may arrive at knowledge.

Socrates is usually counted as the originator of the philosophical method of probing deeply through a sequence of questions. The questions philosophers ask may not have immediate answers, and may even be "unanswerable" in some sense. But this does not mean we should not ask them. Asking questions is the essence of modern research. We see in this Upanishad, the spirit of modern research. In fact, this spirit is the essence of the Upanishads. If modern science has taken the physical universe as its field of investigation, the Upanishads have taken the entire field of experience, both outer and inner, as the field of inquiry. We will see that the act of asking profound and fundamental questions, which lies at the heart of modern science, is the essence of the Upanishadic spirit.

Bertrand Russell wrote:

> Philosophy is to be studied, not for the sake of any definite answers to its questions since no definite answers can, as a rule, be known to be true, but rather for the sake of the questions themselves; because these questions enlarge our conception of what is possible, enrich our intellectual imagination and diminish the dogmatic assurance which closes the mind against speculation; but above all because, through the greatness of the universe which philosophy contemplates, the mind also is rendered great, and becomes capable of that union with the universe which constitutes its highest good. (93-94)

Thus, philosophy may not give definitive answers. It was a profound discovery of the 1930s that even a highly precise subject like mathematics can also pose seemingly accurate questions for which there are no mathematical answers. One of the greatest achievements of twentieth-century mathematics is Gödel's theorem. This theorem is set against the background of what we would call logical thinking and deductive reasoning. When we speak about the truth of a mathematical proposition, we imply that it can be deduced by applying a set of "rules" if you will, or to be more accurate, axioms, to a proposition which we have deemed to be known, to derive the new proposition. Gödel's theorem tells us that reasoning has limitations in the following sense: in any axiom system, one may write down propositions that can neither be proved or disproved. In other words, they cannot be derived by applying the axioms, nor can their negations be so derived.

In the light of Gödel's theorem, is the Upanishad's concern with how one might arrive at all knowledge a mistake? This question can be addressed in various ways. Reading through the Upanishads, it becomes clear that detailed knowledge is not what is meant when one asks for all knowledge. Rather, what is at issue is the essence of knowledge, or the underlying principle of knowledge. To this end, inquiry is a powerful and viable tool, not to be abandoned, even though its limitations are acknowledged in the Upanishads. Language and even the mind are acknowledged as limited for this experience. The claim is made that mind must be transcended through mind by a refinement of inquiry.

Is it possible to arrive at the essence of knowledge? Is it possible to arrive at a condition of mind through which we can understand ourselves and the universe? The word *sraddhā* (faith) is a word we will meet in the Katha Upanishad and it refers to this quality of the mind. "Faith" is a poor translation of the word. It may be more accurate to say it is a feeling that there is structure in this universe, and that we have the ability to discover it. The Upanishadic claim that is implicit and in some cases explicit is that it is possible to arrive at such a point not by objective reasoning, but rather by an inner experience that lies beyond language and beyond explanation. We shall explore this when we come to a detailed study of the Upanishads.

The method of analogy is a method of knowledge. We will find that the sages, often frustrated in their attempt to put their experiences into language, resort to poetry and the method of analogy. For instance, in the same Mundaka Upanishad quoted earlier, we find the following: "As a spider sends forth and draws in its thread, as herbs grow on the earth, as the hair grown on the human head and body, so also from the Imperishable arises this universe" (1.1.7). The sages at the same time never refrain from telling us that "That" which they are trying to describe is beyond mind and speech.

AN OUTLINE OF INDIAN PHILOSOPHY

In broad outline, we may divide the development of Indian philosophy into five historical periods: the Vedic period (2500 BCE to 600 BCE), the Epic period (600 BCE to 200 CE), the Sutra period (200 CE to 600 CE), the Scholarly period (600 CE to 1700 CE) and the Modern period (1700 CE to the present). The writings on which we base our study are all written in Sanskrit, except for those of the Modern period, where in nearly all cases, they are written in English. Knowledge of Sanskrit is not essential for our introductory study of Indian philosophy since we will use several reliable translations to get a proper sense of meaning of the texts. However, it may be appropriate to give a brief introduction to Sanskrit to enable the reader to understand its role and historical context.

Sanskrit is an ancient language whose relationship to the languages of the Indian subcontinent is somewhat akin to the relationship of Latin to the European languages. The discovery of Sanskrit by European scholars can be traced back to the researches of the English philologist and lawyer, Sir William Jones, who in 1783, was posted to India as a judge of the Bengal Supreme Court. Being interested in languages and wanting to understand the legal code of India, he began an ardent study of Sanskrit with the help of Indian scholars. To his surprise, he noticed several common features between Sanskrit and many of the European languages, most notably Greek and Latin. This led to his theory that language families evolved, and in this way, he laid the foundation for the subject of comparative linguistics. His studies expanded to include comparative mythologies and comparative literature. In 1786, he wrote:

> The Sanskrit language, whatever be its antiquity, is of a wonderful structure; more perfect than the Greek; more copious than the Latin, and more exquisitely refined than either, yet bearing to both of them a stronger affinity, both in the roots of verbs and in the forms of grammar, than could possibly have been produced by accident; so strong indeed, that no philologer could examine all three, without believing them to have sprung from some common source, which, perhaps, no longer exists. (Cannon, 245)

This language source that no longer exists from which have sprung Sanskrit, Greek, Latin and other European languages has been labelled by modern linguists Proto-Indo-European (McFetridge, 29). Jones did extensive research and translated many of the Sanskrit literary works into English. Through these writings, the intellectual community in Europe became aware of a new dimension in linguistics.

Sanskrit is a highly structured language with precise rules of grammar. It is phonetic, in the sense that the writing corresponds precisely to the pronunciation. Some English words and Sanskrit words can be traced back to a common Proto-Indo-European root. For instance, the English word "mother" can be compared with the Sanskrit *mātar*, the Latin *māter* and the Greek *meter* (McFetridge, 31). To take a more complicated example, the English word "is" is related to the Sanskrit word, *asti*.[2] This becomes

2 For the very complicated etymology of "is," see the *Oxford English Dictionary* entry.

clearer when we trace it to the Proto-Indo-European root, *esti* and compare it with the corresponding Latin word *est* and the German word *ist*.

Jones's discovery of Sanskrit led to a flurry of translations. Though these early translations conveyed the general sense of the ancient texts, they were not able to preserve and transmit subtle shades of meaning. In some places, the translations were distorted and casual. In this context, let us look at the Sanskrit word *īs*, which means the cosmic ruling force, or cosmic "glue" to put it more poetically. Thus, one of the principal Upanishads, the Isa Upanishad, is a tribute and analysis of this ruling principle. In the earliest translations, the word *Īsa* of the Isa Upanishad is misleadingly translated as "Lord," implying a dualism—a distinction between God and the world—when no dualism was meant. As we shall see, the Upanishads commonly reject dualisms—a theological separation in this case, or the distinction between consciousness and matter.

Thus, we must proceed with caution and carefully ascertain that the translations are faithful to the original spirit. This can be done partly by comparing several translations and also by studying the etymology of the words.

The writing of the Vedic period consists mainly of the four Vedas (Rg Veda, Yajur Veda, Sama Veda, and Atharva Veda), each of which has four parts known as Mantras, Brahmanas, Aranyakas, and Upanishads. The Mantras (or hymns) can be said to be the foundation of Indian philosophy. In the beginning, these hymns seem to be poetic utterances and adoration of the natural forces. At the same time, we can trace within their structure themes that later pervade the Upanishads. The Brahmanas contain ritualistic instructions. The Aranyakas and the Upanishads constitute the philosophical portions. Sri Aurobindo, in his *Secret of the Veda*, gives a psychoanalytic interpretation for the hymnal portion of the Rg Veda. From a philological and linguistic standpoint, there is some basis for this interpretation.

The word "mantra" is derived from two Sanskrit words, *manas*, which refers to the mind, and *trayate* which means to reflect upon, or to cogitate upon. The word can also be defined as "that which protects." The word, *manush* refers to the human being who has a mind or more precisely it refers to the ability of the human species to reflect. The English word "man" is related to the Sanskrit word *manush*, or *manuh*. The cognate Sanskrit word, *mananam*, which means reflection or meditation, has the same roots. There is no doubt that the early writings have declared the power of the word. In these writings, we see a continuous fascination for the interrelationship between the thought and the word.

The word *brahman* is derived from the Sanskrit root, *brihi*, which means vast and expansive. In the early translations, this word has been incorrectly translated into the word "God" and, naturally, this leads to a great deal of confusion. As signalled before, we must be aware of this imprecision when we study some of these translations. For instance, in some translations, the words *Brahman*, *Brahmin* and *Brahma* are interchanged. *Brahma* is a mythological deity. The word *Brahmin* refers to the priest, or to be more accurate, the scholar. Since many found pure reflection difficult, the Brahmins contrived ways of involving physical actions to facilitate the meditation on the mantras. These rituals were then written down into the Brahmanas. Naturally, over time, much of this degenerated into pure priestcraft.

The Aranyakas and Upanishads comprise the philosophical portion of the Vedas. Here again, it may help us to understand the Sanskrit roots of these words. Firstly, the word *veda* is derived from the root word, *vid*, which means to know. Thus, *vidya* or *veda* means knowledge, taken in its most comprehensive sense. *Aranya* means forest, and *Aranyaka* refers to forest writings. It is an ancient tradition, going back to the Vedic period, that the philosopher must retreat from society into the forest in order to understand human society and in a larger context, the meaning of life. Only by such a retreat can you examine the human species in a clinical fashion and arrive at some objective understanding of the phenomenon of life and gain some comprehension of its mysteries. Thus, whoever had a desire to become a philosopher made such a retreat into the forest and pondered over the fundamental questions of life. After much reflection, they would gain some insight and these insights they recorded in their forest writings. In time, these writings gained currency and attracted students. In those days, unlike today, sages and students thought that knowledge is not found in books. Books can only be a guide but cannot really ignite the torch of knowledge. That must come from a living teacher and the student must sit near an illumined teacher so that the knowledge is transferred to the student by some mysterious process of osmosis. This is the meaning of the word *upanishad*, which literally means "near, below, sit," signifying that knowledge comes by sitting near a learned teacher. Thus, the Upanishads are the essential writings of the forest philosophers, or more precisely, their students.

It is in the Upanishads that we find the dominant theme of non-dualism that is central to Indian philosophy. (We shall discuss this theme later.) One can discern a certain impatience with, and sometimes even explicit denunciation of, the ritualistic portion of the Brahmanas in these writings. Occasionally, some mythological or ritualistic motif does intervene in a few of the Upanishads, but often it is to illustrate a subtle philosophical point. Still, we must be careful to sift out the pure philosophy from the mythology and the aspects of social custom and ritual prevalent at that time. There is no doubt, however, that in all of the Upanishads we find the assertion of the existence of an Ultimate Reality and that this Reality can be experienced through the mental faculties of reason and intuition.

The Epic period refers to the two great epics, the Rāmāyana and the Mahābhārata, written according to tradition by Valmiki and Vyasa, respectively. These epics are comparable to the Greek epics of Homer, the Iliad and the Odyssey. Like the Greek epics, they record history in a poetic narrative. In one sense, however, they differ from the Greek epics. Interspersed in both of these works are large tracts of philosophical discourse. Thus, again, we must be careful to separate the philosophy from the literary narrative. The most significant such treatise is the Bhagavad Gita contained in the Mahābhārata. This treatise ranks as one of the foremost texts in Indian philosophic thought.

To the Epic period also belong the early developments of Buddhism, Jainism, Saivism, and Vaishnavism. Each of these have their own philosophical foundations; Saivism and Vaishnavism grew out of the earlier Vedic tradition, and Buddhism and Jainism developed orthogonally to the earlier traditions.

The Sutra period spanning four centuries gave rise to systematic treatises of various schools of philosophy. One can see the critical attitude in a sophisticated stage of development in this period. Six systems have emerged at this time and they are the schools of Nyāya (logical realism), Vaisesika (realistic pluralism), Sāmkhya (evolutionary dualism), Yoga (disciplined meditation), Pūrva Mimāmsā (preliminary interpretation of the Vedas), and Uttara Mimamsa, also known as Vedānta (synthesis of the Vedic tradition) or alternatively viewed as a deeper or higher interpretation of the Vedas.

The fourth period, called the Scholarly period, extends for a thousand years. During this time, many scholars took up the older texts such as the sutras or the Upanishads, and wrote extensive commentaries upon them. Three great philosophers stand out during this period. They are Shankara, Ramanuja, and Madhva, founders of the philosophies of non-dualism, qualified non-dualism, and dualism respectively.

The Modern period may be said to begin with Vivekananda. Unlike the earlier periods where the writings were mainly in Sanskrit, the writings of the Modern period are mainly in English. Principal contributors to modern Indian philosophy include Sri Aurobindo, Mahatma Gandhi, Jiddu Krishnamurti, Rabindranath Tagore, and Sarvepalli Radhakrishnan. We will give a short survey of the life and thought of these philosophers in the final chapter of this book.

1

THE VEDAS

As mentioned earlier, there are four Vedas: the Rg Veda, the Yajur Veda, the Sama Veda, and the Atharva Veda. Each of the Vedas contains four parts: the hymnal portion (*mantras*), the ritual portion (*brahmanas*), the forest teachings (*aranyakas*), and the philosophical portion (*upanishads*).

It is generally believed that the composition of the Vedas dates back to around 1500 BCE. No one person can be said to have composed them. They are to be viewed as some form of encyclopedic account of the highest thoughts current at that time. This explains the diversity of thought contained in them.

The Rg Veda contains about 1000 hymns and is divided into 10 books (or mandalas). These hymns embody a remarkable poetic tradition and reveal a development of thought which is both instructive and inspiring. Typical of this early period was worship of personified natural forces. In many early translations, scholars have used the word "god" to describe these forces. The Sanskrit word is *deva*, which translates as "shining one" or "luminous force." For example, Indra is the god of thunder and rain, Mitra is the god who regulates the movement of the sun, Varuna is the god of moral order, Agni is the god of fire, Usha the goddess of dawn, and Prithvi is the goddess of earth. Whether these hymns represent worship of natural forces or a deeper impulse is not clear. As first suggested by Aurobindo, there is substantial evidence in the writings for the latter, as we shall see below. Viewed from this perspective then, they represent preliminary thought for the philosophic inquiry of the Upanishads.

The opening verse (1.1.1) of the Rg Veda is worth looking at in some detail.

> *Agnimīle purohitam yajnasya devam rtvijam hotāram ratna dhātamam.*

A faithful and literal translation of this verse is:

> I adore the Fire, the sacrificial priest, luminous vibrations of Truth, the fierce warrior, the bestower of delight.

The Sanskrit word *agni*, fire, is a cognate of the Latin word *ignis* with the same meaning, and with English derivatives such as "ignite." The opening word *agnimīle* can be translated as "I adore the Fire." The word *purohita* is a combination of two words *pur* and *hitam*; *pur* originally meant door, or gate and later came to mean a house, or more generally a city (Aurobindo, v. 11, 448ff.). The cognate Greek word, *polis*, meaning city had the same Proto-Indo-European origins. The word *hitam* is an adjective referring to that which has been put or placed before. Thus, *purohitam* indicates that Fire has been placed before us or planted before us, implying that something other than the Fire has placed it there. Fire, then, likened to a sacrificial priest, should be taken as an intermediary between us and something deeper.

The word *yajna* is a word that recurs in the Vedas and the Upanishads. It is also a prominent word in the Bhagavad Gita that occurs in the Mahābhārata of the later Epic period. As a first approximation, it can be taken to mean "sacrifice." According to Aurobindo, a more accurate meaning can be found by considering the root word *yaj* from which *yajna* is formed. The root word refers to the act of applying oneself quietly and persistently, to master something by focussed attention. Thus, *yajna* refers to the sacrifice that one must make in the mastery of any art. Psychologically speaking, we must invoke the inner fire, the fire of enthusiasm, in order to gain mastery or proficiency.

The word *deva* is derived from the root *div* which means to flash, gleam, or more precisely, to vibrate or sparkle. It later came to mean "a god," or "one who plays with light." Related to this root are "divine" in English, and the Latin word *divus*, and the words for God, *dios* in Spanish, and *dieu* in French.

The word *rtam* refers to cosmic order or universal Truth. The word *rtvijam* is a combination of *rtam* and *vijam*. The latter word is derived from *vij* meaning to vibrate, to be full of ecstatic energy. (Compare the Latin word *vigere*, meaning "to be strong" and the familiar English word *vigour*, both related to the Sanskrit root *vij* [Aurobindo, V. 11, 454].) Putting the meanings together, we obtain that "Fire is a cosmic vibration of universal Truth."

The final part is also open to this sort of analysis. The word *hotāram* is derived from the root *hu* meaning to attack, to slay, as in a battle. This explains why Fire is the fierce warrior. Indeed, the fire of enthusiasm must slay the demon of lethargy before we can gain any insight into higher truths. Thus, comparing fire to a fierce warrior is appropriate.

The word *ratnadhātamam* too can be broken down into *ratna* and *dhātamam*. The word *ratna* can be taken as "jewel" or more precisely, "that which shines" or "that which delights." The second word *dhātamam* is derived from the root word *dhā* meaning to bestow, to give, to create. Hence, Fire is the bestower of delight.

Thus putting everything together, the psychological interpretation of the first verse of the first mandala of the Rg Veda is: "I adore the fire of enthusiasm, the gateway to higher knowledge, the destroyer of lethargy, the bestower of delight."

It is quite an opening for the development of later philosophical thought. Derived from this view is the notion of *tapas* or discipline, the idea that the mind must rise from a lower level to a higher level so that it can gain a deeper understanding of the nature of the universe, and more importantly, the nature of itself. Indeed, *tapas* literally means "to heat," invoking again the image of *agni* or fire. Each of us must awaken the inner creative fire. We are reminded of a famous utterance of Teilhard de Chardin, "Someday, after we have mastered the winds, the waves, the tide and gravity, we shall harness for God the energies of love. Then, for the second time in the history of the world, man will have discovered fire" (87). This idea is presented more explicitly in the Upanishads; we shall consider it in detail later.

It is fitting that this very old utterance addresses a universal problem: laziness. We all feel we are capable of much more than we accomplish and yet, we do not know how to awaken this power within. We easily slip into lethargy. William James wrote, "Everyone knows on any given day that there are energies slumbering in him which the incitements of the day do not call forth.... Compared with what we ought to be, we are only half awake. Our fires are damped, our drafts are checked. We are making use of only a small part of our possible mental and physical resources" (14). The opening verse of the Rg Veda is a prayer to awaken these energies, and rouse up the fire of enthusiasm.

This exemplary verse is enough to indicate the general trend of thought found in the Rg Veda. The ninth verse reads, "O Agni, be easy of access to us, as a father is to his son. Stay with us for our happiness" (Radhakrishnan and Moore, 8).

Other Vedas show a similar development of thought, for example, the following verse from the Yajur Veda (1.5):

Agne vrata pate vratam charishyami tachakeyam tanme
Rādhytām idamaham nrutāthsatyamupaimi

May Agni, the fire of our vows, inspire me to master my lower self. May the fire grant me the strength and make my effort fruitful. (Yatiswarananda, 55)

Reading many of the hymns of the Vedas, we can see that the "fire principle" was recognized early. The sages intuitively knew that Fire—creative energy—lay at the heart of all things. At the same time, we see in the opening passage that though Fire is fundamental it is not the ultimate, but only an intermediary to a deeper level of reality.

The analysis above is based on an exposition of Aurobindo (v. 10, 33ff.) where many of the hymns of the Rg Veda have been analyzed from a psychological perspective with linguistic corroboration. For instance, Indra is not the "god of thunder" but rather that which controls the *indriyas*—the sense organs. Thus, Indra really refers to the power of the mind. For Aurobindo, Fire, or Agni, refers to the cosmic will.

Thus the "gods" are energies of the mind or some psychic aspect of the human being. They are all, in some sense, intermediaries or guardians of a higher Reality. Here are some examples.

Usha represents the dawn. Clearly, the transition from night into day or day into night is not only an event of great beauty but also inspires one into a contemplative mood. As such, it was perceived at the individual level as a transition from a period of rest or contemplation to a period of activity or vice versa. Here again, let us observe that Dawn is an intermediary, the ushering of light, just as Fire was seen as an intermediary between ourselves and the ultimate Reality.

Vāk represents the power of speech and it is given the status of a goddess. The Latin word *vox* and the English words *voice* and *vocal* are related to the Sanskrit words *vāk* and *vakti*. Later, we see how the word *vāk* becomes an intermediary beyond which lies the ultimate Reality.

Vāyu is literally the god of wind, but the reference here can be seen to be a more abstract life principle—compare when we talk about the "breath of life."[1] (Other related ways of talking about the Life Principle in the Upanishads will be considered later.)

1 John H. Lienhard points out that ancient languages often used the same word for wind, for breath, and for soul. "In Sanskrit that word is *atman*; in Latin it's either *spiritus* or *anima*; in Hebrew it's *ru-ach*; and in Greek it's *pneuma*. You find *pneuma* and *spiritus* in air-related words like *pneumatic* and *respiration*. *Atman* shows up again as the German verb *atmen* which means to breathe; and *ru-ach* is probably kin [to] the German word *rauch*, for smoke. The Russian word for spirit, *duh*, has many wind-related cognates. *Duhovyia intrumenti*, for example, means *wind instruments*."

The psychological perspective of Aurobindo is controversial, and one might not want to go beyond the naive viewpoint that these are merely hymns in praise of natural forces. Even though these forces are associated with a multitude of gods, these hymns show development of early naturalistic polytheism into monotheism and finally into monism (seeing the divine as within a unified nature). The evidence is clear in this regard. That is, from the many "gods and goddesses" of natural forces, the sages arrived at the principle of the One and then recognized that it was one supreme, vast, all-pervasive being manifesting in various ways.

Nowhere is this more explicitly stated than in the first mandala, hymn 164:

> *Indram mitram varunam agni māhuradho divyah*
> *Sa suparno garutmān*
> *Ekam sat vipra bahudhā vadanti.* (Rg Veda 1.164.46)

> They call it Indra, Mitra, Varuna, Agni as well as Garutman of heavenly plumage. That which exists is One, sages call it by various names. (Radhakrishnan and Moore, 21. See also Aurobindo, Vol. 10, 53)

The monistic tendency dominant in Indian philosophy is often traced back to this ancient verse. It sets to naught all controversy about many gods, one god or even no gods. "That which exists is One, sages call it by various names." This idea is repeated in many places in the Rg Veda. For example, "That which has become all this" (Rg Veda 8.58.2), and "which the learned and the wise describe through many forms of expressions" (Rg Veda 10.114.5), are two instances that point to the emergence of a monistic theme. This trend culminates in the famous hymn of creation, in Mandala 10:

> Neither non-being nor being was as yet,
> Neither was airy space nor the sky beyond;
> What was enveloped?
> And where?
> And sheltered by whom?
> And was there water?
> Bottomless, unfathomed?
>
> Death did not exist nor life immortal,
> Nor was there any sign then of night or day,
> By its inherent force the One breathed windless,
> Beyond that, indeed, nothing whatever was.

Darkness was there first hidden by darkness,
Undifferentiated surge was this whole world.
That which, becoming, by the void was covered,
That One by force of heat came into being.

In the Principle, thereupon, arose desire,
Which of consciousness was the primeval seed.
Then the wise, searching within their hearts,
Perceived that in non-being lay the bond of being.

Their ray extended light across darkness.
Was there a below?
And was there an above?
There were sowers of seeds and forces of might:
Potency from beneath and from on high the Will.

Who really knows, who could here proclaim,
Whence this creation flows, where is its origin?
The gods were born after this world's creation.
Who therefore knows from where it has arisen?

This flow of creation, from where did it rise,
Whether it was ordered, or whether it was not,
The Observer, in the highest heaven,
That alone knows, or perhaps—It knows it not. (Rg Veda 10.129)

In the third verse, we meet the phrase *tad ekam*, which means "That One." No further elaboration is given, except to indicate the principle of One. The third verse uses the word *tapas*, which literally means heat. But it is more than that. It refers to the fire of austerity, and in the later tradition it becomes synonymous with the power of meditation. The last three verses begin a questioning culminating in the last line suggesting that there may be a limitation to human knowledge. At a deeper level, it signals that "knowing" may be a "lower" stage since a duality is implied by it between the knower and the object of knowledge. This issue is taken up later in the Upanishads.

The theme of the "One" resonates in many places of the Rg Veda. For instance, let us look at 8.58.2 of the Rg Veda:

Eka evāgnir bahudhāsamiddha
Ekah sūryo visvam anu prabhūtah

Ekaivosāh sarvam idam vibhāty
Ekam vaidam vi babhūva sarvam (Rg Veda 8.58.2)

One fire burns in many ways; one sun illumines the world; one dawn dispels the darkness of night; All that exists is One and It has taken all these various forms.

Surya, or the sun, was an object of worship in many of the ancient civilizations. This is not surprising because it is the most striking, important, and pervasive of natural objects. It was worshipped as the bestower of light and energy in many of the early cultures. However, for the Vedic sages, it becomes a powerful psychological symbol for Pure Awareness, for *Brahman.* Just as the sun energizes all life on the planet, but does not participate in the good or the bad, the Pure Awareness animates the energies of our being, and illumines our thoughts and feelings but is not touched by good and evil. Thus, the sun becomes the symbol of *Brahman,* the vast expansive consciousness. This psychological use of the symbol of the sun is apparent in many of the hymns of the Rg Veda. To cite a specific and celebrated hymn, let us consider the famous Gayatri mantra, in the third mandala of the Rg Veda:

Tat savitur varenyaṃ bhargo devasya dhimahi
Dhiyo yo nah prachodayāt (Rg Veda 3.62.10)

Let us meditate on the glory of that Supreme Being that illumines everything. May That illumine our understanding.

The word *dhi,* occurring in *dhimahi* and *dhiyo,* refers to understanding, and its cognate word *buddhi* means the reasoning faculty of the mind implying that by reason we may gain a deeper understanding. The Upanishads will declare later that *buddhi* must be transcended to experience the Ultimate Reality.

Before we conclude this chapter, there are two more hymns that are worth considering from a sociological context. They reflect a recognition that when any group of people gather together, they must live in harmony and not in conflict. The famous "unity hymn" in Mandala 10 seems relevant to the modern age, at a time when technology has brought together all the people from the remote corners of the planet to inhabit a "global village," but conflict, rather than unity, appears to be the rule.

Samāno mantrah samiti samāni
Samānam manah saha cittamesām (Rg Veda 10.191.3)

> Common be your prayers. Common be the end of your assembly.
> Common be your purpose. Common be your deliberations.

The word "same" is related to the Sanskrit word *samah* which is the root of *samānam*. The use of the word in poetic cadence in the hymn resonates beautifully the message of harmony. Society cannot exist without unity, and a common purpose provides unity. This common purpose is the challenge of peaceful co-existence of all races, of all nations, and of all cultures.

Another celebrated hymn occurs in the first book: *Āno bhadrah kratvo yantu visvatah* (Let noble thoughts come from all directions) (Rg Veda 1.89.1). This verse emphasizes the complementarity of human knowledge. It highlights the need to learn from all directions because knowledge is not the monopoly of any single individual or nation or race. The pursuit and expansion of knowledge in the widest sense of the word is a collective human endeavour.

2

THE UPANISHADS

As we saw earlier, the word *upanishad* is a combination of three Sanskrit words *upa*, *ni*, and *shad*, translated "near," "below" and "sit" respectively (Radhakrishnan, *Upanishads*, 19). The idea is that these writings arose from the recorded notes of students sitting "below" or "near" an illumined sage. This is an important idea in the Indian philosophical tradition. Knowledge in its most essential form cannot be taught through books but rather is transmitted by example, by experience, by life. In that ancient tradition, the student would live with the teacher and slowly imbibe an outlook on life that resonates with the sage's teaching. Knowledge is not to be separated from daily life, but must also become practical. Even in our modern world, we see clearly that some form of this tradition enters into our method of transmitting higher learning. For example, the outlook of a graduate student must be different from that of an undergraduate. For the latter, the focus is on learning information and passing various examinations. But the graduate program can be seen as an initiatory rite, in which we try to convey that knowledge is not a finished book and that the activity of scholars is to expand and broaden our horizons of understanding. In this, we try to initiate the students to think for themselves, to question, to probe deeper, and ultimately to make an original contribution to human thought. In essence, we teach them that they too must add new chapters to humanity's book of knowledge.

The sixth-century philosopher Shankara, gives a slightly different meaning to the word *upanishad*. He traces the meaning to the root word *sad*, meaning "to loosen," "to reach," or "to destroy." If this root meaning is taken, Shankara says that the word *upanishad* means "that knowledge which destroys ignorance, or that by which ignorance is loosened" (Radhakrishnan, *Upanishads*, 20).

There are over 200 Upanishads. Of these, 14 Upanishads have become prominent in the study of Indian philosophy. They are: Isa, Kena, Katha, Prasna, Mundaka, Māndukya, Taittirīya, Aitareya, Chāndogya, Brhadāranyaka, Svetāsvatara, Kausītaki, Mahānārāyana, and Maitrī. These are called the principal Upanishads. They were written before the Buddhistic period and are dated around the eighth or seventh century BCE.

We do not know the names of the authors of the Upanishads. The writings are to be thought of as brief jottings by students about the teachings of sages. From their brevity, one can infer that their purpose was only to nudge the memory of the student to reflect and meditate upon familiar teachings. The fact that these verses are poetic is significant. Poetry is not to be read but rather to be savoured and to be meditated upon; and that is indeed the intention of all of the Upanishads. The student must make these his or her own inner realizations, through introspection and reflection. The verses are pithy and pregnant with meaning.

Commenting on the psychology of poetry, Colin Wilson writes that "the central device of poetry is contrast, the change of mood. It aims at creating a shadow-play in the mind, in which forms change shape as easily as in a dream.... A poet is concerned with symbols that can evoke certain feelings, as the mere name of the Divine Mother could plunge Ramakrishna into Samadhi [a deep meditative state]" (49-50). The poetic verses of the Upanishads are full of profound symbols that provide access for the sincere student to deeper meditation.

Apart from poetic beauty, a major portion of these writings is pure philosophy and the modern philosopher would have no difficulty in understanding the drift of thought and would be quite at home with the questioning. Occasionally, we find in them examples that clearly refer to some social custom or mythological tradition of that time. In our study of them, we will be careful to separate those passages from the pure philosophical inquiry.

The central theme of the Upanishads is best illustrated by the opening question of the Mundaka Upanishad (1.1.3) where the student asks the sage, "What is that by knowing which everything is known?" This is a fundamental philosophical question that ignites further questions such as "What is knowledge?" and "What do we mean by knowing?"

The core message of the Upanishads is that there is an ultimate Reality that they label as *Brahman*, derived from the Sanskrit word *brih* which means that which is vast and expansive. A refrain in the Upanishads is *Tat tvam asi*, which means "You are that." That is, at the fundamental level, we are That which is vast and expansive. To indicate that dimension of the ultimate Reality at the individual level, the Upanishads use the word *ātman*. We have already indicated the relationship of this word to the English word "atmosphere," which is derived from the Greek word *atmos* which means vapor or air. This does not mean that the word *ātman* means vapor or air. Rather, the sages used the word to indicate the dimension of the ultimate Reality as reflected in the individual. It is often incorrectly translated as the "soul" in the early translations, but a more accurate English rendering would be "Self." Here again, this is a poor translation since the *ātman* is beyond thought and feeling and cannot be objectified. Thus, one should definitely not confuse it with the ego, which is connected to thought and feeling.

We will therefore be alert to indicate the subtle nuances of the Sanskrit passages. It is important to keep in mind that the dominant theme of the Upanishads is monism, or more accurately, it is non-dualism. Monism implies an underlying "oneness." Non-dualism merely asserts that the underlying theme is "not two." This is a subtle difference that is important in Shankara's philosophy. It is most unfortunate that early translations of the Upanishads have distorted their meaning by introducing the word "God" or the word "Lord" when no such dualism was meant. These words now have precise theological meanings and we must be cautious in reading these translations.

THE ISA UPANISHAD

The Isa Upanishad is one of the smaller Upanishads consisting of only 18 verses. Even though it is short, it is considered to be very important and foremost in giving the trend of thought of all the Upanishads. Thus, we will study it in its entirety. The opening verse of the Isa Upanishad is worth examining in some detail. It is

Isāvāsyam idam sarvam yat kinca jagatyām jagat
Tena tyaktena bhunjīthā mā grdhah kasyasvid dhanam.

Isa is the cosmic ruling force. As indicated earlier, the highly complicated and abstract word "is" in the English language is related to the Sanskrit word *asti*. This is not unrelated to *īsa*. This conveys a clearer idea of what is meant by *īsa*. In many translations, *īsa* is translated as God or Lord (see, for example, Radhakrishnan and Moore, 3) but this is inaccurate. These erroneous translations give the impression of some deity sitting up in the clouds, and this is the opposite of what the Upanishads are trying to convey. As we have emphasized, the underlying theme of the Upanishads is non-dualism.

A faithful and accurate translation of the first verse is as follows:

> The ruling force dwells in everything, in every bit of it, even in anything that is changing or moving. By that renunciation, enjoy. Do not covet the wealth of anyone. (Sarvagatananda, 5)

These verses have to be meditated upon deeply before their inner meaning is revealed. Often, several important ideas are compressed into a terse verse. Each verse is to be reflected upon further. Seldom is it the case that the deeper meanings are instantly revealed.

The Upanishadic sages recognized that there is something holding this universe together, some form of "cosmic glue," the *īsa*, the ruling force. Thus the verse says that the ruling force is in everything, not in a part of everything, but in every bit of it, even in those things that are changing and moving. Thus, it is all-pervasive. At the same time, it is not changing. It is eternal, because anything changing is subject to the laws of decay and death.

The last two lines of the verse are equally profound. "By that renunciation, enjoy. Do not covet the wealth of anyone." The word "renunciation" or *tyaga* is a recurrent word in the Upanishads and later in the Bhagavad Gita, so we must understand its precise meaning. It means to give up the sense of ownership, to be detached, to give up the sense of possession. It does not mean, as is often the view, that we should give up everything and walk away. Nor does it mean we should become cynical and pessimistic. Rather, renunciation is something that arises as a corollary of the main thesis that all of this that we see, including ourselves, is *īsa*, is One. "By that renunciation, enjoy," is the instruction we get from the second line.

In this line, the sage has isolated for clinical study that trait of the human being that is responsible for all the difficulties on the planet, namely, the sense of ownership. Thus, if the first line is an assertion of monism, the second line is a total rejection of dualism, since dualism is rooted in the notion of separation, in the idea of "you" and "me," of "mine" and "not-mine." If this universe is pervaded by the cosmic ruling force, then it follows that nothing belongs to me. Thus, we are to enjoy this world by giving up the sense of ownership. Hence, if the first line states that this entire universe, including ourselves, is pervaded by *īsa*, the next line indicates how we may attain to that realization, namely by giving up the sense of ownership, which is rooted in the idea of duality.

When we take a cosmic perspective, things come into clearer focus. Nothing really belongs to us. This body and this mind are not of our making and are not our possessions. We are simply, for the time being, trustees, of our body and mind. This idea is the meaning of renunciation. When we analyze in life what it is that makes us miserable, invariably we find the idea of possession lurking in the background. We have tried to grasp something and it has slipped from our hands. Or often, it is that someone has bruised our ego, which arises from our mind grasping at the idea of "I," at the sense of individuality, which again is based on duality. Our enjoyments at present seem to be through grasping or possession. However, there is, as this verse indicates, a higher form of enjoyment and that is through renunciation, with the awareness that nothing really belongs to us and that we are merely trustees of whatever we temporarily have.

Vivekananda explains the idea of renunciation as follows. Suppose that in an art auction there are paintings for sale and we go there just to look at them but not to buy anything. "Who enjoys the picture," Vivekananda asks,

> the seller or the seer? The seller is busy with his accounts, computing what his gain will be, how much profit he will realise on the picture. His brain is full of that. He is looking at the hammer and watching the bids. He is intent on learning how fast the bids are rising. That man is enjoying the picture who has gone there without any intention of buying or selling. He looks at the picture and enjoys it. So this whole universe is a picture, and when these desires [of possession] have vanished, we will enjoy the world, and then this buying and selling and these foolish ideas of possession will be ended. (Vol. 2, 149)

The last line, "Do not covet the wealth of anyone" is to emphasize again that it is the covetous attitude that is the source of difficulty, that is the cause of misery. If we give up these ideas, we can enjoy life. Thus, enjoyment in the Upanishadic sense can only be when we give up our mental ideas of ownership. It is not attained by outwardly becoming a mendicant, but inwardly, by giving up all ideas of possession. It is a mental process.

A philosopher in this ancient tradition, after having understood things, tries to carry this understanding into practice. This understanding must transcend the intellect and this can only be done by trying to live the idea. This is really what it means to be a true philosopher. This is not easy to do, because we have been conditioned in many ways, for example, through family and social conventions. To be a philosopher means we must examine how these conditionings have entered our thinking and remove them. It will be noticed that all of these conditionings arise from the notion of duality.

Mahatma Gandhi wrote that the first verse of the Isa Upanishad encapsulates the entire theme of Indian philosophical thought. He wrote "Since *īsa* pervades every fibre of my being and all of you, I derive from it the doctrine of equality of all creatures on earth.... This *mantra* tells me that I cannot hold as mine anything...and if my life and that of all who believe in this *mantra* has to be a life of perfect dedication, it follows that it will have to be a life of continual service of our fellow creatures" (*Collected Works*, Vol. 64, 290).

With this in mind, the next verse becomes more meaningful to us. "Only by doing work should one desire to live here a hundred years. Thus, and in no other way, work will not stain you." That is, work—our purposeful activity—is to be understood as "service to our fellow creatures," and if we act with this view, we will not be attached to our actions and their results. The idea here is that when selfish desire enters our work, we become attached to results. So, in this second verse, we see the emergence of a philosophy of work, or *karma yoga*, that is later amplified in subsequent philosophical writings. It is a theme that occurs later in the *karma yoga* expanded upon in the Bhagavad Gita.

The opening word of the third verse requires careful translation. The word *asurya* is a combination of two parts *a* and *surya*. *Surya* means sun or light, and *asurya* means without light. Thus, the meaning of the third verse is that those who do not understand this life principle, *īsa*, are without light and live in a world of blind gloom, as it were.

The fourth verse indicates the understanding of *īsa* is beyond mind, and the fifth verse, through beautiful poetic style, tries to convey this mystery. "Unmoving, the One is faster than the mind. The sense organs cannot reach It.... It moves and It moves not. It is far and It is near. It is within all this. It is also outside all this."

As *īsa* is animating mind and the sense organs, *īsa* cannot be reached through either the mind or the sensory system. Movement can only be described relative to something that is motionless. If *īsa* animates everything, it clearly moves in this sense, and at the same time, it does not move since there is nothing else you can use as a reference point.

At the level of living things, what is meant by "It" in these verses can be taken to mean awareness, or consciousness. It is this mystery of consciousness that is taken up in the later Upanishads and more fundamentally, in the Kena Upanishad. Consciousness animates the mind and the sense organs. "It" can also be viewed as the principle of life. In fact, the word *mātarisvan* that appears in the fourth verse, is a combination of two words, *māta* and *īsvara* derived from the root word *īsa* that we have already met. The word *īsvara* signifies the principle of existence. The word *māta* brings the mother aspect and the combination thus connotes the maternal principle of existence, the "life principle." That this word is used here is significant since the theme of the mother principle pervades much of the later mythology of India. As mentioned earlier, the English word, "mother" is derived from the Latin word *māter*, which in turn is related to the Sanskrit word *māta*.

Aurobindo translates "*mātarisvan*" as the matrix out of which things evolve; this is a more accurate translation. The word "matrix" is derived from the Latin *mater*. It means the womb, or more generally, a place of origin or growth.[1]

Expanding on his translation of the word, Aurobindo writes,

> *Mātarisvan* seems to mean "he who extends himself in the Mother or container" whether that be the containing mother element, Ether, or the material energy called Earth in the Veda and spoken of there as the Mother. It is a Vedic epithet of the God, Vāyu, who representing the divine principle in the Life-energy, Prana, extends himself in Matter and vivifies its forms. Here it signifies the divine Life-power that presides in all forms of cosmic activity. (Vol. 12, 64)

The sixth verse says, "One who clearly perceives the *ātman* in all beings, and all beings in the *ātman*, does not separate oneself from the cosmic principle." As stated earlier, the Greek word *atmos* signifying vapor, or air, and the Sanskrit word *ātman* are related, though in the latter case, the word indicates the *īsa* principle at the individual level. The next verse expands this theme. "What sorrow, what delusion is there for one who sees intimately the unity of existence and knows all beings to be one's own Self (*Atman*)." Thus, the sage who perceives the underlying unity within and without is free from delusion.

The eighth verse is: "It is all pervasive, radiant, indivisible, without a body, without a scar of imperfection, without sinews. It is pure and uncontaminated by ignorance. The poet is the ruler of the mind, the ruler of nature and self-existent. It has assigned all things properly." The last part is to be interpreted as follows. On one hand, all things seem to have an intrinsic order and arrangement. At the same time, it signals that there is more to this universe than what is perceived.

The next verse seems, at first, rather enigmatic. "They enter into blinding darkness who adore ignorance. Into greater darkness, as it were, they enter who are devoted to knowledge alone." At a superficial level, it means

---

1 The usage of the term in mathematics can be traced back to the nineteenth century, to the fundamental work of Hermann Grassman, who was the first to write the foundational treatise on linear and multilinear algebra. It is curious that Grassman was in fact a Sanskrit scholar and compiled a translation of the Rg Veda before his mathematical work. Apart from being a philologist, he was also a mathematician of the highest rank, as is now evidenced by a study of his works. Unfortunately, during his lifetime, Grassman was not recognized for his mathematical abilities and spent his life as a school teacher. Based on his deep knowledge of languages, it is clear that Grassman's use of "matrix" in mathematics was quite deliberate since it is derived from the Latin word *mater* and the Sanskrit word *māta*, both signifying "mother" or, more accurately, "the womb." The theory of matrices is definitely the womb of mathematics, as any serious student of the subject quickly learns. According to Hermann Weyl, it is "Her All-embracing Majesty, GL(n)," which is at the heart of mathematics (*The Classical Groups*, 136).

to be cautious about the arrogance of knowledge. The message reminds us of a famous poem of Pope:

A little learning is a dangerous thing;
Drink deep, or taste not the Pierian spring:[2]
There shallow draughts intoxicate the brain,
And drinking largely sobers us again.
Fired at first sight with what the Muse imparts,
In fearless youth we tempt the heights of Arts;
While from the bounded level of our mind
Short views we take, nor see the lengths behind,
But more advanced, behold with strange surprise
New distant scenes of endless science rise!

But there is a deeper idea: the more you know, the more you discover that is yet to be known. One can say that this is an illumined form of ignorance.

That we must transcend "the greater darkness" is the import of the next two verses. Taken together, they mean, "One result they say is obtained by knowledge, and quite another by non-knowledge. Thus have we heard from the wise who explained it to us. He who understands both knowledge and non-knowledge, conquers death through non-knowledge and attains immortality through knowledge." Here knowledge refers to the knowledge of the changeless, the ultimate Reality; and non-knowledge refers to knowledge of the changing, phenomenal nature. Thus, we conquer death through knowledge of the changing but transcend both life and death, that is, gain immortality in this sense, through knowledge of the ultimate Reality.

A faithful translation of the next two verses is as follows. "Those who think That is beyond manifestation enter into blinding darkness. Those who say That has form enter into greater darkness, as it were. One result, they say is obtained from the adoration of manifestation and quite another from the adoration of the unmanifest. Thus we have heard from the wise who explained it to us." The meaning is clear here. The human being is conditioned to think in forms and words. Thus, if we are to grasp the ultimate Reality without these methods, we plunge into darkness. Without words, we have no support and nowhere to stand. If on the other hand we insist on thinking only in terms of words and forms, then we plunge into greater darkness as it were, since we will limit our idea of That through definitions.

The last four verses are more like a prayer to the mind. In the process of meditation, we may propel our mind to a higher stage of awareness but fail

2 In Greek mythology, the Pierian Spring is the source of inspiration for art and science.

to maintain that awareness due to our past impressions. Thus, the student is praying this does not happen.

> Like a lid, Thy shining golden orb covers the entrance to the Truth. Please remove it, O Supporter, so that I who am devoted to Truth may behold That. O Nourisher, the sole Seer. O Controller, O Sun, the supporter of all. Gather thy brilliance, draw together thy light. Through your grace, I behold That which is beyond. I am That. Let my life force be merged in the all-pervading Life. Let the body be reduced to ashes. Om. Remember the goal. Remember the goal.

And finally, we have, "O Agni, lead us by the goodly path. You know all the ways. Prevent all distractions from the goal. We salute you again and again."

These verses are attempting to convey the state of mind in deeper stages of meditation. According to the sages, it is possible to completely silence all mental modifications so that one may "perceive" the underlying awareness. True, it cannot be objectified, because to do that would put it in the realm of the mind. However, it can be experienced. This is the meaning of the line "I am That," indicating at that point the student has realized his oneness with the Ultimate Reality. The body and mind are only vehicles for this experience and so the next line says, "Let the body be reduced to ashes."

This experience can be likened to the process of putting a multi-stage rocket into orbit. To escape the gravitational pull of the earth, the booster rockets carry the rocket to the higher regions and then drop off so that the main rocket may ascend higher. A similar process is occurring here. Both the body and the mind are instruments to soar into a higher level of awareness and when the sage (or the student recording this teaching) manages to silence his mind to experience the underlying Awareness, he exclaims, "I am That." But then, lest he (or she) descend again to a lower level of awareness, he reminds himself to focus on the goal again. "Om" is the recurrent symbol of the Ultimate Reality that occurs later in many of the Upanishads as well as the Bhagavad Gita. (We will say more about "Om" in a later chapter.) The final prayer to Agni is thus an invocation to the cosmic Will, so that the student may maintain this higher awareness.

In this short Upanishad, we see the trend of thought that is fundamental to the whole of the Indian philosophical tradition. It is therefore fitting that we begin our survey of the Upanishads with the *Isa*.

3

THE KENA AND KATHA UPANISHADS

THE KENA UPANISHAD

The word *kena* means "by whom?" (the opening words in the Kena Upanishad). The Upanishad is an inquiry into the nature of perception. It is a search for the real power behind the workings of the universe both external and internal. It concludes by indicating that it is the *ātman*, but the way it arrives at this conclusion is worthy of detailed study.

Here is a quick translation of the entire Upanishad. The opening verse begins with some thought provoking questions. "By whom does the mind go forward toward its object? Being directed by whom does the life force, *prāna*, proceed to its function? By whom impelled do the people utter their speech? What luminous force directs the eyes and ears?"

The second verse gives the reply. "It is the ear of the ear, the mind of the mind, the speech of speech, the life of life, the eye of the eye. The wise who separate the *ātman* from the sensory functions become immortal."

The third and fourth verses are as follows. "The eye cannot approach It, neither speech nor mind. We do not therefore know It, nor do we know how to teach It. It is different from what is known and It is beyond what is unknown. Thus we have heard from our teachers who taught us."

Now come verses which are not only wonderfully poetic but enable the mind to go to its own boundaries by the very inquiry. At the same time, we see a negation of formal religion. "What speech cannot reveal but what reveals speech, that is *Brahman*, not what people worship here. What mind does not comprehend, but what comprehends mind, that is *Brahman*, not what people worship here. What sight cannot see but what sees sight, that is *Brahman*, not what people worship here. What hearing cannot hear, but what hears hearing, that is *Brahman*, not what people worship here. What the sense of smell cannot reveal, but what reveals the sense of smell, that is *Brahman*, not what people worship here."

Thus far in the opening verse, we have the student inquiring into the nature of perception. The teacher gives his answers in the subsequent verses. Having explained it in this way, the teacher says: "if you think that you know *Brahman* well, then you know little indeed, for the form of *Brahman* that you see in the living beings and luminous forces is but a trifle. You should inquire further into the nature of *Brahman*." The student replies: "I think I know *Brahman*."

This is an important verse that has relevance to the modern spirit of research. When we say we know something, we have put an end to our knowledge of it. Psychologically, we have closed the apertures of the mind in that direction. Our attitude may determine the extent to which we can open our sensory apparatus, including the mind, in order to gain knowledge.

But the student continues in the next verse. "I do not think I know It well. Nor do I think that I do not know It. He knows It who knows that It is other than the unknown and the known." The teacher's reply is the following. "He knows who knows It not. He knows It not who knows. It is unknown to the one who knows. It is known to the one who does not know."

Again, this verse is highly relevant to the modern research student. Everything around us is infinite. We cannot say that we know everything about even a grain of sand. It reminds us of the lines from William Blake's poem, "Auguries of Innocence":

> *To see the world in a grain of sand, and heaven in a wild flower,*
> *Hold infinity in the palm of your hand, and eternity in an hour.*

We cannot say that our knowledge of anything is complete. Even a grain of sand, or the petal of a flower seems to be infinite. In science and mathematics, it often happens that a fresh perspective can open new vistas of knowledge on aspects that humanity may deem "known" or complete.

In his essay "The Open Secret," Vivekananda writes,

> Whichever way we turn in trying to understand things in their reality, if we analyse far enough, we find that at last we come to a peculiar state of things, seemingly a contradiction: something which our reason cannot grasp and yet is a fact. We take up something—we know

> it is finite; but as soon as we begin to analyse it, it leads us beyond our reason, and we never find an end to all its qualities, its possibilities, its powers, its relations. It has become infinite. Take even a common flower, that is finite enough; but who is there that can say he knows all about the flower? There is no possibility of anyone's getting to the end of the knowledge about that one flower. The flower has become infinite—the flower which was finite to begin with. Take a grain of sand. Analyse it. We start with the assumption that it is finite, and at last we find that it is not, it is infinite; all the same we have looked upon it as finite.... So with all our thoughts and experiences... We see we are finite beings.... What is true of the flower, of the grain of sand, of the physical world, and of every thought, is a hundredfold more true of ourselves. We are also in the same dilemma of existence, being finite and infinite at the same time.... When we want to grasp ourselves, we cannot—we have become the infinite.... Everything in this life is so vast that the intellect is nothing in comparison with it.... We ourselves—this is the greatest mystery of the universe. (Vol. 2, 397-98)

From the standpoint of *Brahman*, the meaning of the verse is that he who thinks he knows *Brahman* has a conception in his mind. Since no conception can capture all of *Brahman*, the individual really cannot say he knows It.

The Upanishad continues by giving a means to realize *Brahman*. He who is aware of It through every pulsation of knowing gains immortality. The *ātman* is the source of strength and vigour and through its awareness, we gain immortality. For one who has realized it here and now, there is true life. For one who has not, great is the loss. Discovering the *ātman* in every being, the wise become immortal.

In these verses, we must understand the meaning of immortality. The reference is to the transcendence of life and death, of change. By realizing the *ātman* we enter the dimension of the unchanging, eternal and thus become immortal. The Upanishadic concept of immortality is distinct from the (simplest) Christian idea of immortality. The latter refers to a continued existence as a reward for prescribed meritorious action and conduct. The Upanishadic idea refers to a transcendence of both life and death, of mind and thought, and all relativity.

Now that the sage has imparted to the student the fundamental teaching, he proceeds in the next two sections to illustrate the idea through a story. The story goes that *Brahman* obtained victory for the *devas*, the luminous energies. Though the victory was due to *Brahman*, the *devas* became elated by it and thought, "This victory is ours, the glory is ours." *Brahman* came to know of their vanity and It appeared before them. But they did not understand what appeared before them. The *devas* asked Agni to go and investigate. Agni hastened to That. It asked, "who are you?" Agni replied, "I am Fire, I can burn anything." That Being then said, "Can you burn this blade of grass?" Agni roused up its enthusiasm and energy but could not burn the blade of grass. He returned to the *devas* and told them he could not fathom That. The *devas* asked Vāyu to go and determine what That is. Vāyu went and on being asked "who are you?" replied, "I am *mātarisvan*, the life force. I can blow away anything." That Being then said, "Can you blow away this blade of grass?" Vāyu then roused up its full force to blow away the blade of grass but could not do so. He returned to the *devas* and told them he could not fathom That. Then the *devas* asked Indra to investigate. When Indra went, That disappeared and in that spot appeared a luminous female form, *Umā*, daughter of the snow-clad mountains. Indra asked her, "Who was That?" She replied, "That was *Brahman*. It was through victory of *Brahman* that you achieved your glory." Through the words of *Umā*, Indra understood That was *Brahman*. Agni, Vāyu, and Indra excel the *devas* since they approached *Brahman*. Indra excels the others since he was the first to know That as *Brahman*.

With these verses the allegorical story is complete. None of the three, Agni, Vāyu or Indra, is able to understand It. Indra however does not see That, but rather *Umā*. Recall that Indra is that power which controls the sense organs, namely, the power of the mind. *Umā* is the combined wisdom of the sages, here symbolized by the snow-clad mountains, the meditative retreat of the philosophers of that age.

The teacher continues. "This is the teaching regarding That. It is like a flash of lightning or the wink of an eye. This is with reference to Its aspect as cosmic manifestation."

This verse is important because it indicates that knowledge of *Brahman* can be gained through the study of external nature but the perception of That is momentary like a flash of lightning or the wink of an eye. The next verse indicates that through the mind, the experience lasts longer.

"The manifestation of That in the human being can be perceived inwardly by the mind. *Brahman* can be remembered and imagined as being nearer than the near in every particle of time. *Brahman* is called the adorable One. It can be meditated upon in that way."

What other relation can we have to That which manifests as energy in the human being and is responsible for all the vital processes since the moment of our conception? In this verse, we get a practical method to contemplate *Brahman*, namely, by being constantly aware of the workings of the mind

(Indra), the Life Principle (Vāyu), and the Fire Principle (Agni), for their workings are due to the power of *Brahman*.

Now comes a rather humorous dialogue. The student has just been taught by the teacher. And the student asks, "Sir, please teach me what is called the Upanishad." The teacher replies, "I have just taught you the Upanishad. I have just imparted to you the knowledge of *Brahman*."

Here, *upanishad* is to be interpreted as inner knowledge. The student has not understood and so asks the teacher to teach it again! The patient teacher continues. "Of the Upanishad, *tapas* (concentration of energies of the mind and the senses), *damah* (self-restraint), and *karma* (dedicated work) form the foundation. The Vedas are its limbs. Truth is its abode. One who realizes That is liberated from ignorance and becomes established in That. Yes, he becomes established in That."

The repetition that occurs in this last verse is, apart from its poetic beauty, significant in several ways. First, it underlines the sage's deep conviction that this is true and a matter of personal experience. In this way, he invites the student to undertake the same adventure. At the same time, the repetition is one that has cosmic reverberations, an utterance that reaches out to the world at large that something profound has been discovered that is universal in its message.

Poets often use this repetitive device. In English poetry the most familiar is the poem by Robert Frost, "Stopping by Woods on a Snowy Evening," where the author writes

The woods are lovely, dark and deep,
But I have promises to keep,
And miles to go before I sleep,
And miles to go before I sleep.

The repetition, apart from its literary effect, resonates in the heart of every human being. In this way, it transcends the individual and assumes a vaster cosmic dimension of meaning. The repetition in the last verse of the Upanishad is similar.

In summary, the Kena Upanishad compels us to inquire how it is that we perceive anything. It confronts us with fundamental questions about the mystery of perception and finally indicates the mystery of ourselves. It concludes by saying that mystery is *Brahman*. It cannot be said to be known since we cannot objectify It. Nor can it be said to be unknown since we experience It every moment, nay, It is the cause of our experience. Thus It is more than the known and the unknown.

THE KATHA UPANISHAD

The Katha Upanishad is a dialogue between a young boy named Naciketas and Yama, the "God of Death." It gained some popularity in the nineteenth century when Edwin Arnold gave a free style translation of it and published it under the title "The Secret of Death." Some may have also heard of Somerset Maugham's "The Razor's Edge." The title is taken from a verse in the Katha Upanishad.

The Upanishad opens in the form of a story with the father of Naciketas performing a seemingly meritorious act of giving sacrificial gifts, where his most valued possessions are given away. We are to infer that his father was performing the sacrifice grudgingly when Naciketas approached his father and asked him, "To whom shall you give me?" At first, the father ignored his son's question, but being asked a second and third time, he replied in a fit of short temper, "I give you unto Death." So the boy went to Yama, the God of Death and waited there three days since Yama was not home. When Yama returned and found Naciketas waiting, he said to him, "I am sorry I was not home and you have waited here three days without food or shelter. To make up for it, I shall offer you three boons." So Naciketas said that his first boon is that his father have peace of mind. Yama said, "So be it." His second boon was to understand the nature of the religious sacrifice his father was performing. His father thought this sacrifice would enable him to go to heaven.

In explaining this part of the Upanishad and commenting generally on the notion of "heaven" found in many cultures, Vivekandanda writes,

> Now we have seen that the oldest idea which we got in the Samhita portion of the Vedas was only about heaven where they had bright bodies and lived with the fathers. Gradually other ideas came, but they were not satisfying; there was still need for something higher. Living in heaven would not be very different from life in this world. At best, it would only be a very healthy rich man's life, with plenty of sense-enjoyments and a sound body which knows no disease. It would be this material world, only a little more refined; and we have seen the difficulty that the external material world can never solve the problem. So no heaven can solve the problem. If this world cannot solve the problem, no multiplication of this world can do so, because we must always remember that matter is only an infinitesimal part of the phenomena of nature. The vast part of phenomena which we actually see is not matter. For instance, in every moment of our life what a great part is played by thought and feeling, compared with the

> material phenomena outside! How vast is this internal world with its tremendous activity! The sense phenomena are very small compared with it. The heaven solution commits this mistake; it insists that the whole of phenomena is only in touch, taste, sight, etc. So this idea of heaven did not give full satisfaction to all. Yet Naciketas asks, as the second boon, about some sacrifice through which people might attain to this heaven. There was an idea in the Vedas that these sacrifices pleased the gods and took human beings to heaven. (Vol. 2, 158)

So Naciketas inquired about details of this social custom of the time, and his second boon was granted.

With the third boon, the Upanishad proper begins. Naciketas asks, "When a man dies, some say he is, others that he is not. I desire to understand the mystery of death." Yama was surprised. He was happy to grant the other boons and so he said, "Even the gods had doubts on this point and it is not easy to understand. Very subtle is the matter. Please choose another boon."

Naciketas does not relent. "You say even the gods had doubts on this point. Where will I find another teacher like you? No other boon will I have except this one!" And Yama replied, "Please choose long life, wealth and health on this planet, heavenly maidens and many more pleasures. I will make you lord of the Earth, but please do not ask this question!" Still Naciketas does not relent. "These things are ephemeral. Even the powers of the body wear away. Keep your damsels, song and dance. Please reveal to me the mystery of death."

In this passage, we see what tremendous determination is needed for one who wants to probe deeper. Naciketas has analyzed the temporal nature of all enjoyment and has rejected it. These verses are trying to convey to us the mental and emotional attitudes with which we must approach this higher knowledge. In this context, it is fitting that the seeker of knowledge is a child yet mature. Naciketas is symbolic of the childlike simplicity needed for a seeker of truth.

Now the Upanishad begins. Yama says,

> The better, *sreyas* is one thing, and the pleasant, *preyas* quite another. Of these two, the wise choose the better rather than the pleasant and the fool chooses the pleasant. I am impressed by your desire for higher knowledge Naciketas. Many are they who living in the midst of ignorance but considering themselves wise, go round and round deluded, like the blind leading the blind. Those that think only the sensory world exists, come under my sway again and again. Even to

hear of the *ātman* is not available to many; many having heard of It cannot comprehend. Wonderful is Its teacher and equally wonderful is Its pupil.

āscaryo vaktā kusalosya labdhā
āscaryo jnāta kusalānusistah.

Yama continues, "The *ātman* is subtler than the subtlest and beyond logic and reason. It cannot be reached by vain argumentation and discourse. The wise relinquish both joy and sorrow and develop meditation on the *ātman*, the ancient effulgent One, hard to see, very profound, hidden in experience, seated in the heart and animating this body." At this point, Naciketas seeks further elaboration on what Yama has just taught. He asks, "You say It is beyond virtue and vice, beyond cause and effect, and different from the past, present or the future. Please explain to me That."

Yama responds, "The goal of which the Vedas speak, the goal for which the sages practice austerities, that goal is Om. This syllable represents *Brahman.* It is the highest syllable. By meditating upon it, one gets nearer to That."

Here we come to an important idea in Indian philosophy, namely the philosophy of the word. Yama introduces the word Om (which is pronounced like "om" in "home") to signify *Brahman.* To be more accurate, the "soundless" aspect of Om symbolizes *Brahman.* In explaining this idea, Ranganathananda writes,

> A word and its meaning are inseparable.... History has shown that human knowledge in various fields has been greatly advanced by the invention and use of symbols. Language itself is a collection of symbols. Quantities and numbers become simplified when expressed through symbols. When ancient Indian scientific thought invented the numerals, including the zero sign, the algebraic symbols and the decimal system, it helped immensely to simplify mathematics and its handling of immense physical quantities. When the Indian sages realised the Absolute and the Unconditioned in the unity of *Brahman* and *Atman*, they felt the need for an adequate symbol to communicate so incommunicable a truth.... In their search, they came across the sound symbol *Om*.... They analysed this sound *Om* and discovered that, of all sounds, it possessed the quality of universality. It is composed of sounds of three letters of *akāra*, *ukāra*, and *makāra*.... Hence the combination of these three sounds into *Om* is also a combination of all sounds that one can possibly utter.... *Om* in its uttered form finally merges into its unuttered form; all uttered

> sound merges into the silence of the soundless. This soundless or *amātra* aspect of *Om* is the symbol of *Brahman* in its transcendental aspect, beyond time, space and causality. (373)

Thus, Om is the matrix of all sounds including the "soundless" aspect of sound.

Yama continues his teaching: "The *ātman* is not born nor does It die. It has not come from anything nor has anything come from It. It is unborn, eternal, ever-lasting and ancient. It is not slain when the body is slain. If the slayer thinks that he slays and the slain thinks himself slain, neither of these understand that the *ātman* does not slay nor is it slayed."

Two verses re-appear later in the Bhagavad Gita, with minor modifications, as verses 18 and 19 in Chapter 2. They have inspired many poets and thinkers. An example is the nineteenth-century American philosopher and writer Ralph Waldo Emerson, who wrote in his poem "Brahma":

> *If the red slayer thinks he slays*
> *Or if the slain thinks he is slain,*
> *They know not well the subtle ways*
> *I keep and pass and turn again.*

In the next three verses, Yama tries to explain to Naciketas the notion of the *ātman*.

> It is smaller than the smallest, greater than the greatest, and is ever present in the heart of all creatures. One who is free from selfish desires realizes the *ātman* through a serene mind and thus becomes free from sorrow. Realizing the *ātman* as bodiless in the embodied, the changeless in the changing, infinite and all-pervading, the wise one does not grieve. This *ātman* is not known through study, nor by the intellect, nor through hearing. It is revealed to one whom It chooses to reveal itself. One who has not desisted from bad conduct, nor one whose senses are not under control, nor one whose mind is not tranquil and concentrated, can ever realise the *ātman*.

The last sentence requires some clarification. There are some necessary conditions for the realization of the *ātman* and these are given in the last verse. But they are not sufficient. That is the import of the second last sentence indicating that the *ātman* reveals itself to one who It chooses. The *ātman* is not bound by any rules.

Now Yama introduces the imagery of the chariot. "The *ātman* is the master of the chariot and the body is the chariot. Know the intellect, *buddhi* as the charioteer and the mind *manas* as the reins. The sense organs, they say, are the horses and the sense objects are roads they travel over. They call the *atman* the 'enjoyer' or 'experiencer' when It is united with the body, senses and the mind."

Yama continues, "For him who is devoid of understanding, with a mind not disciplined, the sense organs become uncontrolled like the unruly horses of the chariot. He does not reach the goal but returns to the world of birth and death again. But he who has proper understanding, mind under control, ever pure, reaches the goal."

In the penultimate verse, we find reference to the theory of transmigration. The idea is that until the final awareness of *Brahman* is experienced, the psyche must travel through the cycle of birth and death. This theory later found its way into other philosophies and cultures, most notably in the writings of Plato.

Now Yama organizes the bodily functions in a hierarchy. He says, "Higher than the senses are the sense objects. Higher than the sense objects is the mind. Reason or *buddhi* is higher than the mind. The *mahat* or awareness is higher than *buddhi*. Higher than the *mahat* is *avyakta*, undifferentiated nature. The infinite Self, *purusa* is greater than *avyakta* and the *purusa* is the supreme goal. There is nothing higher than This."

In the previous verses, we may ask how can the sense objects be higher than the senses? The precise term, *artha*, used in that verse refers not to objects visible to the eye but to their nuclear dimension, the *tanmātra* as the Vedānta philosophy later expresses it. Undifferentiated nature or *avyakta* is that which has not manifested but is said to be the combined energies of all causes and effects. *Purusa* is an alternate name for *Brahman* or *ātman*. Thus, the hierarchy represents a gradation from gross matter to subtle matter, its atomic level and beyond.

"The *atman* is hidden in all beings and is not manifest to all," says Yama.

> But it can be realized by refined reason and inquiry. The seeker of knowledge should merge the speech in the mind, the mind in the *buddhi*, the *buddhi* in the *mahat*, and the *mahat* in the *ātman*, the abode of Peace. Arise, awake and enlighten yourself by approaching the great teachers. The sages say the path is difficult to walk upon, as sharp as the razor's edge. By realizing That which is beyond sound, beyond touch, beyond form, imperishable, beyond taste, eternal, and beyond the sense of smell, without beginning, without end, one is liberated from the jaws of death.

Let us observe here that these verses emphasize that the *ātman* can be realized by transcending reason through inquiry. So we must not abandon reason but push it further. How to do this is learned from the teachers.

Here again, the perennial tradition of how knowledge is handed down from generation to generation emphasizes the theme that only another life can transmit the instruction.

Now Yama begins a detailed exposition. "The sensory organs look outward and thus, there is a tendency to look outward and not within. A certain sage, desirous of immortality, turned his mind and senses inward, and realized the *ātman.* The childish go after external pleasures and fall into the snare of death. But the wise, seeking immortality, do not crave for things in this changing world."

Now begin a series of verses reminiscent of the poetry of the Kena Upanishad.

> That by which one cognizes form, taste, smell, sound and touch. This is verily That. Having realized the *ātman* which perceives the dream and waking states, the *dhira,* sage, does not grieve. The sage realizes the *ātman* as the enjoyer, the sustainer of life, ever near, the knower of the past and the future. This is verily That.... What indeed is here is there. What is there is here. He who sees things differently goes from death to death. By mind alone is this realization to be attained. There is no difference here at all. He who sees things differently goes from death to death.

A series of examples follow that illustrate how we are to meditate upon the *ātman.* Observe again that the instruction is by analogy. Yama says, "Just as fire is one force, but assumes various forms, so also That appears to have various forms. As the air is one but assumes various forms so also That appears to have various forms. As the sun is the eye of the whole world, is never tainted by the faults of the eyes, so also the *ātman* is not tainted by the misery of the world because It is transcendent."

After these illustrations, Yama gives the precise technique that later becomes the philosophy of *yoga.* "When the five senses are indrawn and the mind is silent, and even the *buddhi,* reason, does not stir, the sages say that is the highest state. That state is called *yoga.* The *yogi* must be vigilant, for *yoga* can be had and lost."

Yoga is the general method of concentration. Until we are established in that, we must be vigilant since concentration, as we all know, can be lost when it is not deep enough. In deep concentration, we are not so easily distracted.

Now come two verses that are extremely important. They resonate the theme of *sraddhā* or faith, which we mentioned earlier. But this faith is not a religious faith or belief but rather a two-fold faith of the genuine seeker of knowledge. This is a faith that there is order hidden in the universe and secondly, that we have the ability to discover it. This is the essence of scientific inquiry and echoes the quotation attributed to Einstein, "The most incomprehensible thing about this universe is that it is comprehensible."[1] Yama teaches Naciketas the secret: "It cannot be attained through speech, nor through mind nor through the eye. How can It be known then apart from those sages who say, 'It is'? Between the two views of Reality as existence and non-existence, Reality can be realized through the view of existence alone. Its transcendent nature becomes inwardly revealed to one who approaches It as existing."

At first glance, this may seem to be a form of self-hypnosis. Yet upon closer examination, we find it is actually de-hypnosis since we are already hypnotized through social conditioning. A century ago, when Vivekananda was lecturing at Harvard University, he was asked this very question. He replied,

> You are hypnotised already, and you should... de-hypnotise yourself. "There the sun cannot illumine, nor the moon, nor the stars; the flash of lightning cannot illumine That, what to speak of the mortal fire! That shining, everything else shines" (Katha Up. 2.2.15). That is not hypnotisation, but dehypnotisation. It... is the only system that more or less understands that hypnotism comes with every form of dualism. But the [non-dualist] says, throw away even the Vedas, throw away even the Personal God, throw away even the universe, throw away even your own body and mind, and let nothing remain, in order to get rid of hypnotism perfectly. (Vol. 5, 303-04)

Yama concludes, "When all selfish desires that dwell in the heart are removed from their moorings, the sage becomes immortal and attains *Brahman* in this very life. When, in this very life, all the knots of the heart are rent asunder, the sage becomes immortal. This is the teaching of the Upanishad. Hundred and one are the nerves of the heart; of them, one extends to the crown of the head. Going upwards through that nerve, one gains immortality." The reference to the nerve that "extends to the crown of the head" is the *sushumna* nerve that later reappears in the yoga philosophy of Patanjali that we will discuss in subsequent chapters.

The Upanishad ends with the following verse:

> Receiving this teaching from Yama, Naciketas became free from death and attained *Brahman*. So will others who also realise the *ātman* within.

1 The reference usually given for this is an article Einstein wrote in German, but in the article's first publication, in English translation, the quotation actually is "One may say 'the eternal mystery of the world is its comprehensibility'" (351).

4

PRASNA AND MUNDAKA UPANISHADS

THE PRASNA UPANISHAD

The word *prasna* means "question" in Sanskrit. The Prasna Upanishad is a series of six questions asked by students to the sage Pippalāda. The opening verses are significant. When the students approach the sage for instruction, the sage says to them: "Live with me in this hermitage for one year, practicing self-control and austerity with faith (*sraddhā*). Then ask me questions and if I can answer, I will try to answer."

Even the ability to ask intelligent questions requires mental and physical preparation. We cannot rush into them. After posing the question, we must also have the ability to receive the answer. These abilities, according to the sage, can be acquired through self-control (*brahmācharya*) and austerity (*tapas*). The word *brahmācharya* is often translated as chastity or continence, however, its precise meaning is revealed by breaking the word into its component parts: *brahmā* and *ācharya*. The first word indicates the universal awareness and is one we have met before. The second, is derived from āchāra meaning conduct, or more precisely, a regulated way of living guided by self-discipline. Thus etymologically, *brahmācharya* means regulated self-discipline to realize *Brahman*, or universal awareness. However, there is more to the meaning of this word.

The fundamental teaching of the Upanishads is that the human being is not separate from the universe, but only a part of it, just as a wave is a part of the ocean. Aurobindo elaborates as follows:

> An infinite energy... pervades the world, pours itself into every name and form, and the clod, the plant, the insect, the animal, the man are, in their phenomenal existence, merely more or less efficient *ādhāras* [vehicles, vessels or supports of this energy]. We are each of us a dynamo into which waves of that energy have been generated and stored, and are being perpetually conserved, used up and replenished. The same force which moves in the star and the planet, moves in us, and all our thought and action are merely its play and born of the complexity of its functionings. There are processes by which man can increase his capacity as an *ādhāra*. There are processes by which he can clear of obstructions the channel of communication between himself and the universal energy and bring greater and greater stores of it pouring into his soul and brain and body. (Vol. 3, 332)

Thus, the essential principle of *brahmācharya* is the elimination of distractions and the focussing of energies for a higher purpose. We see this even in modern life. We cannot spend all our time watching television and at the same time expect to prove a great mathematical theorem, or compose a literary epic. Proficiency in anything requires self-discipline and regular practice. This is the message of the sage in the opening verse of the Upanishad.

The first question is "How did creation come into being?" The sage Pippalāda answers:

> The Father of Creation (*prajāpati*) desired offspring and performed austerity (*tapas*) out of which life (*prāna*), or universal energy, and matter (*rayi*) have come. It thought, "The combination of these two will produce creatures in many ways." Thus everything we see is the combination of matter (*rayi*) and energy (*prāna*). The sun is life, matter is the moon. Matter is all this, whatever is formed and formless. Therefore, whatever is formed is matter. The rising sun pervades the east and fills with energy all the beings that are there. Likewise, when the sun's rays fall on the south, the west, the north, the zenith, the nadir, and the intermediate regions, all beings there are energised. *Prāna* is the soul of the universe; it is the light that animates and illumines everything.

Then another student approaches the teacher and asks the second question. "What are the energies that sustain the body?" To him, the sage replies:

> Ether, Air, Fire, Water and Earth, as well as Speech, Mind, Sight and Hearing sustain this body. But all of these are supported by *prāna*,

> the Life Principle. As fire, Prāna burns; as the sun, he shines. As cloud, he rains. As Indra, he rules the gods; as wind, he blows. As the moon, he nourishes all. He is all that is visible and all that is invisible. Prāna moves in the womb. As breath, it lives in the body. As fire, it transports energy to all the organs. Prāna protects us as a mother protects her children.

Ether is to be interpreted as space. The message is that the manifestation of life is everywhere, in the sun, in the clouds, in the wind. The moon symbolizes matter, as signalled in the earlier verse, and so it is that matter, or more precisely, food, "nourishes all." Now the third student approaches the teacher and asks,

> How did *prāna* come about? How did it enter the body? How does it distribute itself there? How does it go out of the body? How does it hold together the body, mind and the sense organs?

This student is clever. He manages to ask several questions and compress them into one. We may assume that this is one of the fruits of his year-long austerity. The sage responds by saying:

> You ask very difficult questions, but since you are a sincere seeker of Truth, I will try to answer. *Prāna* is born of the *ātman* but like a man and his shadow, the *ātman* and *prāna* are inseparable. It enters the body by the action of Mind or *manas*. *Prāna* itself may be divided into five parts, *prāna*, *apāna*, *vyāna*, *udāna* and *samāna*. *Prāna*, the first, dwells in the upper body, in the eye, ear, mouth and nose. The *apāna* dwells in the lower, in the excretory organs, *samāna* dwells in the middle, in the abdomen. In the heart are 101 arteries, from each of which emanate 100 smaller arteries. From each of these emanate 72,000 branch arteries. *Vyāna* dwells in them. In the nerve located in the center of the spine dwells *udāna*, leads the virtuous man upward, the sinful man downward and one who is both into the world of beings.

In explaining these verses, Aurobindo writes:

> Prana manifests itself in five distinct vital powers, to which the names, Prana, Samana, Vyana, Apana and Udana have been given by the ancient writers. Prana, the vital force par excellence has its seat in the upper part of the body and conducts all mental operations, the

> indrawing and outdrawing of breath and induction of food. Samana, seated centrally in the body, balances, equalises and harmonises the vital operations and is the agent for the assimilation of food. Vyana pervades the whole body; on it depends the circulation of the blood and distribution of the essential part of the food eaten and digested throughout the body. Apana, situated in the lower part of the trunk, presides over the lower functions, especially over the emission of such parts of the food as are rejected by the body and over procreation; it is intimately connected with the processes of decay and death. Udana is the vital power which connects bodily life with the spiritual element in man. (Vol. 7, 221)

Thus, the five-fold *prāna* controls the nervous energies of the human being.

Then the fourth student approaches the teacher and asks, "When a man's body is asleep, who is it within that sleeps? Who is awake, and who is it that sees the dreams?" The teacher replies:

> When a man sleeps, the sensory organs are drawn in. However, the *prānas*, the fires of life, sleep not. The mind is led nearer to the *ātman*. In the dream state, the mind revives its past impressions. Whatever it has seen, it sees again. Whatever it has heard, it hears again. Whatever it has enjoyed in various places, it enjoys again. What has been seen and not seen, heard and not heard, enjoyed and not enjoyed, both the real and unreal, the mind sees all and becomes the all.

This passage represents an early attempt at dream analysis. At the same time, it makes the vital point that while we sleep, the digestion, assimilation, circulation of blood and other bodily functions continue, so the *prāna* never sleeps. The last line, "the mind becomes the all" is significant. In the dream state, we forget that we are all the characters of the dream. Modern in-depth psychology has shown that all the dream symbols are aspects of our own mind, whether individual or collective. However, the sage does not seem to attach too much importance to these dream symbols. His main point is to draw our attention to the *prāna* which never sleeps.

The sage continues:

> When the mind is overpowered by deep sleep, it dreams no more. As the birds fly to the tree for rest, even so do all these things fly to the *ātman* for rest. Earth and its subtle essence, water and its subtle essence, fire and its subtle essence, air and its subtle essence, ether and its subtle

> essence, the eye and what it sees, the ear and what it hears, the nose and what it smells, the tongue and what it tastes, the skin and what it touches, the voice and what it speaks, the hands and what they grasp, the feet and what they walk on, the mind and what it perceives, the intellect and what it understands, the ego and what it appropriates, the heart and what it loves, the light and what it illuminates, the energy and what it binds together, are what is meant by all these things. It is the *ātman* that sees, hears, smells, thinks, knows and acts. That is *Brahman*, the essence of knowledge. He who knows this becomes omniscient.

Then the fifth student approaches the teacher with the question, "If one meditates on *Om* until the end of one's life, what does one gain by that?" The master replies:

> Om is the symbol of *Brahman*, both conditioned and unconditioned, the personal and impersonal. By meditating on Om, the wise reach one or the other. If one meditates only on one aspect (ā), the verses of the Rg Veda lead one into the world of beings with austerity, self-control and faith and achieves greatness. If one meditates on two aspects of Om (*au*), the verses of the Yajur Veda lead one to the Lunar world (heaven). But he who meditates on Om with full awareness of all three aspects, the verses of the Sama Veda lead one into union with *Brahman*. He sees the Being that dwells in the body, which is higher than the highest life. That is the highest state, tranquil, unchanging, immortal, fearless and supreme.

This requires some explanation. As we have seen in the second chapter, the hymns of the Rg Veda pertained first to natural forces and then led to an inner psychological significance. The hymns of Yajur Veda were more concerned with sacrificial duties. Neither of these lead us to the highest state, the verse declares. Only the Sama Veda combined with meditation on Om with full awareness leads one to the highest state. When we look at the verses of the Sama Veda, we find an emphasis on the glory of the brain and the workings of the *prānas*. The opening chapter of the Sama Veda is again devoted to the praise of Agni, the Cosmic Will. Thus, to turn the mind inward, one must focus first on the *prānas* and the workings of the brain.

The last student approaches the sage and asks him the following. "A prince once asked me if I knew the person with sixteen parts. I said I knew him not. Then the prince rode away. Can you please tell me where is that person?" To him, the sage replies, "You are the person of sixteen parts.

You are life (*prāna*), faith (*sraddhā*), ether, air, light, water, earth, sensory system, mind, food, strength, austerity, knowledge, works, the world, and in the world, name." As we shall see later in the Sāmkhya system of philosophy, the sixteen parts are said to comprise the subtle body, or *linga sarira*, with some modifications.

> The *ātman* dwells within the body, in every creature. As the flowing rivers tend towards the ocean and on reaching that, merge into it, losing their name and form, so also all living things flow towards the ocean of *Brahman* and merge into That, losing their name and form. That is without parts, and immortal. There is no state higher than this.

The students then make obeissances to their teacher and salute him for dispelling their ignorance.

THE MUNDAKA UPANISHAD

The word *mundaka* is derived from the root word *mund* meaning to shave. The idea is that the Upanishad shaves off our ignorance. This Upanishad begins by making a distinction between higher knowledge *parāvidya* and lower knowledge *aparāvidya*. It then teaches that through *parāvidya*, we can know *Brahman*.

After describing how knowledge has been handed down from generation to generation, we are told that a respected householder, Sounaka, approaches the teacher Angiras with the question: "Sir, what is that by knowing which everything else becomes known?" The sage replies:

> The knowers of *Brahman* declare that there are two kinds of knowledge, one higher and the other lower. The knowledge of the Vedas, phonetics, grammar, etymology, astronomy and so forth are considered to be lower. The higher is the knowledge of That by which one knows the changeless reality. That transcends the senses, it is uncaused, it is undefinable, it has neither eyes nor ears, hands nor feet, it is all-pervading, subtler than the subtle, and the wise perceive it as the source of all. As the spider sends forth its thread and draws it in, as herbs grow on the earth, as hair grows on the body of a living person, so also this universe arises from *Brahman*.

As emphasized earlier, one of the fundamental themes of the Upanishads is to arrive at the essence of knowledge. The question "What is that by knowing which everything else becomes known?" is taken up again in the Chāndogya Upanishad.

The sage continues:

> Abiding in the midst of ignorance, wise in their own esteem, thinking themselves to be learned, the deluded go round and round, like the blind led by the blind. Ceremonials and meritorious work do not lead to a knowledge of That. The wise, who are self-controlled and tranquil, who are contented in spirit, who practice austerity and meditation in solitude and silence realise the changeless Self. Let a person devoted to spiritual life examine carefully the ephemeral nature of worldly enjoyment, whether here or hereafter, and then give no thought to these transient things. Let him then approach a learned teacher (*guru*) who is devoted to *Brahman*. To such a disciple who approaches reverently, the learned sage imparts the knowledge of the changeless Self.

In these verses, some prerequisites are delineated. Though the student may not understand knowledge, it is expected that he recognize ignorance, which is here defined as that which is changing and transitory. The student must genuinely seek knowledge, not as a diversion for a day, but as a passionate lifelong quest. His direction must be fixed and he must be ready to practice austerity and meditation, the Upanishad says.

The sage continues:

> As innumerable sparks fly upward from the blazing fire, so also all things have come from the Imperishable. That Being is self-luminous and formless. It dwells within and It dwells without. It is unborn, pure, greater than the greatest, without breath, and without mind. From That are born breath (*prāna*), mind, the sensory organs, ether, air, fire, water and the earth and It binds all these together. Fire is Its head. The sun and moon, Its eyes. The regions of space, Its ears. Its speech is that which is revealed in the Vedas. The air is Its life. The universe, Its heart. Out of Its feet, the earth is born. Indeed, It is the innermost self of all beings. That is to be known, so therefore, know That.

As an introduction to the higher teaching, the sage begins with images the student is already familiar with and reveals their cosmic dimension. How to go deeper? The sage Angiras continues:

> Taking as the bow the great weapon of the Upanishad, one should place the arrow of devotion, and drawing it with a mind absorbed in

> meditation on That, know that That is the target. The syllable Om is the bow, the arrow is the individual being and *Brahman* is the target. Merge the arrow in the target. The arteries of the body merge together at the center of the heart like the spokes of a wheel merge at the center. The Self dwells within the center. Meditate on That as Om. That is the light of lights. The sun does not illumine That, nor the moon, nor the stars, nor the lightning, nor the fires kindled upon the earth. That is the one light that gives light to all. That shining, everything shines. *Brahman* is spread everywhere and is indeed this universe. That is the supreme.

The essential idea is that *Brahman* is not something remote and distant, but rather something we have all been familiar with and have been intimate with. We are to meditate on the symbol Om and recognize the energies manifesting both within and without our body are from That.

To convey a clearer idea of our relation to *Brahman*, the sage proceeds to give the following celebrated example:

> Two birds of golden plumage are perched upon the tree of life. Of these two, one eats the sweet and bitter fruits of life. The other, tasting neither, observes calmly. The former is the individual self, deluded by forgetfulness of its identity with the Supreme Self. Bewildered by the ego, it is sometimes happy and sometimes sad. The latter is the *ātman*. When the former realises its identity with the latter, it grieves no more. The *ātman* is the life shining in every creature. It is within this body and is of the nature of light and purity. It is attainable by austerity, by self-control and by the practice of truth. Truth alone conquers, not untruth. By truth is stretched the pathway to the gods (*devas*), or luminous energies. It is vast, divine, beyond any mental conception, subtler than the subtle, farther than the far, nearer than the near. Yet, It can be perceived, for It is here, hidden in the secret heart. The *ātman* is not seen by the eye. Speech cannot grasp It nor the sensory organs. Neither can it be attained by austerity, or by work. However, when one's nature is refined and purified through meditation, It can be perceived. The subtle self is to be known by thought. Our thoughts are pervaded by the sensory impressions. When the thought is purified, the *ātman* shines forth. He who entertains desires, brooding over them, is born again and again. But he who has gone beyond desire, attains liberation in this very life.

In case the student feels that the way of going beyond desire is through inaction, or any form of mortification, the sage warns us: "The *ātman* cannot be attained without strength": *nāyam ātmā balahīnena labhyah.*

> It is not attained through heedlessness, nor through austerity without a definite aim. But he who strives through proper means can enter the abode of *Brahman.* Having known the Self, the sages are filled with joy. Blessed are they who are tranquil, free from passion. Realizing the all-pervading *Brahman* everywhere, the sages enter into That, the Self of all.

And now in verses that are reminiscent of the verses in the Prasna Upanishad, the sage continues:

> The fifteen parts and the sensory organs, as well as the deeds, merge into the Self. Just as the flowing rivers merge into the ocean casting off name and form, even so the knower of *Brahman* merges the individual awareness into the universal awareness, that luminous Being, higher than the highest.

5

THE MĀNDUKYA, TAITTIRĪYA, AND CHĀNDOGYA UPANISHADS

THE MĀNDUKYA UPANISHAD

This Upanishad is named after the sage *Māndūkya* who taught about the four states of consciousness, namely, waking, dreaming, deep sleep and the fourth, *turīya*, which is the highest. All four are explained through the mystic syllable Om, but the Upanishad is very careful not to call *turīya* a state, for that would be defining it. With this understanding, we should proceed.

The Māndukya Upanishad is the shortest, comprising only 12 verses. Apart from its subtle teaching, it has become famous because of Gaudapada's commentary upon it, entitled the *Kārika*. Gaudapada lived in the sixth century CE and is said to be the guru, or teacher, of Govindapada who was teacher of the more famous Shankaracharya. Though the philosophy of *advaita*, or non-dualism, is the message of the Upanishads, the elaborate exposition and its systematization belongs to Shankara's school, whose philosophy we will discuss in later chapters.

Here is the text in free translation:

> Om. This syllable is all this. All that is past, present and future is also Om. And whatever is beyond this threefold time, that too is Om. All this is verily *Brahman*. The Self within is *Brahman*: *ayam ātmābrahma*. The Self has four aspects. The first is the waking state (*jāgrat*), outwardly cognitive, having seven limbs, nineteen mouths and experiencing the gross material objects.

The seven limbs do not pertain to the human body but to the "cosmic body" named *vaisvānara*. They are enumerated in verse V.18.2 of the Chāndogya Upanishad (further discussed below): "The heavens are his head, the sun his eyes, the air his breath, the fire his heart, the water his stomach, the earth his feet, and space his body." These, the seven limbs referred to in the opening verse of the Māndukya Upanishad, encompass the manifested universe. The nineteen "mouths" are the five sense organs, the five organs of action (walking, talking, expelling, procreating, and handling), the five *prānas*, the mind, the intellect, the ego sense, and thought (*citta*).

The Māndukya Upanishad continues. "The second is the dream state (*svapna*), inwardly cognitive, also having seven limbs and nineteen mouths. In this state, one experiences the subtle impressions of the mind." The verse informs us that in the internal dream world, there are counterparts to everything we meet in the external. Whatever we experience in the waking state, we can also experience in the dream state, but clearly not with the same apparatus.

> The third state is deep sleep, or dreamless sleep (*prājna*). As the darkness of night covers the day and the visible world seems to disappear, so also in dreamless sleep, the veil of unconsciousness envelops the thought and knowledge, and the subtle impressions of the mind apparently vanish. It is a mass of cognition, it is blissful, its face is thought. In this state, the person is said to be blissful since neither anxiety or strife are experienced. *Prājna*[1] rules over all, knows all things and is the inner controller. It is the origin and goal of all. The fourth, *turīya*, is not inwardly cognitive, nor outwardly cognitive, not both-wise cognitive. It is not a cognition mass, not cognitive, not noncognitive, unseen, incapable of being spoken of, ungraspable, without any distinctive marks, unthinkable, unnameable, the essence of the knowledge of the one self, that into which the world is resolved, the peaceful, the benign, the non-dual. That is the *ātman*. That is to be realised.

Here we see for the first time, a word to indicate a state beyond deep sleep. The stages of waking and dream states are bound by cause and effect. *Prājna* or deep sleep state is cause alone. The final, *turīya*, is beyond cause and effect. In his *Kārika*, Gaudapada writes, "*Prājna* or the deep sleep state does not know itself; it does not know anything else either. It does not know the real or the unreal. It does not know anything. *Turīya*, the fourth, however,

1 Prajnā (p. 73) refers to universal intelligence. It is different from Prājna used here to denote the deep sleep state.

knows everything and knows it always." In the *prājna* state, we are totally unconscious. In the *turīya*, you are beyond consciousness and unconsciousness. You are "superconscious." *Prājna* and *turīya* have one thing in common. Neither have perception of the phenomenal world. However, *prajna* is sleep because it involves ignorance while *turīya* is free from ignorance.

After having defined these three states and *turīya*, the "state" that underlies them all and also transcends them, the Upanishad continues,

> This is the *ātman* symbolised by *omkara*, which has four parts. The *akāra*, or the ā sound of Om, represents the waking state and is the root of the words *āpti* meaning "obtaining" and *ādimatvā*, meaning "being first." Whoever knows this obtains all desires and is the best of all. The *ukāra*, or the ū sound of Om represents the dream state and is the root of the words *utkarsa*, meaning "exaltation" and *ubhayatva* meaning "intermediateness." He who knows this excels in his power of understanding, in the continuity of knowledge and becomes equal to that understanding. No one in his lineage is born ignorant of *Brahman*.

This requires some explanation. The waking state includes the manifested universe. If we understand the nature of this universe in its entirety, there is no desire we cannot fulfill. One who understands this universe totally becomes "best of all." So the first part of these verses is clear. The second part is deeper. It involves the knowledge of the dream state. As was pointed out in the previous verses, the realm of cause and effect is contained in the waking and dream states. Modern psychoanalysis has made a serious attempt in trying to understand behaviour by analyzing the dream state. The writings of Carl Gustav Jung in particular point to the "collective unconscious" where archetypal symbols exert a powerful influence over us, whether we are aware of this or not. Thus, to understand the waking state, we need to understand the dream state too, and this is the meaning of "continuity of knowledge." One who understands both, becomes equal to that understanding. The "lineage" referred to in the verse means the succession of students who learn from such an individual. This lineage is aware of a deeper dimension of reality, since neither of these two states of consciousness can explain the phenomenon of life completely.

"*Prājna*," the Upanishad concludes, "is the state of deep sleep and is represented by *makāra*, or the *m* sound of Om. It is derived from the root *mi*, meaning 'to measure' or 'merging.' Whoever knows this measures all this and merges all this into oneself. The fourth, *turīya*, is represented by the silence after Om, the *amātra*, which has no elements, which cannot be spoken of, into which the world is resolved, benign, non-dual. Thus the syllable Om is the *ātman*. Whoever knows this realises *Brahman*."

As remarked earlier, Gaudapada's *Kārika* is important for being the first systematic commentary of the Mandukya Upanishad and at the same time creating the foundation for *advaita* as taught by Shankara. The *Kārika* is famous for its "snake and the rope" example. Gaudapada says that just as we realize upon awaking that the dream images were simply our imagination, so we will realize that this world was simply our mental projection when we "awake" to the awareness of *Brahman*. "In a dark place," Gaudapada writes, "you see a rope, but you are not sure you are seeing a rope. You think you are seeing a snake, a jet of water, or some such thing. All these are illusions. There is nothing but a rope and you have the illusion that the rope is a snake." Because of this illusion, fear comes and a host of other mirages. The snake has no existence independent of the rope. Similarly, the world has no existence independent of *Brahman*." Thus, the relation between the world we see and *Brahman* is precisely the same relation between the snake and rope. As is the gulf between the waking and dream states, so is the difference between all the three states and *turīya*.

THE TAITTIRĪYA UPANISHAD

The Taittirīya Upanishad is often called the "convocation address" since it gives the departing students a list of ethical principles to follow for life. It is also known for its description of five layers, or *koshas* of the human being, namely, food, breath, mind, intellect, and bliss. There is also delineated a "calculus of bliss," leading up to the ultimate *Brahman*.

The Upanishad begins with a prayer for protection for both the teacher and the taught. The second verse talks about pronunciation: "Letters or sounds, pitch, quantity, force or stress, articulation and combination. These are the principles of pronunciation. This world is one of combinations. Here are the great combinations. The earth is the prior form. The heaven is the latter form. The ether is their junction and the air is the connection."

Pronunciation, intonation, word emphasis and combination are important for meaning, for communication between teacher and student. Because language is a matter of combination of words, which are in turn, combinations of sounds, the principles of combination are singled out for further examination. The sage proceeds to show how these principles are manifest in the world around us. He begins with the earth as not being separate from the heavens, but rather connected with it by the link of the atmosphere.

As emphasized earlier, the message of the Upanishads is the teaching of *Brahman*. Though it is beyond mind, one can enlarge one's view of oneself and the world around so as to experience It. "Now as to knowledge," the sage continues, "the teacher is the prior form, the student is the latter form, knowledge is their junction and instruction is the connection." In this verse, the sage conveys a cosmic image to the student with regards to instruction. It is not an isolated event, but part of the cosmic process. We are to be aware of this dimension of meaning.

Then come verses that have given this Upanishad its subtitle as being a "convocation address." The sage instructs, "Practice virtue, do not refrain from study and teaching. Practice truth, do not refrain from study and teaching. Practice austerity (*tapas*), do not refrain from study and teaching. Practice self-control, do not refrain from study and teaching. Practice tranquility, do not refrain from study and teaching." The repeated message, *svādhyāya pravacane ca*, is important for all of us. An echo of this can be heard in the famous saying of Socrates, "An unexamined life is not worth living." We must always examine ourselves and the world around us, and never refrain from learning. At the same time, we must realize that we are part of a connecting, organic link in the transmission of knowledge so we must not refrain from passing on that legacy of learning to future generations.

Having taught the importance of study and teaching, the sage instructs his students not to be negligent of social duties,

> *Mātr devo bhava,*
> *pitr devo bhava,*
> *ācārya devo bhava,*
> *atithi devo bhava.*

> Let your mother be a god to you, let your father be a god to you, let your teacher be a god to you and let your guest be a god to you.

Here is an instruction about human relations, the essence being that we must treat people with respect. We often forget that for at least the formative years of our life the mother is our only support, our sole protector, our first teacher. Then comes the father, the teacher, and the guest. Here is also the seed of a teaching that comes later in the Bhagavad Gita in the form of *karma yoga*, whose fundamental message concerns the science of action.

Rather humbly, the sage instructs his students, "Behave properly. Do not imitate our defects. Imitate only what is good in our practices. Whatever you give, give with faith, with modesty, with sympathy. If any doubt or question arises concerning any matter, seek out the advice of the learned, the wise and after reflection, act accordingly. This is the teaching." Thus, we must not be rash in our behaviour. If any doubt arises, we may consult the wise (not the otherwise, as Plato says), and then act upon reflection. In addition to the proverbial three "Rs," reading, writing and arithmetic, we must be taught reflection.

Now the sage begins his elaborate teaching on the five-fold nature of the universe:

> From food (*annam*) have come all creatures. By food alone, they live, so food is called the healing herb. Those who worship *Brahman* as food, obtain food. The breath (*prāna*) is the life of all beings. Those who worship *Brahman* as life, attain life. Beyond the breath is the mind (*manas*), from where words return unable to attain *Brahman*. Beyond mind is understanding (*vijnāna*). All the gods worship *vijnāna* as *Brahman*. But beyond *vijnāna* is *Brahman*, the source of all things.

Here are described the five layers of personality. The outer layer is the physical body (*annamaya kosha*), the next layer, is the breath body (*prānamaya kosha*), sometimes referred to as the etheric, vital, or subtle body. The third layer is the mental body (*manomaya kosha*), beyond that is the wisdom body (*vijnānamaya kosha*), and after that is the blissful body, (*ānandamaya kosha*). To provide understanding of the extent of the bliss of *Brahman*, the sage gives us the following "calculus of bliss." He says, "Let there be a handsome youth, who is well-read, very strong, very quick and let this entire earth be his domain. We will call this one unit of bliss. A hundredfold is the bliss of the *gandharvas*, the muses of joy and pleasure. A hundredfold times more is the bliss of the divine *gandharvas*." The Upanishad continues its hierarchical succession of levels, until it reaches the bliss experienced by Indra, and then Brhaspati, and then Prajāpati. Finally, it comes to the tenth level, the bliss of *Brahman*, which is 10^{10} times more than the bliss experienced by the strong, handsome youth who has all the worldly wealth. "But equal to the bliss of *Brahman* is the bliss of a knower of *Brahman* who is not smitten by desire."

When we think of ourselves, we tend to think in terms of our bodies or at best, our minds. But there are other layers of our personality that we should reflect upon and "feed." The wisdom "sheath" or layer is very close to the "blissful sheath" and this is something we are aware of. The Upanishad thus teaches us that *Brahman* is not something very distant, but very near.

THE CHĀNDOGYA UPANISHAD

The name of the Chāndogya Upanishad is derived from the word *chandas*, which refers to a poetic metre in which it is written. Poetically expressed, the message of this Upanishad is the importance of speech and song in life. "Speech yields milk," it teaches. After having pointed out the "internal singing" that goes in our breathing system, it emphasizes that in all our singing and chanting, we must be aware of this. Otherwise, it says humorously, "our head will fall off," if we do things "heedlessly."

This is one of the longer Upanishads interspersed with many stories to illustrate its teachings. Just as the Māndukya focụssed on the meaning of Om, so also this Upanishad begins with an instruction that one should meditate on Om, as a loud chant, the *udgītha*. "The essence of all beings is the earth," it continues, "the essence of the earth is water, the essence of water is plants, the essence of plants is a person, the essence of a person is speech, the essence of speech is the hymn of the Rg Veda, the essence of the hymn is the chant, the essence of the chant is the *udgītha* which is Om. Speech and breath are held together by Om."

While the Upanishads teach us that *Brahman* is beyond mind and speech, they at the same time tell us it is very close, nearer than the near, in the world around us and in every breath of our life. The essence of a person is speech; what we think, know, and feel is revealed in our speech. In speaking, breathing plays a vital role. Speech and breath are held together by the "internal chant" of Om.

> In this body, there is an interplay of both light (*deva*) and darkness (*asura*). The gods thought that *udgītha* is the sense of smell, but as we can smell things which are both good and bad, that cannot be It. Then the gods thought *udgītha* is speech, but as we can utter both good and bad words, that cannot be It. Then the gods thought *udgītha* is the sense of sight, but as we can see both good and bad, that cannot be It. Then the gods thought *udgītha* is the sense of hearing, but as we can hear both good and bad, that cannot be It. Then the gods thought *udgītha* is mind, but as we can imagine both good and bad, that cannot be It. Then the gods thought *udgītha* as life (*prāna*) and realised that darkness could not enter *prāna*.

In this sequence of verses, we see that the student is led to see how everything is afflicted with duality, by good and bad, but finally, *prāna* is not and so we are able to understand an aspect of *Brahman* in this way.

The Upanishad continues with some specific instructions on how to meditate on this instruction:

> One may meditate on the sun as *udgītha*. Just as the *udgītha* knows no darkness, the sun knows no darkness. One should meditate on the breathing as *udgītha* since it is constantly chanting Om. As the *vīna* [a stringed instrument] sings, so is the song of the *udgītha* within. The song is all around us also. The song is in the rain. The song is in the waters. The song is in the seasons. The song is in the sounds of birds and the animals. As all leaves are held together by the branch, so also is all speech held together by Om. All this is verily Om.

The central thesis of the Upanishad is that "song" is very much a part of life and that one must commune or become one with the song. The poetic mood is a means to a higher awareness. This experience transcends knowledge. The Bengali poet and Nobel Laureate Rabindranath Tagore explains,

> Does one write poetry to explain something? It is a feeling within the heart that tries to find outside shape in a poem.... That words have meaning is just the difficulty. That is why poets have to turn and twist them in meter and rhyme, so that meaning may be held somewhat in check and feeling allowed to express itself. (*Omnibus 2*, 220-21)

He also writes:

> The main object of teaching is not to give explanations but to knock at the doors of the mind.... I can recollect many things which I did not understand, but which stirred me deeply.
>
> I was pacing the terrace of our house late in the afternoon.... I could see at once that...the effect of the evening...had come within me; its shades had obliterated my *self*.... Now, that the self was put into the background, I could see the world in its own true aspect...full of beauty and joy. (*Omnibus*, 215)

Reminiscent of the Prasna Upanishad, the sage continues, "The heart has five openings. The upward breath is *prāna*, the diffused breath is *vyāna*, the downward breath is *apāna*, the equalised breath is *samāna* and the final one is *udāna*. One should meditate on this.... Verily, a person consists of purpose. According to the purpose, that he becomes."

Then come some illustrative examples. A young boy desiring knowledge went to a sage to be taught. The sage asked him, "What is the name of your father?" The boy replied, "I do not know the name of my father. I was born while my mother was serving various people. I only know that my name is Satyakama and my mother is Jabala." Then the sage replied, "None but a *brahmin* can speak such damaging truth about oneself. As you have not deviated from truth, I shall teach you." Here we see an important feature of that time period. Nowadays, a Brahmin is a member of a superior caste; then, with its earlier meaning, the word meant a sincere seeker of truth.

Now comes a peculiar method of instruction of the sage. The sage gives Satyakama four hundred lean cows to be taken to the forest and says, "When they are a thousand, bring them back." After several years, one of the cows speaks to Satyakama, "We are a thousand now so take us back to your teacher. I will now teach you about *Brahman*." Satyakama was startled and said, "Please teach me." The cow replied, "The east is *Brahman* and so is the west. The north is *Brahman* and so is the south. Fire will now continue the teaching." So Satyakama went to the fire, and said, "Please teach me." Fire then said, "The earth is *Brahman*, so are the sky and ocean. Now the birds will teach you." So Satyakama went to the birds and said, "Please teach me." The birds then spoke, "The sun and the moon are part of *Brahman*, as well as the lightning. Breath is *Brahman* and so are hearing, sight and mind." When Satyakama brought the cows back to the teacher, the sage inquired, "Your face shines like a knower of *Brahman*. Who has taught you?" "Beings other than men, but I wish that you now teach me." Then the sage taught him and nothing was left out.

In explaining to us the meaning of this story, Vivekananda writes about the voices emanating from the cows, the fire, the birds and so forth:

> The great idea of which we here see the germ is that all these voices are inside ourselves. As we understand these truths better, we find the voice is in our own heart.... The second idea that we get is that of making the knowledge of *Brahman* practical.... The truth was shown through everything with which the students were familiar.... The earth became transformed, life became transformed, the sun, the moon, the stars, the lightning, everything became transformed and deified.... The principle that underlies all these stories is that invented symbolism may be good and helpful, but already better symbols exist than any we can invent.... This world spoke to the early thinkers. Birds spoke to them, animals spoke to them, the sun and the moon spoke to them and little by little they realised things, and got into the

> heart of nature. Not by cogitation nor by the force of logic, not by picking the brains of others and making a big book, as is the fashion in modern times, not even as I do, by taking up one of their writings and making a long lecture, but by patient investigation and discovery they found out the truth. Its essential method was practice, and so it must be always.... It is practice first, and knowledge afterwards. (Vol. 2, 311-17)

Next is asked the question that is reminiscent of the opening question in the Mundaka Upanishad. The student asks, "Sir, what is that by knowing which everything becomes known?" The sage replies, "Just as by knowing a clod of clay, all the clay becomes known, so is this teaching. Of this mighty tree, if someone should strike at the root, it would bleed, but still live. If someone should strike at the middle, it would bleed but still live. Being pervaded by the *ātman* it stands firm, drinking in its moisture and rejoicing. Bring to me the fruit of the *nyagrodha* tree." The student brings it and says, "Here it is, Sir." "Break it." "It is broken, Sir." "What do you see?" "Extremely fine seeds, Sir." "Break one of those seeds." "It is broken, Sir." "What do you see?" "Nothing, Sir." "My dear, out of that 'nothing,' this great *nyagrodha* tree has arisen. The *ātman* is subtle, imperceptible, out of which this whole universe has arisen."

Then comes an instruction on progressive meditation. The sage Narada went to another sage called Sanatkumara and said, "I have studied all branches of learning, art, science, music, philosophy as well as the sacred scriptures. But I have gained no peace. I have heard from great teachers like you that only he who knows his Self finds peace." The venerable sage Sanatkumara replies, "What you have studied is name only. Meditate on name as *Brahman*."

What a superb teaching! Observe that the sage does not say all that Narada knows is useless. He transforms it, deifies it by asking him to meditate on that as *Brahman*. Now Narada asks, "Is there anything higher than name?" The sage replies, "Yes, speech is higher than name. It is through speech that we come to know the many branches of learning. Meditate therefore on speech as *Brahman*."

"Is there anything higher than speech?" Narada asks. "Yes," the sage replies, "mind is higher than speech. Mind can hold both name and speech. Meditate on mind as *Brahman*."

"Is there anything higher than mind?" asks Narada. "Yes, will is higher than mind. When one wills, then one reflects, then utters speech, and then utters the name. Thus, meditate on will as *Brahman*."

"Is there anything higher?" asks Narada. "Yes, thinking is greater than will. Even though one may know many things, but does not know how to think, people will say he is nobody, whatever he may know. Meditate on thinking as *Brahman*."

"Is there anything higher sir?" asks Narada. "Yes, contemplation is higher than thinking. The earth contemplates, as it were. The heavens contemplate as it were. The mountains contemplate as it were. Whoever has achieved greatness in this world has done so through contemplation. Meditate on contemplation as *Brahman*." Contemplation involves a detached observation of a sequence of thoughts.

In this context, it is enlightening to quote Thomas Merton on the meaning of contemplation. He wrote:

> Contemplation is the highest expression of man's intellectual and spiritual life. It is that life itself, fully awake, fully active, fully aware that it is alive. It is spiritual wonder. It is spontaneous awe at the sacredness of life, of being. It is gratitude for life, for awareness and for being. It is a vivid realization of the fact that life and being in us proceed from an invisible, transcendent and infinitely abundant Source. Contemplation is, above all, awareness of the reality of that Source. It *knows* the Source, obscurely, inexplicably, but with a certitude that goes both beyond reason and beyond simple faith. (1)

Narada now asks "Is there anything higher sir?" "Yes, insight and understanding are higher. Meditate on insight and understanding as *Brahman*." From detached observation, patterns emerge and this is called understanding, namely, the perception of a pattern or a "law."

"Is there anything higher sir?" "Yes, strength is higher than insight and understanding. A man of both physical and mental strength can make a hundred men of understanding tremble. By strength, verily, the earth stands. By strength, verily, the mountains stand. By strength, verily, the world stands. Meditate on strength as *Brahman*." Here, "strength" should be thought of as sustained endeavour.

"Is there anything higher sir?" "Food is greater than strength. For without food, neither physical strength or mental strength is possible. Thus meditate on food as *Brahman*."

"Is there anything higher sir?" "Water is greater than food. Water is in the earth, the atmosphere, the sky, the mountains, the plants and all living things. Water is indeed all these forms. Thus meditate on water as *Brahman*."

"Is there anything higher sir?" "Heat is greater than water. Without the convection of heat, it will not rain, and there is no water. Meditate on heat as *Brahman*."

"Is there anything higher sir?" "Space (*ākāsa*) is higher than heat. For nothing can exist without space. In space reside the sun, moon and the stars. Meditate on space as *Brahman*."

"Is there anything higher sir?" "Memory is higher than space. Meditate on memory as *Brahman*."

"Is there anything higher sir?" "Yes, desire is greater than memory. Without desire, memory does not proceed. When kindled by desire, memory learns. Meditate on desire as *Brahman*."

"Is there anything higher sir?" "Yes, life (*prāna*) is higher than desire. *Prāna* moves the breath. *Prāna* is all this."

Here we come to interesting and very subtle ideas, ones in need of clarification. By memory, one does not mean the individual memory, but rather the cosmic memory. In Indian cosmology, there is the theory that creation occurs in cycles (*kalpas*). There is dissolution (*pralaya*) of the present universe and then creation (or more precisely, projection) of another universe. The process goes on cyclically according to the theory. In between dissolution and creation, the universe resides in memory. We may want to call it the "collective unconscious" as Jung does, but the idea remains the same. Where do the archetypes reside before they manifest in the waking or the dream worlds? They reside in memory.

In his essay on cosmology, Vivekananda gives some further clarification of some of these points:

> All motion, everything in this universe, can be likened to waves undergoing successive rise and fall. Some of these philosophers hold that the whole universe quiets down for a period. Others hold that this quieting down applies only to systems.... When it quiets down, what becomes of the universe? It exists, only in finer forms, in the form of cause.... There is in the Rg Veda, the oldest human writing in existence, a beautiful passage describing creation, and it is most poetical—'When there was neither aught nor naught, when darkness was rolling over darkness, what existed?' and the answer is given, 'It then existed without vibration.' This *prāna* existed then, but there was no motion in it; *ānidavātam* means 'existed without vibration.' Vibration had stopped. Then when the *kalpa* begins...the *ānidavātam* (unvibrating atom) commences to vibrate, and blow after blow is given by *prāna* to *ākāsa*. The atoms become condensed and as they are condensed different elements are formed. We generally find these things very curiously translated; people do not go to the philosophers or the commentators for their translation, and have not the brains to

understand them themselves. A silly man reads three letters of Sanskrit and translates a whole book. They translate the elements as air, fire, and so on; if they would go to the commentators, they would find they do not mean air or anything of the sort. The *ākāsa*, acted upon by repeated blows of *prāna*, produces *vāyu* or vibrations. This *vāyu* vibrates, and the vibrations growing more and more rapid result in friction giving rise to heat, *tejas*. Then this heat ends in liquefaction, *āpah*. Then that liquid becomes solid.... All that we know in the form of motion, vibration, or thought is a modification of the *prāna*. (Vol. 2, 335-36)

6

THE BRHADĀRANYAKA AND OTHER UPANISHADS

THE BRHADĀRANYAKA UPANISHAD

This is the longest of the Upanishads and the name *Brhadāranyaka* literally means "the vast forest." It is known for the long discourse between the philosopher Yājnavalkya and his wife Maitreyi. Some traces of the society of that time period can be seen in the Upanishad. Many questions are posed by female students, and one can deduce that there was no exclusive masculine privilege of gaining knowledge.

Despite its length, the message of this Upanishad is the same as the earlier ones, namely, it teaches of the underlying reality called *Brahman*. It is curious that the Upanishad repeats itself in places, as in the case of the conversation between Yājnavalkya and Maitreyi. In later parts, there are verses that are literally taken from some of the earlier Upanishads such as the Isa and Kena. However, the Upanishad does have the virtue of giving us further meditations on the *ātman* and *Brahman*.

The Upanishad is most famous for its "*neti, neti*" doctrine, or the "not this, not this" principle that has come to occupy a central place in the *advaita* philosophy (the philosophy of non-dualism). We will give free, but faithful, translations of the passages and occasionally pause to highlight significant points.[1]

> The world existed first as seed, which as it grew and developed took on names and forms. As fire is hidden in wood, the Self dwells in all

1 Most of these translations have been taken from Prabhavananda and Manchester.

> forms and beings, even to the tips of the fingers. Yet the ignorant do not know That, for behind the names and forms, the Self is hidden. When one breathes, one knows him as breath. When one speaks, one knows him as speech. When one sees, one knows him as the eye. When one hears, one knows him as the ear. When one thinks, one knows him as the mind. All these are but names related to the acts of the Self. And he who worships the Self as one or another of them does not know the Self, for of them, It is neither one or another. The Self is the goal of all beings. For by knowing the Self, one knows all. This Self, which is nearer to us than anything else, is indeed dearer than a son or daughter, dearer than wealth, dearer than all beside.

So far, this is an echo of the message we have heard in the earlier Upanishads. But now comes the entry of the "philosopher-king," an ideal that was to dominate Indian philosophy of the later periods. The boastful sage Gārgya meets King Ajātasatru and says to him that he will teach him about *Brahman*. The king humbly submits. Then follows a rather interesting dialogue that reveals that the king had advanced further in the path to *Brahman*. Repeating the outer message of the Upanishads, Gārgya begins, "He who is the being in the sun and at the same time the being in the eye, Him I meditate upon as *Brahman*. He who is in the moon and at the same time in the mind, Him I meditate upon as *Brahman*. He who is in the lightning and at the same time in the heart, Him I meditate upon as *Brahman*." The king replies, "Please do not speak thus of *Brahman*. That Being, I worship as the transcendental, luminous, supreme, infinite, power." Gārgya continues, "He who is the being in the sky and at the same time in the heart, Him I meditate upon as *Brahman*. He who is in the wind and at the same time in the breath, Him I meditate upon as *Brahman*. He who is in the fire and at the same time in the heart, Him I meditate upon as *Brahman*." The king replies, "Please do not speak thus of *Brahman*. That Being, I worship as all-pervading, changeless, effulgent, invincible, forgiveness, harmony, life force and supreme will."

In this dialogue, we see the contrast between concrete symbols and abstract concepts that have no physical symbols. The king, by his reverential attitude to higher knowledge has gone beyond the preliminary stage of meditation on *Brahman* through symbols around him. He has entered the realm of the abstract, whereas the sage was trapped in the realm of symbols. The sage had come to realize this in the course of their dialogue, and so he asks the king, "Sir, please accept me as a disciple and teach me of *Brahman*." Then the king took Gārgya by the hand and arose. The two walked side by side and they came upon a sleeping man. Now comes a discussion that can be said to be a continuation of the Māndukya Upanishad on states of consciousness.

The king tried to wake the sleeping man, but the man did not stir. Then he rubbed the hand of the sleeping man, and slowly the man awoke. The king asked Gārgya, "This man, who is a conscious, intelligent being, where was he when he was thus asleep, and how did he thus wake up?" Gārgya was silent. The king continued:

> When this man, who is a conscious, intelligent being, is thus in deep sleep, he enters into the Self, within the lotus of the heart, having withdrawn into himself both his senses and his mind. When the person withdraws the senses, he is said to be asleep. When the breath is restrained, speech is restrained, the eye is restrained, the ear is restrained and the mind is restrained. He enters the dream state. Just as a king moves about his own country as he pleases, so also in the dream state one moves about one's own body as one pleases. Beyond the dream state is the state of deep sleep.[2] In this state he knows nothing. He enters into the seventy-two thousand nerves which go out from the lotus of the heart.... As the spider moves along its web, as small sparks come forth from the fire, even so the Self moves forth through the *prāna*, through all worlds, through all beings. This is the essence of the Upanishad. *Prāna* is the truth and the Self is the truth of that. That is the truth of truth (*satyasya satyam*).

In many of the Upanishads, the sun and the heart are seen as similar. Just as the many rays of light radiate from the sun and energize the world, so also many rays of nerves radiate from the heart energizing the parts of the body. The network of nerves is compared to a spider's web. The spider can only travel along the threads of the web. Similarly, the Self "moves" along the nerves as *prāna*. We can know truths about *prāna* and more generally its manifestation, this world, the verse says. But beyond that, the "truth of truth" or the "meaning of the meaning" is *Brahman*.

This passage is significant for many reasons. The subtle teaching comes from the lips of a king, indicating that the kings were deeply interested in the teachings of the Upanishads. Their interest was not academic, but rather, practical. This becomes a dominant theme in the later philosophical treatises, the most celebrated being the Bhagavad Gita, where Krishna appears as the ideal "philosopher-king." Another reason why these verses

2 For some unknown reason, Prabhavananda and Manchester reverse the order of dream and deep sleep, though in the original Upanishad it is in the order we have given in the translation above.

are important is the use of the phrase "truth of truth" (*satyasa satyam*), indicating that we can know truths about the world we see, but there is a deeper layer of truth behind it. But perhaps the novel feature of this Upanishad is its physical account of the dream and deep sleep states. The senses are withdrawn from the outer world and the awareness seems to reside in the *pranamaya kosha*, the nervous network of the human being. If we think of the mind as the cognizer, a part of its activity is to give cohesion to all our sensory impressions and "interpret" it so that we may understand. The verses of this Upanishad suggest that a similar process is taking place with respect to neural impressions in us when asleep. They may be given form and "interpreted" in the form of dream.

A good portion of this Upanishad is dominated by the personality of the sage Yājnavalkya. He says to his wife that he will leave for her all his wealth as he is about to renounce the world and begin a life of exclusive meditation. What we see here is that one need not be a mendicant or a stern ascetic to embrace the life of meditation. It is a natural event that comes from maturity and after one has gone through the various phases of life and its teachings. The Upanishadic age refrained from making such compartmental divisions either to society or to life.

Yājnavalkya's wife, Maitreyi, then replies to him, "What will I do with wealth. Your goal is also my goal. Teach me that which will enable me to transcend death." Yājnavalkya is delighted for he has now found a fit pupil:

> Verily, it is not for the sake of the husband that the husband is dear to the wife but for the sake of the *ātman* that she loves him. It is not for the sake of the wife that the husband loves the wife but for the sake of the *ātman* that he loves her.... None loves a thing for that thing's sake. It is only for the sake of the *ātman*. This teaching must first be heard, then reflected upon and then meditated upon. When the *ātman* is seen, then all becomes known.

This requires some explanation. Why do we love anything? It is because the light of the *ātman* animates it. The beauty that shines through the eyes is the beauty of the *ātman*. Thus, the beauty that we enjoy is the bliss of *Brahman*, even though we are not aware of it. Our difficulty arises when we try to narrow the experience through only one person or one thing. This teaching is similar to the earlier teachings of the Upanishads where something familiar is taken and a cosmic aspect of it is revealed. Here the familiar idea taken up for reflection is love and beauty.

In explaining these verses, Vivekananda writes:

> As soon as you are attached to anything in the universe, detaching it from the universe as a whole, from the *Atman*, there comes a reaction. With everything we love outside the Self, grief and misery will be the result. If we enjoy everything in the Self, and as the Self, no misery or reaction will come. This is perfect bliss. (Vol. 2, 418)

Now how can we enlarge our vision and gain this cosmic perspective for everything we encounter? Yājnavalkya explains:

> As when a drum is beaten, one is not able to grasp the external sounds, but by grasping the drum or the beater of the drum, the sound is grasped, similarly when one grasps the Pure Self, all things and beings become known. They have no existence apart from the Self. All knowledge is the breath of the eternal.... As a lump of salt thrown into water becomes dissolved in the water and one cannot separate it, so also the infinite is mingled with all that you see. Everything is permeated with intelligence. This universe arises out of That and goes back to That.

The imagery here is brilliant. Can we catch the sound? Only by going to the source of the sound can we do so. Similarly, as long as we perceive diversity but no unity behind that diversity, we are confused and subject to the oscillations of pain and pleasure. "Everything is permeated with intelligence," just as salt is dissolved in water and permeates that water. But this teaching confuses Maitreyi and she asks, "What will become of individuality? It looks like it will disappear. Will there be then no one to love, no one to recognize? What will become of us?"

Then Yājnavalkya replies:

> My dear, let nothing I say confuse you. As long as there is duality, one sees the other, one hears the other, and so forth. But where everything has become the Self, who is seen by whom, who is heard by whom? The Pure Awareness that reveals all, by what shall It be revealed?

Individuality is, upon closer examination, a myth. The body is constantly changing. The mind is constantly changing. Medical science informs us that the body is composed of about 10^{12} cells and these cells have different life spans. Blood cells are changing every few seconds. The surface of the cells lining the stomach changes every few minutes. These cells are completely transformed within a few hours. Stomach lining cells live only for about two days, a skin cell lives about two weeks, a red blood cell lives for about two months, liver cells live about two years, whereas heart and brain cells last a lifetime.

Expanding on this theme, Vivekananda writes:

> The body and the mind are continually changing, and are, in fact, only names of series of changeful phenomena, like rivers whose waters are in a constant state of flux, yet presenting the appearance of unbroken streams. Every particle in this body is continually changing; no one has the same body for many minutes together, and yet we think of it as the same body. So with the mind; one moment it is happy, another moment unhappy; one moment strong, another weak; an ever-changing whirlpool. That cannot be the Spirit which is infinite. Change can only be in the limited.... These are old delusions, however comfortable they are, to think that we are little limited beings, constantly changing. (Vol. 2, 79)

In his inimitable humorous style, Vivekananda continues:

> People are frightened when they are told they are the Universal Being, everywhere present.... They will again and again ask you if they are not going to keep their individuality. What is individuality? I should like to see it. A baby has no moustache; when he grows to be a man, perhaps he has a moustache and beard. His individuality will be lost if it were in the body. Then a drunkard should not give up drinking because he would lose his individuality. A thief should not be a good man because he would thereby lose his individuality. No man ought to change his habits for fear of this. There is no individuality except in the Infinite. That is the only condition which does not change. Everything else is in a constant change of flux.... Neither can individuality be in memory. Suppose on account of a blow on the head, I forget all about my past; then, I have lost all individuality; I am gone. I do not remember two or three years of my childhood, and if memory and existence are one, then whatever I forget is gone. That part of my life which I do not remember, I did not live. That is a very narrow idea of individuality. (Vol. 2, 80)

Next in the Upanishad, comes a sequence of verses that highlight the symbiosis between the human being and the world around. "The earth is honey to all beings and all beings are honey to the earth. They both help each other. The sweetness in all things is the *ātman*. The water is honey to all beings and all beings are honey to the water. They both help each other. The sweetness is the *ātman*." The idea here is that the things we see around us are not separate from us; rather, we are interconnected. The enjoyment that you experience is a particle of the bliss of *Brahman*. The symbols of sweetness offered by the Upanishad are fire, air, space, sun, moon, lightning, and thunder.

From these concrete symbols, the Upanishad continues, "The law is honey to all beings and all beings are honey to the law. They both help each other. The essence of both is *Brahman*." Now we have entered the abstract. The word *dharma*, translated here as "the law," is a complicated word. An accurate translation is "social order, social justice." Though *dharma* is not directly perceived, its effects are perceived and we are to reflect upon that. Here we see the beginnings of a theme that later pervades the Mahābhārata, the philosophy of social justice or *dharma*. An individual is not separate from the state; they both help each other.

The Upanishad now moves toward more abstract notions:

> Truth is honey to all beings and all beings are honey to truth. They both help each other. The essence of both is *Brahman*. Humanity is honey to all human beings and all beings are honey to humanity. They both help each other. The essence of humanity is *Brahman*. The *ātman* is honey to all beings and all beings are honey to the *ātman*. The essence of both is *Brahman*. As the spokes of a wheel are held together by the hub of the wheel, so also all beings are held together by the *ātman*. *Brahman* has entered all forms. *Brahman* is without cause, without effect, without inside and without an outside. This *Brahman* is the *ātman*, the all perceiving. (*Ayam ātma brahma*.)

The purpose of these verses is to give the student a progressive series of meditations. We begin with concrete symbols such as the earth, the sun, the moon, the air and so forth. Then we move to subtler meditations like humanity, *dharma*, truth, and *Brahman*. These meditations culminate in the philosophical equation that the *ātman* is *Brahman*. In science, a mathematical equation compresses a vast history of thought and establishes an identity between two seemingly different expressions. Through that one equation, the scientist, in a single glance, can comprehend the diverse and complicated phenomenon the equation describes.

Now comes a revealing section of the Upanishad, showing us, among other things, that knowledge and learning were highly valued at that time and that all people, from the peasant to the king, were interested in gaining some insight into the nature of *Brahman*. King Janaka held a royal court and invited learned scholars for a philosophical debate. He offered a thousand cows as the prize for the winner of the debate. Yājnavalkya enters the court and sits next to the other sages and the debate begins. A sage stands up and asks the question, "What is the means of overcoming death?" Yājnavalkya responds, "By fire, by speech, we overcome death."

Here, as we have seen, speech is symbolic of the "word" or the miracle of language. Language is the means for gaining higher knowledge. Fire is symbolic of the will. Thus, by combining learning and the will to learn, one overcomes death.

In the course of the debate, the sage is asked a series of questions and Yājnavalkya emerges victorious in the discussion. We are to infer that the assembly consists of many learned sages, both male and female. The challenges to Yājnavalkya come from all sides. He continues, in terms somewhat reminiscent of the Kena Upanishad:

> He who dwells in speech, yet is within speech, whom speech does not know, whose body is speech, who controls speech from within, that is the *ātman*. He who dwells in the eye, yet is within the eye, whom the eye does not know, whose body is the eye, who controls the eye from within, that is the *ātman*.... It is unseen, but It is the seer. It is unthought, but It is the thinker. It is unknown, but It is the knower.

King Janaka is pleased with the debate and comes to reward Yājnavalkya. Janaka asks, "Did you come here for cattle or philosophy?" The sage replies, "For both. But before I accept your reward, I would like to hear what your teachers have taught you." Then, Janaka says, "I was taught that word is *Brahman*." The sage expands:

> It is true that word is *Brahman* since the legacy of learning, first from the mother, then the father, and then the sages, is through the power of the word, the power of sound, the *sabda brahman*. The organ of speech is its abode, the space its support. Meditate on sound as pulsating with knowledge.

Yājnavalkya then takes Janaka through a progressive series of meditations:

> When the sun has set, the moon has set, the stars have set, the fire is out, what illumines the world? Speech (sound) illumines the world and when that is not there, what illumines the world? It is the light of *Brahman* that illumines the world.

Consciousness is the ultimate source of light. The famous autobiography of Helen Keller brings this message to us with impressive force in the chapter entitled "The Seeing Hand." Blind, deaf, and mute since infancy, she wrote,

> My hand is to me what your hearing and sight are to you.... The hand is my feeler with which I reach through isolation and darkness and seize every pleasure, every activity that my fingers encounter.... In all my experiences and thoughts, I am conscious of a hand. Whatever moves me, whatever thrills me, is as a hand that touches me in the dark, and that touch is my reality.... The delicate tremble of a butterfly's wings in my hand, the soft petals of violets.... My world is built of touch sensations devoid of physical colour and sound; it breathes and throbs with life.... Remember that you, dependent on your sight, do not realize *how* many things are tangible.... A tangible object passes complete into my brain with the warmth of life upon it and occupies the same place that it does in space, for, without egotism, the mind is as large as the universe.... The silent worker is imagination which decrees reality out of chaos. (*World*, 6-7)

Apart from its literary beauty, this passage is important for us, as students of philosophy, for several reasons. The passage suggests that in our waking life, with sensory impressions coming from many directions, the impressions are received pell-mell by our brain. The imaginative faculty gives order to these diverse impressions and fashions for us some view of the world. Most of this is happening too fast for us to "listen" to the "inner symphony" being played. When, as the Upanishads instruct, we withdraw the mind from the outer world and observe within, we find a subtler layer of experience. In the case of Helen Keller, the energy expended through the faculties of sight, speech, and sound has been eliminated and she finds still a richer world revealed through the sense of touch. In her essay on optimism, she wrote, "Once I knew only darkness and stillness... my life was without past or future... but a little word from the fingers of another fell into my hand that clutched at emptiness, and my heart leaped to the rapture of living" (*Optimism*, 13). This highlights the non-verbal language of touch and how one can still understand and experience the world. Equally amazing is that the mind can still fashion through imagination an idea of the world outside that gives her meaning.

With verses that seem to be echoes of the Taittirīya, Isa, and Kena Upanishads, the sage teaches:

> But beyond is *Brahman*, the One without a second, beyond duality.... When one is healthy, wealthy and has lavish enjoyments, this is said to be the highest bliss of human beings.... But the bliss of the knower of *Brahman* is the greatest.... According as one acts, according as one behaves, so does he become.... As is his desire, so is his will. As is his will, so is the deed. Whatever deed he does, that he attains.... When all the desires of the heart are cast away, then he attains *Brahman*.... Into blinding darkness they enter, who worship ignorance. Into greater darkness than that, they enter, as it were, who delight in knowledge.... They who know the life of life, the eye of the eye, the ear of the ear and mind of the mind, realise *Brahman*. Only by the mind is it to be perceived. In it there is no diversity. Let the seeker of *Brahman* practice the means to wisdom. Let him not reflect on too many words, for that only gives rise to weariness of speech.

In conclusion, the Brhadāranyaka Upanishad teaches us that whatever we enjoy in this world and find dear is through the bliss of *Brahman*. Thus, joy, with which we are all familiar, is associated with *Brahman*. Next, it tells us that one may meditate on physical symbols as *Brahman*, but there is a higher meditation, on the formless, through mental abstraction. Forgiveness, joy, harmony, humanity, social justice, power, truth, and meaning are all without form, and yet we continuously experience their manifestations. After speaking about the various states of consciousness, it teaches us how to progressively withdraw our consciousness from the outer world and focus on the inner. One of its powerful symbols is its comparison of the heart radiating its network of veins and arteries to the sun radiating its rays of light and energy. As a spider is limited in its movement to the threads of the web it has spun, so also the individual experiences the world only through the network of nerves. By withdrawing the senses, one may enlarge the experience. One may say that this Upanishad makes explicit the physical dimension of the meditative experience more than any other Upanishad.

A BRIEF LOOK AT SOME OTHER UPANISHADS

We will conclude our survey of the Upanishads by highlighting significant verses from some of them. In the Aitareya Upanishad, we find the phrase *prajnānam brahma*, which translates as "intelligence is *Brahman*." Here, "intelligence" is not to be interpreted as a function of the mind, but rather as "pure consciousness." "The world is guided by intelligence. *Brahman* is intelligence" (Radhakrishnan, *Principal*, 523). In other translations, we find different meanings ascribed to the word *prajnā*. Aurobindo translates it as "wisdom" (Vol. 12, 364), others translate it as "pure consciousness" (Prabhavananda and Manchester, 97), or as the "intellect" (Radhakrishnan and Moore). However, there is a general consensus that the word indicates the principle of intelligence that pervades all life. In referring to this hidden principle, Aurobindo writes:

> We see it as *prajnā*, the universal Intelligence, conscious in things unconscious, active in things inert. The energy of *prajnā* is what the Europeans call Nature. The tree does not and cannot shape itself, the stress of the hidden Intelligence shapes it. (Vol. 3, 363)

A tree is shaped by its genetics, but the word *prajnā* encompasses more than that. Intelligence is that which forms cosmos out of chaos and gives cohesion to the world. Helen Keller referred to it as "imagination," but it is clear from her writing that it is the principle of intelligence to which she refers. This principle is "all-pervasive" (*sarvagatah*). Even the minutest cells in our body "know" what to do and how to function. They even have some form of "cellular telepathy" and can communicate with faraway cells of the body. Our body is not just a bunch of cells and chemicals put together. There is a principle of intelligence that pervades it and this is the message of this particular upanishad.

The Svetāsvatara Upanishad is named after the sage Svetāsvatara. Its teachings find greater expression in the Sāmkhya and Yoga philosophies of a later period. One can see clearly delineated here the essential principles of *raja yoga*, or what has been called the "kingly path" to *Brahman*. Here is a general account of its essential ideas.

Beyond matter (the object of enjoyment), mind (the enjoyer), and Maya (that which connects the two) is the infinite Self. When all three are known as one with *Brahman*, then the Self is realized. The truth is that we are always united with the Self, but we must *know* this. The way to do this is by meditation on Om. As fire is latent in sticks and it comes out when they are rubbed together, so also is the Self hidden in all beings. It is realized through the heat (*tapas*) of meditation on Om. Holding the body steady with the chest, neck and head erect, the sense organs and the mental activities must be silenced. Let the yogi practise meditation in a solitary place free from all distractions. By regulating the breathing and neural currents, let the yogi meditate on the syllable Om. The mind is thus trained in inwardness. As you go deeper, you will realize the infinite dimension of the eternal Self. At this point, the sage Svetāsvatara goes into a paean of song.

> *srnvantu visve amrtasya putrā āye dhāmāni divyāni tasthuh... vedāham etam purusam mahāntam āditya varnam tamasah parastāt tam eva viditvāati mrtyum eti nānyah panthāvidyate ayanāya.* (Svet. Up. 2.5, 3.8)

> Hear ye, children of immortal bliss, even those that reside in the starry heavens. I have found the Supreme Being, luminous and beyond all darkness. Only by knowing the Supreme Self is the way out of the cycle of life and death. There seems to be no other way.

> The sage continues:

> That Being is everywhere. It resides in the hearts of all beings, *sarva-gata sivah.* Truly, It is what has been, what is, and whatever will be.

> *Sarvatah pāni pādam tat, sarvato'ksi siro mukham, sarvatah sruti malloke, sarvam āvryta tisthati.*

> Its hands and feet are everywhere. Everywhere, Its eyes, ears, heads and faces on all sides. It envelops the whole cosmos. It is smaller than the smallest, larger than the largest. It is not female, it is not male, it is not neuter either. That is hidden in all beings and in all things, whatever there is. The wise perceive That as their own Self. Then only one may have ever-lasting contentment.

By the power of austerity (*tapas*) and by the grace of the divine, Svetāsvatara spoke about the nature of *Brahman.* May all sincere seekers of Truth benefit from this teaching of the highest mystery.

The final Upanishad we will survey is the Maitrī Upanishad, named after the sage responsible for it. The teaching here goes into some detail on the meaning of Om. Here are a few central verses.

> By austerity (*tapas*) one achieves goodness. Through goodness, you can take hold of the mind. Through the mind, one can realise the Self. As fire, when its fuel is spent, comes to rest in its source, even so the mind, when the thoughts are silenced, the mind returns to its own source. The mind is the key. Here is the eternal mystery. What you think, that you become (*yac cittas tan-mayo bhavati guhyam etat sanātanam*). (Maitrī Up. 6.34.3)

The essential sense of this is that whatever thought we hold, the mind tries to take the shape of that thought, or become that thought, as it were. Through that process we gain understanding.

The essential message of the Upanishads as a whole is that there is a changeless reality behind the changing. The substratum is *Brahman*. Though it is beyond mind and speech, has no form or shape, and is beyond any form of mental conceptualization, the Upanishads tell us with conviction that It can be realized and experienced. Using familiar symbols, they suggest meditation on symbols around us; they transform them. We can no longer treat the sun in the same way as before. The sun becomes a symbol of *Brahman*. When we look at the moon, that becomes a symbol of *Brahman*. When we look at the sky, we are reminded of the vastness of *Brahman*. We have recovered an ancient kinship with the world around us. We can no longer walk upon the earth without feeling some affinity to it. And more importantly, we become aware of the Infinite Spirit, or the Pure Awareness, peering through every eye of every living thing. In fact, the value of a deep study of the Upanishads is that it changes the way we look at the world around us, the way we look at others, and more importantly, the way we look at ourselves. It widens our view from the narrow limited view of ourselves, to a larger view, that we are all part of the Infinite. It changes our thought and energizes the mind. And as the Maitrī Upanishad teaches through insightful poetry, whatever we think, that we become. Thus, when we contemplate the Infinite, the Infinite we become.

7

THE BHAGAVADGĪTA

THE HISTORICAL AND LITERARY BACKGROUND OF THE GITA

The Epic period in India (1000-600 BCE) is so called because of the epics that appeared during this time, the greatest of which are the Rāmāyana and the Mahābhārata, written by the two sages Valmiki and Vyasa, respectively. It is conjectured that they were written down in the sixth century BCE, though they describe events of an earlier period. For the most part, they are history, written in poetic style, but they also delve deeply and at length into philosophical questions. The Rāmāyana has 25,000 verses; the Mahābhārata, with 100,000 verses, is considered the longest poem written in any ancient civilization.

The Rāmāyana records the life of Rama, one of the earliest examples we have of a philosopher-king. Taught by the sages Vasishta and Visvamitra, Rama tried to bring the sages' high ideals into the administration of the country. His idealistic rule was successful for some time; one refers to it, even now, as *rāma rājya*, indicating a just rule of the country in which everyone's voice is heard and fair decisions made. We may view this epic as the first record of an experiment in democracy. However, as one can imagine, such idealism in one or a few persons cannot survive unless it is shared by the multitude. It is this conflict that is explored in the *Rāmāyana*.

The Mahābhārata centres on a conflict between two people vying for the throne. It describes the psychological, philosophical, moral, and political struggles of various philosopher-kings who try to put the Upanishadic teachings into practice. By and large, the epic can be regarded as addressing the problem of social justice (*dharma*) from an idealistic standpoint. A central theme of the work is the struggle between good and evil.

After the Upanishadic age, the most challenging question addressed by the philosophers and sages was how does the teaching of the Upanishads, most notably the omnipresence of *Brahman*, fit into our daily life? How can we explain good and evil? Most importantly, is the Upanishadic message only for the recluse in the forest, or can it actually help people in daily life? We have already seen some of these issues parenthetically touched upon in some of the later Upanishads. But now, these questions are addressed directly in a long poem, about 700 verses, a portion of the Mahābhārata known as the Bhagavadgīta. Over the centuries, the appreciation of the value of the Bhagavadgīta (or Gita, for short), has grown, and it now occupies the sacred status of a scripture. The word *Bhagavadgīta* is composed of two syllables, namely, *Bhagavān* ("God"), and *Gīta* ("song"), so the word literally translates as "The song of God." The original meaning of *Bhagavān* was one who is fortunate, or blessed. Over time, this meaning morphed into its current theistic connotation.

It may help to briefly delineate and describe some of the events that led to the dialogue recorded in the Gita. The clan of the Kurus, led by the blind king Dhritarāshtra, ruled over Kuruksetra (literally meaning the land of the Kurus), which was a region near present-day Delhi, in northern India. As the king was about to step down, he decided to hand over the throne to Dharmarāja, who was well known for his virtue and wisdom, instead of to his own son, Duryodhana. Indeed, the name Dharmarāja literally means "king of social justice." Dhritarāshtra's decision irritated Duryodhana, who felt that the throne should be rightfully his. Clearly, the king would very much have liked to have had his own son on the throne, but to be fair and just he selected Dharmarāja since it was a choice the people would also accept. Naturally, a conflict arose. Dharmarāja and his four brothers (collectively called the Pandavas), the most notable of whom was Arjuna, the great warrior, stood firm and considered the king's decision as final. Duryodhana resorted to various assassination attempts to eliminate the brothers. They all failed. Finally, he invited the brothers to a meeting of reconciliation, where together with various scheming friends he planned to use Dharmarāja's virtue as a weapon to eliminate him and his brothers. He invited Dharmarāja for a game of dice, and thinking that Duryodhana had finally come around to walk the path of virtue, Dharmarāja accepted. The dice were loaded, and the conspirators were relying on Dharmarāja's penchant for the game, along with his reputed resolve to fulfill any promises he made. Dharmarāja lost repeatedly, and in the confusion of the game, forfeited his right to the throne and agreed to banishment from the kingdom for him and his brothers for a period of 13 years. After the period of banishment, the Pandavas return and Dharmarāja felt that he had a right to the throne. Duryodhana did not accept his offer and declared war. The nation became divided. This is the background for the Mahābhārata war.

In the course of the 13 years of banishment, the Pandavas befriended the philosopher-king Krishna. His sage advice and counsel on many issues were adopted by the Pandavas on numerous matters. In fact, it was clear to the Pandavas that Krishna was one who has inwardly realized the teachings of the Upanishads, not only intellectually, but also as personal experience. The knowledge of *Brahman*, or *Brahmajnāna*, was clearly revered in the scholarly circles. *Abhyāsa* (practice) is a recurrent theme in the Mahābhārata and the sincere seekers of higher knowledge (*parāvidya*) were well aware that it is through practice that one enters into the higher realms of the teaching. From the episodes recounted in the Mahābhārata, it was clear that Krishna was not only a knower of *Brahman* and had realized the Upanishadic ideal, but somehow had even gone beyond it. Thus, in the eyes of the Pandavas, he not only became their teacher, but even acquired god-like status. Krishna became the embodiment of the teaching of the Bhagavad Gita; his presence indicates that the philosophy of the Upanishads can be put into practice in daily life.

When Duryodhana declared war, the Pandavas wondered how to respond. They consulted Krishna, who advised them that they must first explore all ways of making peace before any such drastic action was taken. So Krishna offered to mediate and bring about a reconciliation. However, when he went to the court of Duryodhana, he was captured and tied up. Krishna escaped and returned to the Pandava camp, informing them that war seemed inevitable despite his best efforts to avert it.

A curious episode is related in the Mahābhārata concerning the period just before the war. As Krishna was himself a king, he commanded an army and had a formidable force at his disposal. Duryodhana was urged by his mentors to somehow acquire Krishna's military arsenal. So he went to Krishna to ask for his military force. At the same time, Arjuna also approached Krishna with a similar request. To be fair to both, Krishna made the following offer. The passage is quite humorous. "One of you can have my military arsenal. The other can just have me. But mind you, I will not fight. I will assume no military position. I will be the charioteer of one of you. Occasionally, I may give you unsolicited advice, and that too if I feel like it. Since Arjuna is the younger of the both of you, I will let Arjuna choose first." Duryodhana protested that the offer was unfair. He had come there first, he insisted, so he should get the first choice. But Krishna was firm and asks Arjuna, "Have you listened carefully? I will not fight. I will merely drive your chariot according to your instruction. I will pick up no weapon. I may give occasional advice and that too if and when I feel like it." Duryodhana mused to himself. "What kind of offer is this? Who would be a fool to refuse the weapons, the armies and the means to secure a victory in war? Arjuna will choose the weapons and I will be left with nothing!" But then, Arjuna refused the weapons and chose Krishna. Duryodhana was elated and so too was Krishna, of course. Krishna had just given the first test to Arjuna and he passed it. It foreshadowed the teaching about to take place on the battlefield, and the teacher had tested the fitness of the disciple.

Let us also observe the imagery of the chariot that reappears here reminiscent of the symbol used in the Katha Upanishad. Recall that there, the charioteer was *buddhi* or illumined reason. The mind was symbolized by the reins, the horses, the sense organs, and the road, the world around us. The rider in the chariot is the *ātman*, or the individual soul, here represented by Arjuna. The fact that Krishna is the charioteer signifies that the Upanishadic teaching can be put into practice by uniting the reasoning faculty to the higher ideal so that it is transformed into *buddhi*, or illumined reason.

The towering personality of Krishna dominates the Mahābhārata. Over the centuries, he has acquired mythic dimensions and even acquired the status of "God," which many religious sects have formed around his name and teaching. On this point, Vivekananda writes:

> It is human nature to build round the real character of a great man all sorts of imaginary superhuman attributes. As regards Krishna, the same must have happened, but it seems quite probable that he was a king. Quite probable I say, because in ancient times [in India]... it was chiefly the kings who exerted themselves most in the preaching of *Brahmajnāna*. Another point to be especially noted here is that whoever might have been the author of the Gita, we find its teachings the same as those in the whole of the Mahābhārata. From this, we can safely infer that in the age of the Mahābhārata some great man arose and preached the *Brahmajnāna* in this new garb to the then existing society. (Vol. 4, 104)

The opening scene of the Bhagavadgīta is the hesitation of Arjuna the warrior to go into battle. The armies are lined up and the battle is about to begin, but Arjuna became despondent. He had been reluctantly drawn into war and his mind was in turmoil. There was no doubt in Arjuna's mind about whether he could win the war or whether he was fit to fight, since he was aware that he had won many battles before with opponents more formidable than those arrayed before him. He did not question his abilities.

He was wondering about the propriety of the whole thing. "How can I slay these people?" he asked Krishna. "These are the people I have grown up with. Some of them were my teachers in my formative period. I cannot fight them. It is better to live the life of a mendicant than to slay these honoured teachers." Saying this, Arjuna threw away his mighty bow and arrows and sat down in his chariot, overwhelmed by sorrow.

This important opening chapter represents the recurrent predicament of every human being. At every step of our life, we must make choices, we must decide what course of action to take. Especially in moments of crises, we must think clearly. The fact that this is the fundamental human challenge is singled out in the opening scene.

At such moments, it is human nature to come up with noble and lofty reasons for taking the easy way out. "It is better to live the life of a mendicant than to slay these honoured teachers," Arjuna says. Thus, the opening chapter brings into bold relief two features of human psychology. When confronted by a crisis, we often do not think clearly. We try to run away from the problem and rationalize our behaviour. I think we can all identify with this phenomenon.

Vivekananda writes:

> For all of us in this world, life is a continuous fight. Many a time comes when we want to interpret our weakness and cowardice as forgiveness and renunciation. There is no merit in the renunciation of a beggar. If a person who can [give a blow] forbears, there is merit in that. If a person who has, gives up, there is merit in that. We know how often in our lives through laziness and cowardice we give up the battle and try to hypnotise our minds into the belief that we are brave. (Vol. 1, 459)

The opening scene has a deeper symbolic significance. Arjuna has to battle his own kith and kin and he shirks from this task. If we view the battle as taking place within ourselves, we find that we must battle our own shortcomings, our own bad habits, symbolically, our own kith and kin. In *Gitanjali*, Tagore has a beautiful poem reflecting this dilemma. He wrote:

> When it was day they came into my house and said,
> "We shall only take the smallest room here."
> They said, "We shall help you in the worship of
> Your God and humbly accept only our share of his grace";
> And then they took their seat in a corner and
> They sat quiet and meek,
> But in the darkness of night I find they break

> Into my sacred shrine, strong and turbulent,
> And snatch with unholy greed
> The offerings from God's altar. (*Omnibus 1*, 87)

The opening scene is universal in its significance and addresses psychological issues faced by everyone when they look at themselves and find both the good and the bad, the positive and the negative, and must now take the necessary steps to improve the situation. This is the meaning of Arjuna's despondency.

Krishna now realizes it is time for his "advice." This forms the bulk of the Bhagavad Gita. Krishna begins by telling Arjuna,

> Arise. Yield not to despondency. You grieve about people for whom you should not grieve. The wise do not grieve either for the dead or the living. Never was there a time when I was not, nor you, nor these people here. Nor will there ever be a time when we shall all cease to be. The drama of life is a process of growth. Just as one grows in this body from childhood, youth and old age, even so, one moves from death to birth, by taking on another body. The sage is not perplexed by this.

Before we give an explanation of these opening lines, we need to have some background of the philosophic thought current at the time of the Bhagavadgīta. The Sāmkhya system and the Yoga system are constantly referred to in the Gita. These are the precursors of the later systems of philosophy with the same names. Kapila is said to be the founder of the Sāmkhya system, and Patanjali of the Yoga system.

The Sanskrit word *sāmkhya* means "enumeration" and its basic starting point is to analyze perception and resolve it into its component parts. It begins with the axiom that there are two universal and indestructible principles whose inter-relation is the cause of the universe. These principles are called *Purusha* and *Prakriti* and can be approximately translated as Pure Awareness (inactive) and Creative Energy (active). (Observe that *prakriti* and the English word "procreate" are cognates. Sometimes, *prakriti* is incorrectly translated as "nature," but this is incomplete since it includes external nature of matter and the internal nature of thought and mind as well.) In later philosophies, these principles are called *Shiva* and *Shakti*. All experience is said to be a combination of these two, *Purusha* (the knowing subject) and *Prakriti* (the known object). Thus, there is an inherent duality in the system. *Prakriti* is said to be composed of three modes of energy, or three *gunas*: *tamas* or inertia, *rajas* or activity, and *sattva* or equilibrium of the other two energies. Everything in the universe is said to be the combination of these three modes of energy. In the Gita, these words are also used to describe the qualities of inertia, activity and harmony, respectively. Thus, according to Sāmkhya, everything in the cosmos is only a combination and recombination of these three essential modes of energy. These combinations give rise to 23 *tattvas*, or cosmic principles. (It is important to remember that *tattva* in Sanskrit means "thatness.") They are the five elements of nature, namely, ether, air, fire, water, and the earth. These are to be viewed as the subtle conditions of material energy out of which the gross manifestations arise. They are "nowhere to be found in their purity in the gross material world. All objects are created by the combination of these five subtle conditions or elements" (*Aurobindo*, Vol. 13, 66). Each of these five is again the basis for five subtle energies of sound, touch, form, taste, and smell representing the energies the mind uses to cognize objects. In addition to these *tattvas*, there are a further thirteen: Pure Intelligence (*Mahat* or *Buddhi*), Ego (*Ahamkāra*), Mind (*Manas*), together with its ten sensory functions, five of knowledge and five of action.

According to Sāmkhya, the Purusha has become identified with Prakriti through the "ego-sense" or *ahamkāra*. As there are many individuals, whose experiences are varied, the original Sāmkhya postulates a plurality of Purushas, and only one principle of Prakriti. This curious arrangement will be discussed later, when we take up Vedānta. For the present discussion, it is sufficient if we understand the sense in which the terms "Sāmkhya" and "Yoga" are used in the Gita. We have briefly explained the former term earlier. However, in the Gita, the term is used generally to refer to the philosophy of the Upanishads, and more specifically, the method of *jnāna yoga*, or the yoga of knowledge. Now let us discuss the term "yoga" as it appears in the Gita.

As explained in an earlier chapter, *yoga* is derived from the Sanskrit word *yuj*, which means "to yoke." From the Upanishadic standpoint, any method that enables us to become aware of the *ātman* or *Brahman* is referred to as a "yoga" in that it unites us with the infinite dimension within. However, in the Gita, the term "yoga" refers to a combination of *karma yoga*, or the yoga of work and *rāja yoga*, the yoga of psychic control. The yoga philosophy of Patanjali forms the basis for the system called *rāja yoga*. The Gita's original contribution may be said to be a delineation of the basic principles of *karma yoga* as well as *bhakti yoga*, or the yoga of love and devotion. It is a masterly synthesis of the entire Upanishadic thought and three systems of philosophy, namely, Sāmkhya, Yoga, and Vedānta.

Krishna begins by delineating the theory of reincarnation. Life is a process of psychic growth, he says. According to Sāmkhya yoga, the goal of every individual is to realize the *ātman*. Consciously, or unconsciously, we are all moving towards this goal. The process does not terminate with death.

Krishna continues:

> Life is a combination of both cold and heat, pleasure and pain. They come and go and do not last forever. So when pain comes, learn to endure it. The sage is the one who can rise above the duality of pain and pleasure. That which pervades all this is indestructible. Of this immutable being, no one can bring about its destruction. Therefore fight!

This message must be understood from two standpoints. The first is from the standpoint of Arjuna, to whom the message is addressed. As already emphasized, the philosophy of *dharma*, or social duty, was a dominant framework of thought for the Pandavas, as Dharmarāja, the eldest among them was a strong proponent of it. Thus, in the immediacy of the battle, the strongest argument Krishna could put forward was from the standpoint of one's duty, and the preservation of social justice (*dharma*). He, however, combines this notion familiar to Arjuna, with the indestructible nature of the *ātman*.

Elaborating on this, Aurobindo writes:

> The Gita is ... addressed to a fighter, a man of action, one whose duty in life is that of war and protection, war as a part of government for the protection of those who are excused from that duty, debarred from protecting themselves and therefore at the mercy of the strong and the violent, ... and by a moral extension of this idea, for the protection of the weak and the oppressed and for the maintenance of right and justice in the world.... Although the more general and universal ideas of the Gita are those which are most important to us, we ought not to leave out of consideration altogether the colouring and trend they take from the peculiar Indian culture and social system in the midst of which they arose. That system differed from the modern one in its conception. To the modern mind, man is a thinker, worker, or producer and a fighter all in one, and the tendency of the social system is to lump all these activities and to demand from each individual his contribution to the intellectual, economic, and military life and needs of the community without paying any heed to the demands of his individual nature and temperament. The ancient Indian civilisation laid peculiar stress on the individual nature, tendency, temperament and sought to determine by it the ethical type, function and place in the society. Nor did it consider man primarily as a social being ... but rather as a spiritual being in process of formation and development and his social life, ethical life, ... as means and stages of spiritual formation. Thought and knowledge, war and government, production and distribution, labour and service were carefully differentiated functions of society, each assigned to those who were naturally called to it and

> providing the right means by which they could individually proceed towards their spiritual development and self-perfection. (Vol. 13, 45-46)

The second standpoint from which to understand Krishna's opening message is more cosmic in its scope. The message is for humanity at large. Life is a battle, not necessarily against others, but rather against our own weaknesses. Each of us has a tendency to shrink from the challenges of life, and then to sanctify our behaviour as moral virtue. An important theme emerges from this message. It is not the action that determines virtue, but rather the motive behind the action. Vivekananda explains this as follows:

> In all matters, the extremes are alike.... When the vibrations of light are too slow, we do not see them, nor do we see them when they are too rapid.... Of like nature is the difference between resistance and non-resistance. One man does not resist because he is weak, lazy and cannot, not because he will not; the other man knows that he can strike an irresistible blow if he likes; yet he not only does not strike, but blesses his enemies. The one who from weakness resists not commits a sin, and as such cannot receive any benefit from the non-resistance; while the other would commit a sin by offering resistance. Buddha gave up his throne and renounced his position, that was true renunciation; but there cannot be any question of renunciation in the case of a beggar who has nothing to renounce. So we must always be careful about what we mean when we speak of this non-resistance and ideal love. We must first take care to understand whether we have the power of resistance or not. Then, having the power, if we renounce it and do not resist, we are doing a grand act of love; but if we cannot resist, and yet, at the same time, try to deceive ourselves into the belief that we are actuated by motives of the highest love, we are doing the exact opposite. (Vol. 1, 38-39)

Echoing the famous lines of the Katha Upanishad, Krishna continues:

> He who thinks that this slays and he who thinks that this is slain; both fail to perceive the truth; this one neither slays nor is slain.... It is never born. Nor does It ever die. It is unborn, permanent and eternal. It is not slain when the body is slain. Just as one discards worn-out garments and puts on others that are new, even so does the embodied soul cast off worn-out bodies and take on others that are new. Weapons do not cleave It. Fire does not burn It. Water does not make It wet. The wind does not dry It.

All of this argument is from the standpoint of the Sāmkhya philosophy. "For one that is born, death is certain and for one who has died, birth is certain. This is a process. What is there to grieve about? The *ātman* within is eternal and can never be slain." Now Krishna changes tone and becomes more pragmatic. He appeals to Arjuna's sense of duty.

> Besides, you are a warrior and it is your duty to defend the innocent. Happy are the warriors for whom a war comes of its own accord. If you abandon your duty, people will forever recount your actions, and this is worse than death. If you fight and emerge victorious, then you can enjoy the victory. If on the other hand, you are slain fighting, you will attain heaven. Therefore arise, and be resolved in battle.

Thus, in these opening verses, we see Krishna's argument made from three viewpoints. The first is simply an urge to snap out of depression. But since Arjuna does not comply, Krishna brings in the philosophical arguments of the Upanishads and Sāmkhya. He reminds him that life is a process of psychic evolution and that for the *ātman*, there is no death or birth. Pain and pleasure are part of life and we must receive both with a balanced mind. Then, suddenly, Krishna changes strategy and argues from the standpoint of Arjuna's reputation, hoping that would lift him out of despondency. When even this does not seem to work, Krishna begins his marvelous contribution to philosophy, the yoga of work, or *karma yoga*. This we shall discuss in the next section.

AN OVERVIEW OF THE BHAGAVADGĪTA

The setting of the Bhagavadgīta is symbolic of the battlefield of life but perhaps more importantly, it is symbolic of the battlefield within all of us. Our life is a constant turmoil between our positive impulses and negative impulses, between the pleasant and the moral, between our likes and dislikes, between the good and the bad. As such, the Gita addresses questions that arise in the heart of every human being. Thus, even though the Gita is the record of a dialogue that occurred ages ago, it is relevant to the modern age (or any age), as it addresses fundamental questions and tries to provide answers to them. Through the vista of epic literature, we are able to hear and see the sacred dialogue between Arjuna and Krishna. Arjuna's despondency is our own despondency. Arjuna's questions are our own questions. As we read the Gita, it is as if we are in direct communion with the great sage embodied in the personality of Krishna.

In the last section, we saw Krishna's immediate response to the dejection and despondency of Arjuna on the battlefield. He began by telling him to snap out of it. "This is not the behaviour of a great warrior," he told him. Normally, if the depression is mild, such words of encouragement do have an effect. In this case, however, the problem is deeper. So Krishna immediately resorts to the highest teaching he can give, namely the essence of the Upanishads teaching us of the immortality of the Supreme Self. "Life and death are part of the cosmic process. But the Self is indestructible and immortal. It is not slain when the body is slain."

We must remember here that a battle is just about to begin. All avenues of diplomacy have already been tried. The work to be done is clearly before Arjuna, yet at the eleventh hour, he has become doubtful of his role. Thus Krishna teaches Arjuna about the *ātman* and instructs him that he should keep this awareness while engaged in battle. But even this highest teaching cannot lift Arjuna out of his depression. Then, Krishna comes down and makes a plea from a worldly perspective. "If you abandon your work, people will forever recount your abandonment, and living such a life is worse than death. Therefore, stand up and fight!"

This exhortation still does not energize Arjuna to go into battle. So Krishna begins his brilliant discourse on the theory of work, known as *karma yoga*. This is one of three original contributions to Indian philosophy that we find in the Gita, the other two to be described later in this chapter.

It is good to begin with Vivekananda's explanation of the meaning of *karma yoga*. He says:

> The word *karma* is derived from the Sanskrit *kri*, [meaning] "to do"; all action is *karma*. Technically, this word also means the effects of actions. In connection with metaphysics, it sometimes means the effects, of which our past actions were the causes. But in *karma yoga* we have simply to do with the word *karma* as meaning work.... Thus we are all doing *karma* all the time. I am talking to you: that is *karma*. You are listening, that is *karma*. We breathe, that is *karma*.... Everything we do, physical or mental, is *karma*, and it leaves its marks on us.... We are responsible for what we are; and whatever we wish ourselves to be, we have the power to make ourselves. If what we are now has been the result of our own past actions, it certainly follows that whatever we wish to be in future can be produced by our present actions; so we have to know how to act.... But there is such a thing as frittering away our energies. With regard to *karma yoga*, the Gita says that it is doing work with cleverness and as a science, by knowing how to work, one can obtain the greatest results. (Vol. 1, 27-31)

Krishna says:

> In the path of *karma yoga*, no effort is ever lost and no obstacle prevails. Even a little practice of this yoga saves one from great fear. The resolute understanding is single. Thoughts of the irresolute are many-branched and endless. Firmly fix the thought on the Supreme Self, and relinquish all selfish desire. To action alone, you have the right, but not to the fruits of action. Don't let the fruits of action be your motive. Neither should you be attached to inaction. Fixed in this yoga, do your work, abandoning attachment and being of even mind in both success and failure. Evenness of mind is called *yoga* [*Samatvam yoga ucyate*]. (Bhagavadgīta, 2: 48)

The first thing in *karma yoga* is to fix the thought on the realization of the Supreme Self. Thus the teaching of the Upanishads has made the foundation on which the yoga is built. The next step is to act but not with a selfish motive. This is a difficult message to comprehend. If we examine our life, we find it is full of self-interest. How can we work if we are not motivated by self-interest? Does this mean we should abandon work? Krishna emphatically says no. You should not resort to inaction either. The ideal is to work with an evenness of mind in both success and failure. Is this possible?

Vivekananda gives us a personal view on this matter.

> I have been asked many times how we can work if we do not have the passion which we generally feel for work. I also thought in that way years ago, but as I am growing older, getting more experience, I find it is not true. The less passion there is, the better we work. The calmer we are, the better for us, and the more the amount of work we can do. When we let loose our feelings, we waste so much energy, shatter our nerves, disturb our minds, and accomplish very little work. The energy which ought to have gone out as work is spent as mere feeling, which counts for nothing. It is only when the mind is very calm and collected that the whole of its energy is spent in doing good work.... The man who gives way to anger, or hatred, or any other passion, cannot work; he only breaks himself to pieces, and does nothing practical. It is the calm, forgiving, equable, well-balanced mind that does the greatest amount of work. (Vol. 2, 293)

So we see from this explanation that it is not that we must extinguish our passions, but rather the passions must be given a higher direction. Often, we waste energy through negative emotions. Krishna elaborates on this higher direction of emotion later in his exposition of *bhakti yoga*, or the yoga of devotion.

Krishna continues.

> Action should be guided by intelligence, not by self-interest. One who has joined himself to *buddhi*, or illumined reason, and works, is said to be skillful in action. Yoga is said to be this skill in action [*Yogah karmasu kausalam*].

In these verses, Krishna outlines his theory of work and gives two definitions of *yoga*. One is that it is evenness of mind, and the other that it is skill in action. Both of these have to be combined to gain a proper understanding of this philosophy of work. In all our actions, we must work with full attention, with a calm mind and be skillful in action. At the same time, we must not be attached to the fruits of our work.

At this point, Arjuna asks for a description of such a perfect sage. His question is indicative that slowly Arjuna is coming out of his despondency and depression. Krishna answers, "When all the desires of the mind are put away and the spirit is content in itself, the sage is said to be of settled intelligence (*sthitaprajna*). He is untroubled in the midst of sorrow and is free from eager desire amid pleasures. He from whom passion, fear and rage have passed away is called one of settled intelligence. He who draws away the senses from the objects of sense just as a tortoise draws in its limbs into the shell, his intelligence is said to be firmly set."

Now begins Krishna's masterly analysis of how attachment comes about.

> The objects of sense turn away when one abstains from feeding on them. The taste for them, however, remains, and only disappears when the *ātman* is realised. The senses are impetuous and can carry the mind away by force, if one is not careful. By thinking about sense objects, attachment to them is formed. From attachment, arises a desire to possess them. When this is not gratified, anger comes. From anger comes confusion. From confusion, loss of memory. From loss of memory, the destruction of intelligence. From the destruction of intelligence, one perishes.

Thus, it is clear from this verse, that when Krishna refers to passion as being destructive, he is referring to violent destructive passions. In Chapter 12, he outlines how the passions should be given a higher direction in the form of *bhakti* yoga (or the yoga of devotion). In this verse, he is highlighting the destructive power of negative emotions.

Modern psychoanalysis has theorized that anger is a manifestation of repressed or suppressed desire. Modern medicine has established the damage to internal physiology caused by excessive anger. In all forms of conflict, when we analyze them carefully, we find these principles at work. How often is it the case, that in moments of anger we are confused and bring in issues that have no bearing on the circumstances, only to add further confusion. In such confusion, we forget many things: the purpose of our life, our roles, our goals, and most importantly, the necessity of peaceful co-existence with others and of respect for their feelings.

This important verse describes how the mind falls into error, and how, if this error is not corrected, it falls into destruction. Literature is replete with examples of this one psychological phenomenon: how selfish desire can possess the mind and lead it to annihilation. This is the fundamental theme in the drama of human life. The aim of a life of moral choice can be achieved only when guided by intelligence, by illuminated reason (*buddhi*).

Krishna continues:

> But one who is of disciplined mind, who moves among objects of sense with the senses under control, free from attachment or aversion, such a one attains purity of spirit. For the uncontrolled, however, there is no intelligence, nor is there the power of concentration. Without concentration of mind, there is no peace. For the unpeaceful, how can there be happiness? When the mind runs after the roving senses, it carries away all understanding just as the wind carries away a ship on the waters. What is night for all beings is the time of wakefulness for the sage. What is the time of wakefulness for all beings is night for the sage.

The meaning of the last part is an indication of priorities. When the world is dazzled by the glitter of sense objects, the sage is focussed on understanding reality and on touching the very substance under life's phenomena. Thus the mind of the sage is asleep to what the world is awake to. Conversely, the world is asleep to what the sage is awake to.

In a masterly stroke of psychoanalytic insight, Krishna indicates that "the sage does not hug desires when they arise. Nor does he agitate the mind to create them. He is indifferent to them. As waters enter the sea, though ever being filled, is ever motionless, so is the mind of the sage with respect to desires." From his spiritual vantage point, Krishna sees desires as part of a psycho-biological process. Arjuna intervenes and asks, "If you think the path of understanding (*jnāna yoga*) is better than the path of action (*karma yoga*), then why do you urge me to fight? I think you have only confused me by this teaching. Tell me for certain which path I should follow."

Here begins Krishna's outline of the theory of work. To many contemporary thinkers, such as Mahatma Gandhi, this is considered to be the major contribution of the Bhagavadgīta to philosophic thought. In response to Arjuna's question, Krishna replies,

> One may lead a life of contemplation, or a life of action. Both properly done lead one to illumination. But one must understand that freedom from work is not gained by abstaining from work. By mere renunciation of work, you do not attain perfection. It is impossible to maintain even one's life without doing some work. One who restrains the organs of action but continues to brood over sense objects is said to be a hypocrite and only brings about misery and delusion on oneself. But he who controls the senses by the mind and engages the organs of action in the path of work is superior.

Here is the beginning of Krishna's brilliant fusion of both *jnāna yoga* and *karma yoga*.

In order to refrain from falling into error, one is tempted to refrain from action altogether. But this is definitely not the way. Vivekananda describes this error in a humorous way. "The cow never tells a lie, and the stone never steals, but nevertheless, the cow remains a cow and the stone a stone. Man steals and man tells lies, and again, it is man that becomes a god" (Vol. 5, 451).

The Teacher instructs:

> Do thou thy allotted work, for action is better than inaction. Even to maintain physical health, one must work. But learn to work free from attachment. This world is an interdependent world. All creatures support each other through mutual co-operation. Join your mind to a higher cause that enables the welfare of all. It is in this way that the great ones of the past have attained perfection through work alone. Whatever a great person does, others follow. Whatever standard is set by such a one, the world rises to that standard. Look at me Arjuna. There is not for me any personal gain from the work I do, yet, I continue to work. If I did not engage in work unwearied, people would follow my example and the world will fall into ruin. Just as the ignorant act from attachment to work, so should the learned act, but without any attachment and with a desire for the welfare of the world. The enlightened person acts in a spirit of yoga and thus sets others to act as well.

Here is the main message of the Gita. Often we are tempted to take up a life of exclusive meditation, but this is not an option to be followed according to Krishna. Few have the capacity for sustained concentration and so most of the time is spent in idleness. The classical adage, "An idle mind is the devil's workshop" summarizes the dangers of such an option. The ideal is to join the mind to a wider vision, a worthy cause that enjoins the welfare of all, and then to engage the mind and body in work.

This does not mean that we must abandon our present work and take up something that has been certified hugely important by the world at large. "Do thou thy allotted work," enjoins Krishna. "Repressing or suppressing desires is not desirable for then, these energies only become subconscious to manifest later in all their fury. The energies and passions must be given a higher direction as I have indicated. Better is thought and action consonant with one's own abilities and aptitudes than that which is not. Even though this may not be done perfectly, it is better because acting contrary to one's psychological disposition often leads to great fear." Thus, we see that we must take our own abilities and give them a higher direction. For this, we need not go anywhere. It is our own view that must be adjusted and enlarged.

Krishna goes on to say:

> What is action, what is inaction and what is non-action? Even the wise are confused on these points. He who sees action in inaction and inaction in action, he is the yogi. For one whose actions are free from selfish desire, every work culminates in wisdom. Such an individual holds his life as an offering, a sacrifice, to a higher ideal. Knowledge as a sacrifice is greater than any material sacrifice since all works without exception culminate in wisdom. Learn that by humble reverence, by inquiry, by concentration and by service.

Mere physical action is not action according to Krishna. Real action is the process by which we refine wisdom from the crude ore of experience. One may be silent, reflective, outwardly performing no action, but acting inwardly introspective and thereby gaining insight and wisdom. All experiences, good and bad, can be used to distill wisdom through humble reverence, inquiry, concentration, and service. This brings us to the second major contribution of the Gita, namely, the union of the path of devotion, or *bhakti yoga* and the path of concentration *rāja yoga*. Krishna now indicates that we must infuse feeling into whatever we do, and this must be a feeling of humble reverence. At the same time, we must practice concentration of mind.

The mind must learn to concentrate; it must be trained to do so by engaging the will. What exactly is will? It is love converted into power. Thus, the same mechanism that leads one to a downfall can be used to rise to a higher awareness. The mind should be fixed on the desire to realize *Brahman.* "As a lamp in a windless place does not flicker," Krishna says, "so also is the mind fixed on the Supreme Self that is not disturbed by selfish desire. Let him gain little by little, tranquility by means of reason controlled by steadiness, and having fixed the mind on the Self, let him not think of anything else. Whenever the mind wanders, let him restrain and bring the mind to the focus of concentration." Arjuna intervenes and says, "This control of mind that you describe is very hard indeed. It is as difficult as trying to control the wind." Krishna replies:

> Yes, but it can be done with steady practice. Wonderful things can be accomplished through steady practice. It becomes easier if we constantly remind ourselves of the goal to be attained. Thinking of That, directing one's whole conscious being to That, making That their whole aim, with That as the sole object of their devotion, they reach that supreme state. Even here on earth, the world of duality is transcended by one whose mind is established in equality.

As the discourse continues, Krishna's mind ascends in awareness. His speech begins to reveal that he is now teaching from the universal awareness as taught by the Upanishads.

> I am the taste in the waters. I am the light in the moon and sun. I am the syllable Om. I am the fragrance in the earth and brightness in the fire. I am the life in all existence. I am the origin of all. From Me [the Universal Self] the whole creation proceeds. Knowing this, the wise worship Me, with their thoughts fixed on Me.

As Krishna's mind ascends to a higher level of awareness, Arjuna asks if he too can have such an awareness. "If you think It can be seen, then please reveal It to me." Then Krishna says, "It cannot be seen by the human eye. I will give you the divine eye by which you can see." In the eleventh chapter of the Gita is described this cosmic form, *visva rūpa*, of Krishna. Arjuna is, at first, frightened. "If a thousand suns were to rise simultaneously in the morning sky, that might resemble the splendour of that vision," says the poet.[1] Arjuna says:

---

1 Robert Oppenheimer, the American physicist often called the father of the atomic bomb, said he thought of this verse during the first test explosion of the bomb on July 16, 1945. Indeed, the explosion was "brighter than a thousand suns." He also says he thought of the next line, "I am become death, the destroyer of worlds" (sometimes quoted as the "shatterer" of worlds). But the correct translation is, "I am time, the devourer of worlds." Indeed, time devours everything.

> I behold Thee, infinite in form on all sides. I do not see Thy end, Thy middle or Thy beginning. I see many things. The entire space is pervaded by Thee alone. I see sons of Dhritarāshtra rushing towards destruction. As moths rush swiftly into a blazing fire to perish there, so do these men rush into their own destruction.... I have seen what was never seen before and my heart is shaken with fear. Please show me your compassionate form.

Then Krishna said:

> This universal form is very hard to see and you have seen It. Others too can, through unswerving devotion to the Supreme, attain to the same state of awareness. In the practice of devotion, it is difficult for the mind to focus on the abstract, That which is beyond manifestation, beyond thought, which is changeless, immobile and constant. This is quite difficult for embodied beings. But those who worship Me, meditating on Me, with unswerving devotion, also attain to a higher level of awareness. The essential thing is to give up selfish desire and be dedicated to the welfare of all beings. Real devotion is to not have any ill-will towards any being, to be free from egotism, to be even-minded in pain and pleasure. This is the yoga of devotion (*bhakti yoga*).

This can be said to be the second major contribution of the Gita to the world's philosophic thought. In these verses, Krishna assimilates in a masterly way all dualistic views into the non-dualistic framework. As long as one thinks of oneself as an embodied being, a dualistic view will intervene no matter how hard we try to avoid it. One need not lament about that. The essential thing is "to have no ill-will towards anyone, to be free from egotism, to be even-minded in pain and pleasure." That is the essence of devotion.

From duality, Krishna moves to plurality. In the thirteenth chapter of the Gita, Krishna gives us a detailed view of the Sāmkhya philosophy. As mentioned earlier, this philosophy is based on two eternal principles, *purusha* and *prakriti*, or simply, Pure Awareness and Creative Energy or as Krishna defines it, the Knower of the Field (*ksetrajna*) and the Field (*ksetra*). After elaborating on the 24 cosmic principles of the Sāmkhya, Krishna gives us his insight into the manifestation of the *gunas*, or modes of energy:

> As the one sun illumines the world, so does the *ksetrajna* illumine the entire field of *ksetra*. Those who perceive thus through the eye of wisdom attain to the Supreme. The three modes or gunas are the

cause of bondage. Dullness (*tamoguna*), born of ignorance, deludes all embodied beings and gives rise to attachment to negligence, indolence and sleep. Passion (*rajoguna*) springing from craving gives rise to attachment to selfish action. But goodness (*sattvaguna*) being pure, causes illumination and health, and causes attachment to knowledge. When the light of knowledge streams forth in all the gates of the body, *sattva* is said to increase. When greed, restlessness and selfish activity prevail, *rajas* is said to increase. When delusion, negligence and inertia prevail, *tamoguna* is said to increase. From goodness arises knowledge, from passion, greed and from dullness, ignorance. When one rises above these three modes, one attains the state of *Brahman*. Everything in this manifested universe exhibits this three-fold nature.

Krishna explains:

For example, there are three kinds of work. That work which should be done, performed without attachment to fruits, is said to be of the nature of goodness, or *sattva*. That work which is done in great strain to gratify one's selfish desires is said to be of the nature of passion, or *rajas*. That work which is done through ignorance, without regard to consequences, or to loss and injury, without regard to one's human capacity, is said to be of the nature of dullness, or *tamas*.

Then Krishna makes a final appeal, echoing his earlier message of verses 30 and 31 of the third chapter:

mayi sarvāni karmāni
samnyasyā'dhyātmacetasā
nirāsir nirmamo bhūtva
yudhyasva vigatajvarah
ye me matam idam nityam
anutisthanti mānavāh
sraddhāvanto 'nasūyanto
mucyante te'pi karmabhih

Resigning all your works to Me, with your consciousness fixed in the Self, being free from desire and egotism, fight, free from any mental fever. This is my philosophy of life and whoever follows this teaching will also be released from the bondage of work.

These two verses contain the essence of the Gita.[2] Krishna's use of the term *me matam* is especially important since it means "my philosophy" or "my religion." The human mind has four faculties: thinking, feeling, willing, and restraining. Just as thinking can be taken to a higher state as illumined reason, so also feeling, willing, and restraining can be taken to higher levels. The method for raising each faculty to a higher state is called *yoga* and the four yogas, *jnāna, bhakti, karma*, and *rāja*, correspond to the four faculties of thinking, feeling, willing and restraining. When Krishna refers to "his philosophy," he means the four-fold combination of all these yogas. This is his masterly stroke. This is his magnificent synthesis of all philosophic thought. The human brain should not be developed in a one-sided fashion but must be exercised in this four-fold way giving a higher expression to each of its four faculties.

So Krishna says, "Resigning all your works to Me (*bhakti*), with your consciousness fixed in the Self (*jnāna*), being free from desire and egoism, fight (*karma*), delivered from mental fever (*rāja*)." The Teacher continues, "This wisdom more secret than all secrets, has been given to you by Me. Please reflect upon it and do as you choose."

Here again is the fundamental principle of choice in life. We are given the highest wisdom and now must choose. No one can be coerced into goodness. "Have you listened carefully Arjuna?" Krishna asks. "Would you like me to repeat anything?"

Here again, the Teacher is the embodiment of patience. After receiving the message from Krishna, Arjuna rises, "Gone is my delusion. Through your grace, my doubts have been dispelled. I shall carry out your word."

Thus ends the Bhagavadgīta. So profound and valuable is its teaching that it has acquired the status of an Upanishad, and it is referred to as the Bhagavadgīta Upanishad. However, it can be said to include all the other Upanishads in it as well as much more, encompassing all religious, moral, and philosophical traditions in a universal synthesis.

To reiterate, the Gita's contribution to philosophy is its introduction of *karma yoga*, or the yoga of work, *bhakti yoga*, the yoga of devotion, and its assimilation of all philosophies ranging from the plurality of Sāmkhya to the non-dualism of the Upanishads. As such, it absorbs into it the yoga of reason (*jnāna yoga*) and the yoga of restraining (*rāja yoga*).

What is impressive about the whole piece is the personality of Krishna. He is, as it were, the very embodiment of the universal teaching he is giving. The message is delivered on the battlefield, not in the solitude of a forest hermitage or a secluded mountain cave. Stand in the middle of the battle of

2 This was first pointed out to me by Swami Sarvagatananda of the Vedānta Society of Boston. I am deeply indebted to him for his remarkable insights and interpretations in all matters pertaining to Indian philosophical thought.

life and be calm, think clearly and act from the higher standpoint. That is his message and if one looks at Sri[3] Krishna's life, he is the superb example of the teaching put into practice.

Concerning the personality of Krishna, Vivekananda writes:

> He is the most rounded man I know of, wonderfully developed equally in brain and heart and hand. Every moment of his is alive with activity, either as a gentleman, warrior, minister or something else. Great as a gentleman, as a scholar, as a poet. This all-rounded and wonderful activity and combination of brain and heart you see in the Gita.... Most wonderful heart, exquisite language,... This tremendous activity of the man—the impression is still there. Five thousand years have passed and he has influenced millions and millions.... My regard for him is for his perfect sanity. No cobwebs in that brain, no superstition. He knows the use of everything, and when it is necessary to assign a place to each, he is there.... Then that heart!... That wonderful mind! That tremendously active life!... Krishna preached in the midst of the battlefield. "He who in the midst of intense activity finds himself in the greatest calmness, and in the greatest peace finds intense activity, that is the greatest Yogi as well as the wisest man." It means nothing to this man—the flying of missiles about him. Calm and sedate he goes on discussing the problems of life and death. (Vol. 1, 457-58. The quotation from the Gita is in 4: 18)

How does the message of the Gita relate to our daily life? For each individual, life is a series of choices they have made, partly based on circumstance, environment, outlook, and aptitude. We can all testify that life is not always smooth sailing, but often a stormy journey. The storm is partly within and partly without. During such episodes, there is a psychological tendency in each one of us to abandon whatever it is we are doing and take up something else, simply because difficulties have arisen. It is precisely such moments through which enlightenment can be gained, says the Gita, if one works through it, with a calm mind, giving up egoism with firm determination. Thus, the message of the Gita is a perennial message and millions have been inspired by its teaching. Mahatma Gandhi spoke of it as "his mother," and wrote:

> When disappointment stares me in the face and all alone I see not one ray of light, I go back to the *Bhagavadgīta*. I find a verse here

3 "Sri" is a conventional title of respect for a distinguished Indian.

> and a verse there and I immediately begin to smile in the midst of overwhelming tragedies—and my life has been full of external tragedies—and if they have left no visible, no indelible scar on me, I owe it all to the teachings of the *Bhagavadgīta*. (Radhakrishnan, *Bhagavadgita*, 10)

The Gita has survived countless centuries and it is sure to survive for many more centuries as it addresses the fundamental questions of the human heart.

8

BUDDHISM

THE STORY OF THE BUDDHA

The age following the Epic period in India can be considered as a period of tremendous philosophical ferment, most notably with the advent of Buddha (563-483 BCE).

It was clear to many scholars and thinkers that the pure philosophy of the Upanishads must not reside in forest retreats or mountain caves, but must be brought down to a more practical level so that it can be practised by the people at large. We see such an attempt first made in the synthesis expounded by the Bhagavadgīta. It is common that, with the passing of time, teachings get buried or modified and the pristine purity of the original thought evaporates. Such was the case at the time of Buddha. The pure philosophy of the Upanishads and the practical philosophy of the four yogas as expounded in the Gita became buried and replaced by esoteric and meaningless rituals. In time, people had even forgotten the Upanishadic portion of the Vedas and came to believe that the rituals current at the time were the essence of the Vedas. Society became stifled, as it were, and a caste system of privilege became entrenched. At this time, several systems of philosophy rose to meet the challenge of liberating society from the shackles of priestcraft. These systems can be grouped into two categories: heterodox and orthodox.

The heterodox systems formally reject the Vedas and try to build a philosophy anew. Under this heading are included the Carvaka philosophy, Jainism, and Buddhism. The orthodox systems return to the Vedas and try to renew the vitality of the Upanishads. Under this heading are listed the six systems of philosophy: Nyāya (logic), Vaisesika (atomic theory), Sāmkhya (evolutionary dualism), Yoga (disciplined meditation), Pūrva Mimāmsā (earlier interpretations of the Vedas), and Uttara Mimāmsā (Vedānta or later interpretations of the Vedas).

The life of the Buddha is a source of inspiration for further study. Buddha was born as Prince Siddhartha; astrologers predicted a life of a mendicant and a great world teacher. His father the king was alarmed at this prediction; to make sure this would not happen, he ensured that Siddhartha was kept within the confines of the royal palace and inundated with all the worldly pleasures. So the young prince came to believe that life is one immense pleasure garden. In his late teens, he was married to a beautiful princess and they had a child. The king felt joyous that he had outwitted the astrologers. He had foiled the plans of the gods, he mused. However, the young prince was always wondering what lay beyond the palace walls. One day, Siddhartha with his friend ventured out of the palace secretly and they came across a funeral procession. He asked his friend, "What is this?" "It is a dead body, sir," replied his assistant. "Death is the end of every human body." As they walked further, they came across a lame old man with a wrinkled face. "Why is this man walking so?" "The man is old and not well," replied the friend. "Sickness, disease and aging are also a part of life." Siddhartha became thoughtful. As they walked further, they came across a monk, with a shaven head, a saffron garb, and a serene countenance. "Who is that?" Siddhartha asked. "He is a monk. He lives the life of a recluse." Then the prince stopped the monk and asked him why he had adopted such a life. The monk replied, "To be free of misery." With these encounters, the prince returned to the palace, his mind preoccupied with existential questions. The words of the monk haunted him. Human misery was a fact of life. "Is there a way out?" he pondered. He could no longer be distracted by the song and dance of the palace. That night, he decided to renounce his royal splendour, his beautiful wife, his lovely child, and the security of his regal power, and take up the garb of the mendicant. At the dead of midnight, he rode off on a horse, throwing off his princely robes. He disappeared into the wilderness of the forest. He was 28 at the time.

The next day he joined a group of ascetic monks who believed that the control of mind is the way out of human misery and this control can be achieved through progressive fasting. Young Siddhartha attempted this technique only to find that the craving for food returned with doubled force after the period of fasting was over. He concluded that self-mortification was not the way for achieving this control of the mind. By this experiment, he discovered the "middle path." Neither by indulgence in sensual pleasures nor by austerities of self-denial is the control of mind attained. It is by the equilibrium of these two that the control is gained. These findings echo the teaching of the Bhagavadgīta where Krishna teaches Arjuna:

yuktạhāra vihārasya
yuktacestasya karmasu
yuktasvapnāva bodhasya
yogo bhavati duhkhahā (6: 17)

For one who is temperate in food and recreation, restrained in his actions, with sleep and waking regulated, there ensues a discipline which destroys all sorrow.

Thus Siddhartha discovered for himself the middle path that required *control* of the mental tendencies, not their suppression. This control was to be combined with reasoning and meditation. His brother monks had abandoned him, thinking he had strayed away from the path, whereas in actuality, he had found it. With firm resolve, Siddhartha walked alone to the outskirts of a town called Bodh Gaya. The thought in his mind was to later find expression in the *Dhammapada*:

If you do not find a companion, intelligent, one who associates with you, who leads a good life, lives soberly, walk alone like a king who has renounced his kingdom or like an elephant roaming at will in the forest. It is better to live alone rather than have the companionship of a fool. Let a man walk alone with few wants, like the elephant roaming in the forest. (23: 329-30, "The Elephant")

The elephant is a recurrent symbol in Buddhism symbolizing strength and endurance.

On reaching Bodh Gaya, he seated himself under a Bo tree with a firm resolve that he would not rise until he had solved the mystery of life and found a way out of human suffering. His first discovery was that in order to concentrate the mind and take it to higher levels, he should not have any ill-will towards any being. *Ahimsa*, or non-injury by thought, word, or deed was the foundation of his meditation. It is the foundation of other systems too, most notably, Jainism, as well as the Yoga system of Patanjali and Vedānta. This is again an echo of the teaching of the Gita:

advesta sarva bhūtānām maitrah karuna eva ca…
yo madhbhaktah sa me priyah.

> He who has no ill-will to any being, who is friendly and compassionate, ... he is said to be My great devotee. (12: 13)

Thus Siddhartha began his meditation under the Bo tree with a meditation of peace for all living things. He silenced his senses and, slowly, silenced his thoughts. As he progressed deeper and deeper into meditation, he realized the extent of the sorrow and suffering in the world. He realized that the way the world deals with this issue is by intoxicating itself with pleasure. But pleasure and pain are intertwined. Our pleasures are through attachments. We may think that a person we love will give us happiness. It may be so for a while, but a change comes. Perhaps he or she dies, or has a change of heart. The world will not revolve according to our desires and wishes. Reasoning thus, Siddhartha realized the first noble truth: "Everything in this universe is changing, nothing is permanent. Pleasure, alas, is not permanent. By the same logic, pain too is not permanent."

This may mean that we should take a pragmatic view of life: be happy when things go our way, and bear with it when they don't. But this may also mean that our life is reduced to that of a piece of driftwood moving aimlessly in the river. Control of external events is an impossibility. However, we can be in control of our internal reactions. Pleasure and pain are both caused by desire, or craving (*tanha*), and this is the second noble truth. The conclusion is now inevitable. To remove misery, one must eliminate craving, and this is the third noble truth. How can we eliminate craving? This is the fourth noble truth: the eight-fold way.

The eight-fold way is a process by which the mind is gathered inwards and concentrated: *samyag drishti, samyag samkalpa, samyag vāk, samyag karmanta, samyag ajīva, samyag vyayamā, samyag smriti,* and *samyag samādhi.* In many translations, the word *samyag* is translated as "right." However, the Sanksrit root indicates that this translation is incomplete. A more accurate rendering of the word is "wholesome, total, balanced." So the eight terms mean wholesome view, wholesome willing, wholesome speech, wholesome action, wholesome vocation, wholesome effort, wholesome mindfulness, wholesome meditation.

As the young prince went deeper and deeper into his meditation, he came across the thought of "I." When he examined this notion of "I," the "I" disappeared into *nirvāna.* For seven weeks, he was absorbed in this state of illumination. Siddhartha had become the Buddha (meaning the awakened). After returning to normal consciousness, it is said that he sat silent. He had just discovered the greatest treasure of the universe. He wanted to share it with humanity, but then, who would understand? The whole world was engrossed in the sensory plane. Here he had discovered higher planes of consciousness. Then the idea arose that perhaps his brother monks he had left behind in Sarnath would understand the reality of these higher dimensions. So he walked from Bodh Gaya to Sarnath, a distance of 144 miles, and gave his first sermon to his five brother monks about the eight-fold path.

On careful examination, it becomes evident that the eight-fold path is nothing other than the four-fold yoga. Buddha had re-discovered the teaching of the Bhagavadgīta, not intellectually, but as a matter of personal experience. Buddha was averse to argumentation. He advocated that individuals think for themselves:

> Believe not because some old manuscripts are produced, believe not because it is your national belief, because you have been made to believe it from your childhood, but reason it all out, and after you have analysed it, then, if you find that it will do good to one and all, believe it, live up to it, and help others to live up to it.

Buddha's silence on the nature of the Supreme Being has often been interpreted as atheism. But the fact of the matter is that he knew it cannot be reasoned out. He was averse to argumentation. "Be good and do good," he taught, "and you will get to freedom and whatever Truth there is." Buddha's emphasis was always on love and service. He earned the name of the Compassionate Buddha and lived to a ripe age of 80, it is said, serving humanity till his last days.

He had extraordinary methods of teaching. One day his brother monks gathered around to hear a sermon from him. He noticed that one was missing and asked where he was. They replied that he was sick in bed and suffering much. Buddha immediately rose and went to the bedside of the ailing student and inquired of his welfare. He realized the student had a fever and after speaking to him a few gentle words, began to fan him until the ailing student slipped into slumber. An hour thus passed and Buddha got up. One of his students reminded him of the sermon he was supposed to give. "The sermon?" asked Buddha. "I believe we just had it."

On another occasion, a distraught woman came crying to the Buddha because her son had passed away. Her mind knew no rest. She came to Buddha and asked him to revive her son. Instead of giving her a lecture that death is an inevitable part of life, he simply asked her first to go into the town and fetch a few mustard seeds from a house in which no one has died. So she went running and inquired at every house for a few mustard seeds. When she asked if the house was free from death, no one could say that it was not. In every house, some death had occurred over the years and thus she returned to the Buddha with empty hands and her mind at peace, for she learned that she was not alone in her misery.

The teachings of the Buddha take up the thoughts of the Upanishads and give them a new orientation. Formally, he rejects the Vedas, since by that time the pristine teachings of the Upanishads were forgotten and empty ceremonies had taken over. It is clear that he was a marvellous combination of head, heart, and hand and represented the ideal sage described by the Bhagavadgīta. "Just as the mountain is not agitated by the wind, so also is the wise man, undisturbed by honour or dishonour. To conquer one's lower mind is a greater victory than to conquer thousands in battle" (Bukkyo Dendo Kyokai, 187).

In the course of time, Buddha's life and teachings were interpreted in various ways. One group insisted on individual struggle as the means to *nirvāna*, the state of Buddha. Another insisted that it was a life of service. The latter became known as Mahayāna Buddhism and the former Hīnayāna Buddhism, the words *mahayāna* and *hīnayāna* meaning "great raft" and "little raft," respectively. Viewed from the perspective of the four yogas, we can see that the Hīnayāna path is a combination of *jnāna* and *rāja* yogas. The Mahayāna is a combination of *karma* and *bhakti* yogas. Over the wide span of centuries, a sharp division arose between these two schools. The Hīnayāna school was strictly monastic and also assumed the name of the Theravāda, or the way of the elders. One can trace the monastic traditions of the world to the Theravāda school. Both of these schools of thought spread in their own way across southeast Asia, and northeastward to China, Japan, and Korea. Buddhistic thought also spread to Egypt and westward through Persia and then to Greece. Buddhism, in various forms, pervades the Asian continent today; all this can be traced back to that one moonlit night, when Siddhartha attained illumination under the Bo tree.

ETHICAL PHILOSOPHY OF THE DHAMMAPADA

We will give a brief discussion of some of the ethical principles outlined in the Dhammapada. The word *Dhamma* is a modification of the word *Dharma*, which we already introduced and which was defined as "social justice." But in Buddhism, it is understood as "right action" or "code of conduct." Thus, *Dhammapada* would translate as "The path of virtue." Though it passed through several versions, its verses are said to be of the Buddha. It was very likely used as a code of conduct for the monastic class and this should be kept in mind as one reads the verses. However, the principles outlined are universal in application. We will give below a brief overview of the main ideas. The verses have sublime poetic beauty and stunning simplicity.

> We are the product of our thoughts. Our mental nature is the result of what we have thought.
>
> If a man speaks or acts with an evil thought, sorrow follows him even as the wheel follows the ox which draws the cart. If a man speaks or acts with a pure thought, then happiness follows him like the shadow that never leaves him.
>
> As rain breaks through an ill-thatched house, so passion makes its way into an unreflecting mind. As rain does not break through a well-thatched house, so passion does not make its way into a reflecting mind. (1.1, 1.2, 1.13, 1.14)

These opening verses emphasize the importance of reflection and the role of thinking and its effect. Central in Buddhistic thought is the law of *karma*, interpreted as the law of cause and effect. Our thinking is a factor in the law of causation.

> Vigilance is the abode of eternal life, thoughtlessness is the abode of death. Those who are vigilant (who are given to reflection), do not die. The thoughtless are as if dead already.
>
> When the wise man drives away sloth by strenuous effort, climbing the high tower of wisdom, he gazes sorrowless on the sorrowing crowd below.
>
> Earnest among the slothful, awake among the sleepy, the wise man advances as a racehorse does, leaving behind the hack. (2.1, 2.8, 2.9)

A "hack" is an old worn-out horse. The word "hackneyed" meaning trite or banal is derived from this source. Vigilance is again a form of reflection and lack of vigilance is slothfulness or carelessness. Such inaction has its effect and effective action also has its positive effect. The verse is not intended to imply that the wise man is insensitive and races ahead of humanity. Rather, it is meant to discourage argumentation and debate, both of which stifle a life of solitude and silent reflection.

> Just as a fletcher [arrow-maker] makes his arrow straight, the wise man makes straight his trembling, unsteady thought which is difficult to guard and difficult to restrain.
>
> The control of thought, which is difficult to restrain, fickle, which wanders at will, is good; a tamed mind is the bearer of happiness. (3.1, 3.2)

This last verse is an echo of the verse (Chapter 6, verse 35) from the Gita which says that the mind is difficult to control but it can be controlled with steady practice.

Here is a string of verses using flowers as an image to make a philosophical point in a forceful poetic manner.

> Even as a bee gathers honey from a flower and departs without injuring the flower or its colour, or scent, so let a sage dwell in his village.
>
> Like a beautiful flower, full of colour but without scent, are the well-spoken but fruitless words of him who does not act as he professes to.
>
> But like a beautiful flower full of colour and full of scent are the well-spoken and fruitful words of him who acts as he professes to.
>
> Sandalwood or tagara, a lotus flower or a vassiki, among these kinds of perfumes, the perfume of virtue is unsurpassed.
>
> Little is the scent that comes from tagara or sandalwood, the perfume of those who possess virtue rises up to the gods as the highest. (4.6, 4.8, 4.9, 4.13)

Since the emphasis of the Dhammapada is on the path of virtue, it does not lose any opportunity to reinforce this theme through images of everyday life.

> If on a journey, a traveller does not meet his better or equal, let him firmly pursue his journey by himself; there is no companionship with a fool.
>
> The fool is tormented thinking "these sons belong to me" and "this wealth belongs to me." He himself does not belong to himself. How, then, can sons be his? How can wealth be his?

> That deed is not well done, which having been done, brings remorse, whose reward one receives weeping and with a tearful countenance.
>
> But that deed is well done, which having been done, does not bring remorse, whose reward one receives delighted and happy. (5.2, 5.3, 5.8, 5.9)

These last two verses echo the discourse on the three kinds of work discussed in Chapter 17 of the Gita.

> Engineers (who build canals and aqueducts) lead the water (wherever they like), fletchers make the arrow straight, carpenters carve the wood, and wise people discipline themselves.
>
> Even the gods envy him whose senses are subdued like horses well-tamed by the charioteer, who is free from pride and free from taints. (6.5, 7.5)

The former verse compares character development to an art and a science. The latter verse introduces the imagery of the horses as representing the sense organs, a recurrent image in the Upanishads and the Gita.

In the chapter on the "Thousands," we find the following:

> Better than a thousand utterances composed of meaningless words is one sensible word on hearing which one becomes peaceful.
>
> If a man were to conquer in battle a thousand times a thousand men, and another conquer only one, namely himself, he indeed is the greatest of the conquerors.
>
> Conquest of self is indeed better than the conquest of other persons; of one who has disciplined himself and who always practices self-control, not even the gods can tempt. (8.1, 8.4, 8.5)
>
> Think not lightly of good (saying) that "it will not come near me." Even a water pot is filled by the falling of drops of water. A wise man becomes full of goodness even if he gathers it little by little. (9.7)

This resonates with the verse of encouragement in the Bhagavadgīta (2: 40) that a little bit of practice will save one from great fear. One makes progress by steadfast practice.

> Let no one neglect his own task for the sake of another's, however great; let him, after he has discerned his own task, devote himself to his task. (12.10)

This reminds us of the verse in the Gita (3: 35) where Krishna advises Arjuna that it is better for one to do that work which gives creative expression of one's own psychological disposition rather than taking up another simply for the novelty or its allurements.

> Get up, rouse yourself, do not be thoughtless. Follow the law of virtue. He who practices virtue lives happily in this world as well as in the world beyond.

In the Gita, we find, "Raise yourself by yourself, don't let yourself down. For you are your own friend and you are your own enemy" (6: 5). How can one be one's own friend? How can one be one's own enemy? The next verse responds to this question by saying that if one disciplines one's own mind, you become your own friend. If you leave it to itself, you become your own enemy.

> He who formerly was thoughtless and afterwards became reflective lights up this world like the moon when freed from a cloud. (13.2, 13.6)

Knowledge gained from bitter experience often leads to character transformation arising from reflection. Then, that person's message is indeed powerful and illumines our understanding.

> Even the gods emulate those wise men who are given to meditation, who delight in the peace of emancipation from desire, the enlightened, the thoughtful.

> Difficult is it to obtain birth as a human being; difficult is the life of mortals; difficult is the hearing of the true law, difficult is the rise to buddhahood, or enlightenment. (14.1, 14.4)

This particular verse is interesting since it is practically identical to the opening verses in the *Vivekachudamani*, where Shankara writes that three things are difficult to obtain, namely, a human birth, the desire for liberation, and the instruction from a great teacher: "*manushyatvam, mumukshatvam, mahapurusha samsrayah.*"

> Not reviling, not injuring, practicing restraint according to the law, moderation in eating, dwelling in solitude, diligence in higher thought, this is the teaching of the awakened.
>
> He who takes refuge in the Buddha, the Law, and the Order, he perceives, in his clear wisdom, the four noble truths. Suffering, the origin of suffering, the cessation of suffering, and the noble eight-fold path which leads to the cessation of suffering. (14.7, 14.12, 14.13)

In this verse we find the "trinity of Buddhism," namely, Buddha, Dharma (the Law), and Sangha (the Order).

> Health is the greatest of gifts, contentment is the greatest of wealth; trust is the best of relationships and nirvana is the highest happiness. (15.8)

There is a Bengali proverb that says that we don't know the value of teeth as long as we have them. Similarly, we never count our blessings. In order for the mind to rise to a higher level of awareness, health, contentment and trust are essential.

> He who gives himself to the distractions of the world and does not give himself to meditation, giving up his own welfare and grasping at pleasure, will envy him who exerts himself in meditation.
>
> Let a man overcome anger by non-anger, let him overcome evil by good, let him overcome the miser by liberality, let him overcome the liar by truth. (16.1, 17.3)

In Patanjali's Yoga Sutras, we will encounter a similar idea that the way to overcome one psychological tendency is to produce a counter-tendency. Here we see the germ of this idea.

> But there is an impurity greater than all impurities. Ignorance is the greatest impurity. (18.9)

In Buddhism, there is no idea of "original sin" that we find in Christian theology. The closest we come to such a concept is this idea of ignorance.

> The fault of others is easily seen; our own faults are difficult to see. A man winnows the faults of others like chaff, but his own faults he hides even as a cheat hides an unlucky throw. (18.18)

This verse underlines the difficulty of introspection, of truly looking at ourselves and facing the truth. The journey within is indeed a hero's journey.

> He who does not get up when it is time to get up, who though young and strong, is full of sloth, who is weak in resolution and thought, that lazy and idle man will not find the way to wisdom.
>
> Rouse yourself by yourself, examine yourself by yourself. Thus guarded by yourself and attentive, you will live happy, O mendicant.
>
> For the self is the lord of the self; self is the refuge of self, therefore, curb yourself even as a merchant curbs a fine horse. (20.8, 25.20, 25.21)

These verses echo verses 6.5 and 6.6 of the Bhagavadgīta. Here again, self-discipline implies self-effort. No one can do it for us. The task of self-knowledge cannot be entrusted to someone else. "Be a lamp unto oneself," as the Buddha would say.

THE EXPANSION OF BUDDHIST THOUGHT

The great appeal of the Buddha is his simplicity of teaching and clarity of expression. Both had an impact in generating a great following, first among the monastics, and later among the general public. Even in his own lifetime, Buddha had an immense following. Immediately after his passing away, the senior disciples convened a meeting to compile his teachings. The monasteries grew into universities and acquired a reputation far and wide, the most famous one being the monastery at Nalanda, in modern Bihar, in northern India. In fact, the word *Bihar* is a modification of *vihara*, which means monastery, or a place for meditation. The state of Bihar was populated with many Buddhist monasteries.

Shortly after Buddha's passing away in 483 BCE, the First Council at Rajgraha, Bihar, was organized by King Ajatasatru between 483 and 486 BCE. The Second Council was organized at Vaishali in 383 BCE. Ashoka (304-232 BCE) ruled from Afghanistan to present-day Bangladesh from 269-232 BCE. After seeing the horrors of war, he embraced Buddhism and dedicated his life to its propagation. Through his patronage, many monasteries and universities were built to spread the message of the Buddha. H.G. Wells, in *The Outline of History*, writes:

> Amidst the tens of thousands of names of monarchs that crowd the columns of history, their majesties and graciousnesses and serenities and royal highnesses and the like, the name of Ashoka shines, and shines, almost alone, a star. (25.4)

The Ashoka chakra, or "Dharmachakra" adorns the Indian flag today and is symbolic of the message of the Buddha. Ashoka endorsed the spread of Buddhist ideas into the Middle East and southern India.

In later centuries, many scholars arose and founded new schools of Buddhistic thought. Sometime between 150 CE and 250 CE, Nagarjuna developed the Madhyamaka school, leading to Mahayāna Buddhism. He expounded the philosophy of *sunyata* often incorrectly translated as "emptiness." A more accurate translation would be "insubstantial."

Buddhism entered China around 200 CE via the Silk Road and then spread to Korea, Japan, and southeast Asia.

A most startling discovery was made in the twentieth century in connection with the spread of Buddhist ideas in China. In 1907, the world's earliest printed book called the Diamond Sutra was discovered in China. Scholars say it was printed in 868 CE, approximately 600 years before the Gutenberg bible. This sutra, written in Chinese, is a translation of the original work in Sanskrit called *Vajrachedika Prajnaparamita Sutra*, or more precisely, "The Diamond that cuts through illusion sutra." It records a conversation between the Buddha and his disciple Subhuti who asks how one should discipline the mind, to which the Buddha replies: "Subhuti, this is how. The disciple should practice compassion and charity. Why? Because practicing compassion and charity without attachment is the way to reaching the Highest Perfect Wisdom, it is the way to becoming a living Buddha."[1] This was the message of karma yoga and *bhakti* yoga, and the verse highlights that through these yogas, one disciplines the mind.

Later in the Sutra, the Buddha underscores that we use concepts only temporarily and that we should not get attached to them. "As a raft is used to cross a river, and once crossed, the raft is of no use and should be discarded, so also, all words, concepts, symbols must be discarded on being illumined." This is familiar for students of the Gita, where Sri Krishna declares that for the realized being, the Veda becomes "Aveda," that is, irrelevant. *Veda aveda bhavati.* It also reminds us of the classical example given in Vedānta where one uses a thorn (of knowledge) to remove another thorn (of ignorance) that is stuck in the foot and afterwards, one throws both thorns away. That is, one transcends both knowledge and ignorance.

Then in a strange reversal of roles between the teacher and the student, the Buddha asks questions to his disciple, Subhuti. "Does a Buddha say, 'I have attained enlightenment?'" to which Subhuti replied, "No, if he were to say so, he would be admitting that he had an identity and thus would not be enlightened."

In many places of the Sutra, there are very grandiose verses on the merit that one would accrue simply by reciting a fraction of the Sutra. The idea behind such verses is to underline the value of the message and to highlight their power to transform character.

1 Translations of the Diamond Sutra by Nhat Hanh.

9

NYĀYA AND VAISESIKA

NYĀYA

Nyāya is one of the six orthodox systems of Indian philosophy. These systems are called *darśanas* in Sanskrit.[1] The Nyāya system is a philosophy of logic. It is also a system of epistemology. Though it was first formally written down by Akṣapāda Gotama in the third century BCE, its history extends over twenty centuries as the original writings were expanded upon by subsequent writers and commentators. Most notable are the contributions of Udayana in the tenth century CE, who wrote a treatise entitled *Nyāya Kusumānjali* that attempts to use the Nyāya system to establish the existence of God. Essentially, it is a treatise expounding the argument from design.

The word *nyāya* literally means that by which the mind is led to a conclusion. We are led to conclusions by reason and by argument. The popular usage of the word *nyāya* means "right" and so Nyāya as a system has come to mean the science of correct reasoning.

According to Nyāya, there are four methods of gaining knowledge (*pramāna*): direct perception (*pratyaksa*), inference (*anumāna*), comparison or analogy (*upamāna*), and verbal knowledge or testimony (*sabda*). In everyday experience, one uses any or a combination of these four methods to gain knowledge.

The Nyāya Sūtras define each of these methods as follows:

1 The "orthodox" schools are those that accept the Vedas as authoritative scriptures. In addition to Nyāya, they are Sāmkhya, Vaisesika, Mimasa, Vedānta, and Yoga, a system incorporating several elements of the others. The "heterodox" schools are Buddhism, Jainism, and Cārvāka.

> Perception is that knowledge which arises from the contact of a sense with its object, and which is determinate [well-defined], unnameable [not expressible in words], and non-erratic [unerring, that is, not illusory].... Inference is knowledge which is preceded by perception, and is of three kinds, viz., *a priori* [knowledge of the existence of unseen effects on the basis of perception of their causes],[2] *a posteriori* [knowledge of the existence of unseen causes on the basis of perception of their effects] and "commonly seen" [knowledge of the existence of something unseen on the basis of perception of something known to be simultaneously associated with it].... Comparison [analogy] is the knowledge of a thing through its similarity to another thing previously well-known.... Word (verbal testimony) is the instructive assertion of a reliable person. (359)[3]

Suppose we see billowing smoke on the hill. This is visual perception and we *know* there is smoke on the hill. We infer that the smoke is caused by fire and conclude that there is a fire on the hill. This is knowledge by inference. The hill is shaped like a pyramid. This is knowledge of the shape of the hill through comparison or analogy. Historical texts say that the hill has been there for the last five centuries. This is knowledge of the age of the hill from reliable verbal testimony.

About ten years ago, several of my doctoral students asked me to explain how one does scientific research. I realized that the art of research is really the art of asking probing and relevant questions. So I tried to write down some general methods by which one may generate such productive questions. I ended up by writing down eight methods by which we may generate questions and gain some knowledge. These methods, corresponding to the four *pramānas* of Nyāya, are: Survey of relevant literature, Observation of patterns, Conjecturing theorems, Re-interpretation of existing theorems, Analogies, Transferring ideas from one area to another, Induction, and Checking converse propositions. (The acronym "SOCRATIC" is just an accident!) It is easy to see that each of these really falls into one of the four methods outlined by the Nyāya system. The method of survey is part of verbal knowledge. Observation is part of direct perception. Conjecture, induction, checking converse propositions are part of the process of inference. Finding analogies and transferring ideas are part of the process of analogy. Finally, re-interpretation is a combination of direct perception and inference. This is really the art of seeing something familiar from a new perspective.

2 Note that the translators use the terms "a priori" and "a posteriori" in a slightly old-fashioned way different from what contemporary philosophers mean by them.

3 Translations in this chapter are from Radhakrishnan and Moore.

Examples can be enumerated for each of these methods of knowledge in any particular field. Here are striking episodes from the history of science. In 1859, Dmitri Mendeleev was 25 and was a poor school teacher in Siberia. The knowledge of chemistry was meagre at that time and the natural elements were slowly being classified. Mendeleev decided to organize these elements according to their properties and atomic number, that is, the number of protons in the nucleus. As he began to place the elements in columns, he discovered a periodicity in their properties and could correlate them to their atomic number. Mendeleev had stumbled on a mathematical key to the chemical elements. It was a moment of "Eureka" because at the time of Mendeleev, only 63 out of 92 natural elements were known and it was inevitable that there would be gaps in his listing.

> The conception of gaps or missing elements was a scientific inspiration. It expressed in practical terms what Francis Bacon had proposed...the belief that new instances of a law of nature can be guessed or induced in advance from old instances.... In science we do not simply march along a linear progression of known instances to unknown ones. Rather, we work as in a crossword puzzle, scanning two separate progressions for the points at which they intersect: that is where the unknown instances should lie in hiding. Mendeleev scanned the progression of atomic weights in the columns, and the family likenesses in the rows, to pinpoint the missing elements at their intersections. By doing so, he made practical predictions, and he also made manifest (what is still poorly understood) how scientists actually carry out the process of induction. (Bronowski, 205)

Mendeleev's discovery organizes past knowledge by using analogies based on careful observations. Thus, direct perception (*pratyaksa*), analogy (*upamāna*), and past knowledge (*sabda*) are all involved. What is brilliant about it is the "gaps" in the table that point to new elements. This is the method of inference (*anumāna*). Thus, this episode is a good illustration of a combination of survey, observation, conjecture, and induction methods applied to gain knowledge.

An excellent example of the method of transfer (illustrative of using analogy to gain new knowledge) is given by an episode in the life of Archimedes. As he stepped into the bath tub, he observed that a certain amount of water was displaced proportional to his own weight. He conjectured what is now called the principle of buoyancy. The moment he realized he could transfer this idea to the problem the king had given him of determining whether the goldsmith had cheated the king of his gold when he made the crowns without destroying the crowns, it is said that Archimedes ran naked through the streets of Syracuse shouting "Eureka," for he had indeed found the solution to the problem he was thinking about.[4]

A spectacular example of the method of re-interpretation is Einstein's theory of gravitation. In the Newtonian view, gravity was a force, but for Einstein, it is the curvature of space. In Einstein's theory, space itself is warped by the nearby presence of a massive body. Thus, a massive body like the sun would distort the space around it and the smaller bodies, like the planets, would have to move along the curved space. Einstein then used the tensor calculus and differential geometry to describe the precise equations of curvature of space-time. His theory includes Newton's theory but goes beyond it and explains observations that were inexplicable through the Newtonian model. For example, the anomalous advance of Mercury's orbit around the sun and the existence of black holes, both of which are due to the bending of light in large gravitational fields, are two instances of why Einstein's theory is now accepted.

A superb illustration of the method of analogy and converse is given by the discovery of electromagnetism. In 1813, the Danish physicist Hans Christian Oersted wrote:

> One has always been tempted to compare magnetic forces with the electric forces. The great resemblance between electrical and magnetic attractions and repulsions and the similarity of their laws necessarily would bring about this comparison. An attempt should be made to see if electricity has any action on the magnet as such. (Glashow, 333)

What Oersted proved by his researches was that electricity produces magnetism. This led the British physicist Michael Faraday[5] to ask if the converse was true: does magnetism produce electricity? He devised an experiment to show that this was indeed the case and this led to the mathematical theory of electromagnetism. Thus, we see how analogy and converse methods of inquiry can lead to profound discoveries.

There is another theme in the Nyāya philosophy that is worth highlighting before we conclude our brief survey. This concerns the relation between perception and language. When we see a cow, for example, we not only see the individual cow in front of us, but awaken within our mind the general

---

4 This often-told story is at least somewhat historically inaccurate, but it serves as a nice illustration of our principles anyway.

5 When Michael Faraday gave a demonstration of his discovery of electricity to the prime minister, the latter apparently asked him of what use is it, to which Faraday replied, "I don't know, but someday you will tax it!" (Another amusing but probably apocryphal story.)

shape or form of the cow and become aware of the class or genus of all cows. Thus, perception has this three-fold component to it. This is also the case even if the cow is not in front of us, but we say the word "cow." That is, even the usage of words in everyday language has this three-fold aspect: the individual word, the image or "shape" the word evokes, and the genus or universal suggested by both of these.

In verses 59-69 of Book 2, Chapter 2 of Gotama's Nyāya Sūtras, we find:

> There is doubt as to what a word (noun) really means, as it invariably presents to us an individual, form and genus. Some say that the word (noun) denotes [only an] individual, because it is only in respect of individuals that we can use [the demonstrative] "that."... [But] a word (noun) does not denote an individual alone, because it is not restricted to the latter. What is denoted by the word "cow" is not the mere individual by itself, without any qualifications, and as apart from the universal (to which it belongs), but the individual as qualified by (and along with) the universal.... [Nor] is it the genus [universal] alone that is meant by a word (noun), because the manifestation of genus depends on the form and individual. The meaning of a word (noun) is, according to us, the genus, the form and the individual. An individual is that which has a definite form and is the abode of particular qualities. The form is that which [indicates or] is called the token of the genus. The "universal" is the cause (or basis) of comprehension and cognition. (369-70)

There has been a great deal of discussion throughout the history of Western philosophy about universals—abstract entities, for example, *redness*), that are supposed to explain the similarity of particular things; thus red particular objects are classified together because they instantiate—exemplify—the universal. (Similarly, sets of three particular things are alike in that they instantiate the universal *three*.) But do we really need to think of the population of the universe as containing redness in addition to particular red things? Nyāya emphasizes the interdependence of universals and their particulars. The notion of forms and universals in the Nyāya philosophy is highly reminiscent of Plato's theory of ideas and forms. Just as Plato exalts the dialectic and ultimately arrives at the "Idea of the Good," the Nyāya system also tries to arrive at some notion of "God" through logic. "From effects, combination,... an everlasting omniscient Being is to be established" (383). This is the age-old "argument from design." Consequently, it can be seen as a "dualistic" view of the universe as opposed to the later systems like Vedānta, which present a "non-dualistic" view of the world. Dualism here (as explained earlier) is the view that there is an abstract Being separate from the manifested world. Non-dualism does not posit an external Being separate from the world.

The Nyāya Sūtras also devote a considerable portion to the art of debate and discussion. Since the goal of Nyāya was to sharpen the process of logical reasoning, minute attention was given to the subtleties of argumentation. In the course of time, its finer observations regarding the theory of perception and its contributions to the theory of knowledge were over-shadowed by excessive attention to the art of debate and Nyāya philosophy became synonymous with argumentation. However, as can be seen from our brief survey, the Nyāya Sūtras are full of deep psychological insights and their study enhances our view of the universe.

VAISESIKA

The Vaisesika philosophy derives its name from *visesa* meaning "particularity." Its emphasis is on the theory of particulars, and thus is pluralistic in its view. It is older than the Nyāya school and was founded by Kanāda around 300 BCE. Essentially, it is an early attempt at an atomic theory of the universe and consequently does not mention "God," but later commentators felt that the atoms by themselves could not have created an orderly universe so they postulated a "God" regulating the activities of the atoms. Below, we will give a brief survey of the original sutras of Vaisesika.

Before we begin, it is important to understand that the tenor of the Vaisesika system is really the beginnings of the scientific method. The word "science" can be traced back to the Latin word *scire*, meaning "to know"; this is possibly related to *scindere*, meaning "to cut, to dissect, to analyze, to take apart."[6] The word "scissors" can be traced back to *scindere*. By contrast, the word "religion" is sometimes thought to be derived from a Latin word meaning "to bind, to put together, to unify." This suggests that, from an etymological perspective, the words "science" and "religion" are opposites. "Science" refers to analysis and "religion" to synthesis. In the Vaisesika theory, both methods of analysis and synthesis are needed for an understanding of ourselves and the world around us. In the scientific method, we proceed by analysis, by subdivision, by refining our understanding of the component parts. At the same time, in science, we try to unify.

6 The origins of *scindere* can be traced back to the Greek word *schizein* meaning "to split" and this in turn is related to the Sanskrit word *chinatti* meaning "he splits." The etymological connection between "science" and "scissors" is, however, highly conjectural. See http://www.biotech.wisc.edu/education/genwords.html for an example of this sort of conjecture.

But that unity is gained by a simultaneous perception of both the whole and its component parts.

The mathematician Emil Artin expresses this idea when he wrote:

> We all believe that mathematics is an art. The author of a book, the lecturer in a classroom tries to convey the structural beauty of mathematics to his readers, to his listeners. In this attempt, he must always fail. Mathematics is logical, to be sure, each conclusion is drawn from previously derived statements. Yet the whole of it, the real piece of art, is not linear; worse than that, its perception should be instantaneous. We all have experienced on some rare occasions the feeling of elation in realizing that we have enabled our listeners to see at a moment's glance the whole architecture and all its ramifications. (534)

In its attempts to understand the nature of knowledge, the Vaisesika philosophy delineates "particulars" and, at the end, uses the term *samavāya* or coherence to refer to the instantaneous perception of the whole that Artin has referred to in the above passage.

This system divides the universe into six categories or *padārthas* called *dravya* or substance, *guna* or quality, *karma* or action, *sāmānya* or that which constitutes a genus, *visesha* or that which constitutes its uniqueness or individuality, and finally, *samavāya* or coherence. Each of these categories is again subdivided into further sub-categories. Without going into too much detail, we will only touch on two of these sub-categories. For instance, substance is divided into nine sub-categories of earth, water, light, air, ether, time, space, self, and mind (*manas*). The substances cannot exist without qualities of which there are 17: colour, taste, smell, touch, number, extension or quantity, individuality, conjunction, priority, posteriority, thought, pleasure, pain, desire, aversion, and will. The substances are affected by five kinds of action: upward motion, downward motion, contraction, expansion, and movement from one spot to another. The first four qualities, namely, colour, taste, smell, and touch are made up of indivisible atoms that have no dimension.

Let us begin by examining the six categories in some detail. Unlike the Nyāya system which gave a three-fold view of perception, Vaisesika gives us a six-fold view. Consider the example of Beatrice, the cow. When we see Beatrice, we see a cow (substance), we observe her colour and shape (quality), we see her grazing (action) in the pasture. In addition, we are aware that Beatrice is a member of a larger family (genus) of cows, and at the same time, we are aware of Beatrice's uniqueness (perhaps she has a beauty spot on her face) and finally, the unification of all these, a certain coherence.

In this brief overview, we will highlight some of the essential verses of Kanāda's Vaisesika. "Substance," the treatise claims, "is not annihilated either by effect or cause" (388). The subsequent chapters begin with an exposition of the theory of cause and effect, proceeding then to the manifold aspects of matter together with a detailed discussion of its qualities; and next, the deduction of the existence of mind. "The appearance and non-appearance of knowledge, on contact of the self with the senses and the objects are marks of the existence of the mind" (391). In a remarkable verse, it deduces that there is only one mind per organism: "From the non-simultaneity of volitions, and from the non-simultaneity of cognitions, it follows that there is only one mind in each organism" (392). Some clarification is needed here. If there was no mind, the self would be inundated by many cognitions simultaneously. Thus, there must be something called mind (*manas*) that prevents this from happening. After indicating that there can be only one mind, in subsequent verses, the treatise deduces the existence of the self or *ātman* from the action of the life breath. All of this, it says, is *adrista*, unseen or invisible. "The circulation of water in trees is *adrista*. The sun's rays and their action on convection of wind is *adrista*. However, the action of air and fire is explained by the action of the earth. The action of the mind is explained by the action of the hand" (393). Finally, in verses that seem to echo the Bhagavadgīta, we find, "Pleasure and pain result from the contact of the self, senses, mind and object. Non-origination of that follows on the mind becoming steady in the self; after it, there is non-existence of pain in the embodied self. This is that *yoga*" (393).

What we have here is something like an atomic theory; but it runs into this problem: Where does the knowledge of the combinations of atoms reside? That is, what gives the individual atoms different characteristics and the power of combination? This is its ultimate question. "Unique particularities reside in the ultimate substances. They are the factors that make for ultimate distinctions among these substances" (399). That is, mind and matter are interdependent, so matter must have a mental nature as well. Radhakrishnan explains:

> Countless millions of unthinking atoms cannot produce the marvellous unity in variety of the world. They are incapable of taking counsel together or carrying out a common plan of evolving a spiritual commonwealth. The logical minds of the Vaisesika thinkers were not favourable to the hypothesis of mere chance. They soon realised that the atoms, however immutable and eternal, were of no avail unless their activities were regulated by a presiding mind. (Vol. 2, 206)

These words seem to echo the sentiments of a twentieth-century physicist, Max Planck, who wrote:

> As a man who has devoted his whole life to the most clear headed science, to the study of matter, I can tell you as a result of my research about atoms this much: there is no matter as such. All matter originates and exists only by virtue of a force which brings the particle of an atom to vibration and holds this most minute solar system of the atom together. We must assume behind this force the existence of a conscious and intelligent mind. This mind is the matrix of all matter.

Another feature of the treatise is how time, space, *ātman*, and *manas* are classified under substance. Several sections of the writing are devoted to an inquiry into the nature of time and space. Its deduction of the existence of "an intelligent agent" seems to resonate with Planck's position above:

> As from the motion of the chariot, we infer the existence of an intelligent guiding agent in the shape of the charioteer, so also we infer an intelligent guiding agent for the body.... The intelligent agent is also inferred from the actions of breathing.... From the fact of the wounds of the body being healed up, we infer the existence of the agent who would be like the master of a house repairing it. (405)

What is impressive about the work is its attention to detail concerning very abstract concepts. We have already mentioned how the notions of time and space are discussed. Another chapter is devoted to the discussion of the concept of "number" and how the mind apprehends such an idea.

In conclusion, the Vaisesika system indicates the beginnings of a scientific method in investigating both the external world and the internal world of the mind. In later systems, this attitude is expanded and amplified.

10

SĀMKHYA AND YOGA

SĀMKHYA

The Sāmkhya system is very ancient, thought to have been systematized by the sage Kapila around 550 BCE, but to have existed before that. The earliest available text on this philosophy is the commentary written by Isvara Krishna during the third century CE. The system is most notable for its theory of evolution and for its reduction of the numerous categories of Nyāya and Vaisesika to two fundamental ones, namely, *purusha* and *prakriti*, the former being understood as Universal Awareness and the latter as Universal Energy. Prakriti is often translated as "Nature." However, it is clear from the writing that Kapila meant something more particular: creative energy. For him, "Nature" is part of the Universal Energy.

The Universal Energy has three modes (or *gunas*) of manifestation, according to Sāmkhya. As explained in Chapter 8, these are *sattva*, *rajas*, and *tamas*. *Tamas* indicates inertia, *rajas* indicates activity, and *sattva* is the equilibrium of the two. Everything that we see or experience in this world is the combination and re-combination of these three *gunas*. When these three universal vibrations are held in equipoise, there is no action according to the theory. It is only when there is a disturbance of the equilibrium that evolution begins. Universal Energy or Prakriti is unconscious and it is only through the presence of the conscious Purusha that evolution begins.

The process of evolution then follows a hierarchy of 23 categories or *tattvas*. (In Sanskrit, *tattva* literally means "thatness.") *Mahat* is the first product. It is a non-material mode of energy, and is the basis of the principle of Universal Intelligence. Just as we have, in the Upanishadic philosophy, distinguished between universal Self (*Brahman*) and individual

Self (*ātman*), though there is no "individuality" attached to the *ātman*, the Sāmkhya finds it convenient to designate Universal Intelligence by *mahat* and individual intelligence by *buddhi*. *Buddhi* is that mode of energy that operates as intelligence and is the basis of all mental processes. Next in the hierarchy is *ahamkāra*, or Ego, the self-sense. Three branches of evolution arise from *ahamkāra*. From its *sattva* aspect evolve *manas* (or mind), the five organs of perception, five organs (or instruments) of action. From its *tamas* aspect evolve the subtle elements of nature, namely ether, air, fire, water, and earth as well as the corresponding sensory vibrations of sound, touch, form, taste, and smell. The *rajas* aspect provides the energy for this evolution.

The word *sāmkhya* in Sanskrit indicates "number" and the system is distinguished by its emphasis on enumeration of creative principles. The two principles of *Purusha* and *Prakriti* are its foundation. This is followed by the principle of three *gunas*. The five organs of perception together with *manas* and *ahamkāra* (making a total of seven) form the basic individual. *Manas*, together with its organs of perception and organs of action, make a total of 11 principles that form the basis for all mental experience. These 11 together with *ahamkāra* and *buddhi*, making a total of 13, is the complete individual. If we consider *ahamkāra* and *manas*, the ten organs of perception and action, together with the five subtle elements of sound, touch, form, taste, and smell, we get 17 principles. These 17 together with *buddhi* and *Prakriti* give us 19. Finally, the number of principles evolving out of *Prakriti* is 23.

In this system, sentiency arises only from the presence of the Purusha. Prakriti is not an "unfoldment," but *mahat*, *ahamkāra*, together with the five subtle elements (sound, touch, form, taste, and smell) are unfoldments—that is, they have come out of Prakriti and the five gross elements (ether, air, fire, water, and earth) have come out of these. We must remember that the latter five do not refer to any "material" elements, but rather the principles represented by them.

In contrast to the method of knowledge listed in Nyāya, the Sāmkhya lists only three: perception, inference, and valid testimony as the means. The Sāmkhya philosophy states that the method of comparison or analogy has been explicitly left out since it is included in the method of inference:

> Knowledge of objects beyond the senses comes from inference based on analogy.... Non-perception may be because of extreme distance, extreme proximity, injury to organs, non-steadiness of the mind, subtlety, veiling, suppression and blending with what is similar. The non-perception of Prakriti is due to its subtlety, not to its non-existence, since it is perceived in its effects.[1]

1 Translations of Sāmkhya in this chapter are by Radhakrishnan and Moore.

Prakriti is material and it includes everything seen and unseen. Vivekananda explains:

> What we call matter in modern times was called... *bhutas*, the external elements. There is one element which according to them, is eternal; every other element is produced out of this one. It is called *ākāsha*.... Along with this element, there is the primal energy called *prāna*. *Prāna* and *ākāsha* combine and recombine and form the elements out of them.... The *ākāsha*, acted upon by the repeated blows of *prāna*, produces *vāyu*, or vibrations...giving rise to heat, *tejas*. Then this heat ends in liquefaction, *āpah*.... All that we know in the form of motion, vibration, or thought is a modification of the *prāna*,...and everything that we know in the shape of matter,...is a modification of the *ākāsha*.... You have never seen force without matter, or matter without force; what we call force and matter are simply the gross manifestations of these same things, which, when superfine, are called *prāna* and ākāsha. *Prāna* you can call...life, the vital force; but you must not restrict it to the life of man; at the same time you must not identify it with Spirit, *ātman*.... Creation cannot have either a beginning or an end; it is an eternal ongoing. (Vol. 2, 435-36)

From the union of *purusha* and *prakriti*, Sāmkhya says, the insentient *prakriti* appears sentient. After stratifying the mental processes of cognition into various categories, the theory says:

> Just as a picture does not exist without a substrate, or a shadow without a post or the like, so too the cognitive apparatus does not subsist supportless, without what is specific, that is, a subtle body (*linga sarira*). Formed for the sake of the spirit's purpose, the subtle body acts like a dramatic actor, on account of the connection of "causes and effects" and by union with the all-embracing power of *prakriti*.... This evolution from the will down to the specific elements, is brought about by the modifications of *prakriti*. This work is done for the emancipation of each spirit, and thus is for another's sake, though appearing as if it were for the sake of *prakriti* herself. (439-42)

Vivekananda amplifies this passage from Sāmkhya as follows:

> Why does nature do all this? Nature is undergoing all these changes for the development of the soul; all this creation is for the benefit of the soul so that it may be free. This immense book which we call

> the universe is stretched out before man so that he may read; and he discovers eventually that he is an omniscient and omnipotent being. (Vol. 2, 439)

Thus, according to Sāmkhya, the *purusha* has somehow become identified with *prakriti* and this is the source of bondage. The role of *prakriti* is to liberate us from this identification. Kapila, the author of Sāmkhya, says there is no need to postulate the existence of "God," if we take this word to mean "The First Cause." Causation is a concept and as such is a mental evolute. In this sense, *purusha* and *prakriti* are both eternal as they are not mental evolutes. Such a startling conclusion in this ancient period is fascinating in itself. It echoes the conclusions of modern astrophysics. In his book, *A Brief History of Time*, the celebrated physicist Stephen Hawking writes:

> The idea that space and time may form a closed surface without boundary also has profound implications for the role of God in the affairs of the universe. With the success of scientific theories in describing events, most people have come to believe that God allows the universe to evolve according to a set of laws and does not intervene in the universe to break these laws. However, the laws do not tell us what the universe should have looked like when it started—it would still be up to God to wind up the clockwork and choose how to start it off. So long as the universe had a beginning, we could suppose it had a creator. But if the universe is really completely self-contained, having no boundary or edge, it would have neither beginning nor end: it would simply be. What place, then, for a creator? (140-41)

Thus, Sāmkhya denies the "creation theory." The *purusha* somehow has identified itself with *prakriti* and appears to be bound. The purpose of *prakriti* is to liberate the spirit (or *purusha*) from this apparent identification. The third-century CE commentator Isvara Krishna writes in his explanation of Sāmkhya:

> Verily no spirit is bound; nor does any migrate; nor is any emancipated. Nature alone, having many vehicles, is bound, migrates, and is released. Bondage, migration and release are ascribed to the spirit, in the same manner as defeat and victory are attributed to the king, though actually occurring to his soldiers, because it is the servants that take part in the undertaking, the effects of which—grief or profit—accrue to the king. In the same manner, experience and

> emancipation, though really belonging to Nature, are attributed to the spirit, on account of the non-discrimination of spirit from Nature. (444)

YOGA

The Yoga philosophy of Patanjali, founded in the second century BCE, accepts the Sāmkhya metaphysics, with only one difference. Namely, it introduces a "First Teacher" called Isvara, and in this sense, may be classified as theistic. On the whole, however, the philosophy is a practical discipline for the mind rather than metaphysical speculation; the majority of the treatise focuses on meditation and psychic control. It is often called *rāja yoga*, or the kingly path, and brief references were made in the Bhagavadgīta, as part of the four-fold yoga.

The work lays the foundations for a science of the mind. According to Patanjali, all knowledge comes through the power of concentration of the mind; the Yoga Sutras describe the art and science of mental concentration. Vivekananda writes in his characteristic humorous style:

> Every science must have its own method of investigation. If you want to become an astronomer and sit down and cry "Astronomy! Astronomy!" it will never come to you. The same with chemistry. A certain method must be followed. You must go to a laboratory, take different substances, mix them up and compound them, experiment with them and out of that will come knowledge of chemistry. If you want to be an astronomer, you must go to an observatory, take a telescope, study the stars and planets, and then you will become an astronomer.... It is comparatively easy to observe facts in the external world, for many instruments have been invented for that purpose, but in the internal world, we have no instrument to help us. Yet we know we must observe in order to have a real science. Without a proper analysis, any science will be hopeless—mere theorizing. And that is why all the psychologists have been quarrelling among themselves since the beginning of time, except those few who found out the means of observation. The science of raja yoga...proposes to give us such a means of observing the internal states. The instrument is the mind itself. (Vol. 1, 129)

The Yoga Sutras begin with the following definition of yoga: *yoga chittavritti nirodhah*, which means "yoga is the restraint of mental modifications." Here, the word "yoga" is being used in the sense of mental concentration, and this controls thought and feeling, referred to here as "mental modifications."

> They are restrained by practice and non-attachment (*abhyāsa* and *vairāgya*). Practice is the repeated effort to follow the disciplines which give permanent control of the thought-waves of the mind. It becomes firm when it has been cultivated for a long time, uninterruptedly, with earnest devotion. Non-attachment is self-mastery; it is freedom from desire for what is seen or heard. (Prabhavananda, 10)

The emphasis in these verses is on practice, or repeated effort guided by an eager view of the end to be attained. The end is the knowledge of the Self, the *ātman*. Patanjali says that the human mind is usually in one of five general states: wandering (*ksipta*), forgetful (*mūdha*), occasionally steady or distracted (*viksipta*), focussed (*ekāgra*), and restrained (*niruddha*). It is the last two states of mind that are essential for the realization of the *ātman*. As will be explained below, the last two states form part of an eight-fold process to take the mind to higher levels of awareness. Normally, our minds only experience the first three states. The highest state of mind, transcending all five others, according to Patanjali, is the state of *samādhi*, or perfect understanding. It is said to be of two kinds, "with image" (or *savikalpa*) and "without image" (or *nirvikalpa*). The last state is characterized by the fact that there is no thought wave in the mind, it is perfectly still and supremely aware of itself. Thus, it is an identity with the state of *Brahman* described in the Upanishads. It is most unfortunate that many modern expositions of the work translate *samādhi* as "trance" and this is totally inaccurate for it is not a state of stupor or daze as is commonly connoted by the word, but rather a state of higher consciousness, or as Vivekananda would say, "superconsciousness."

The treatise now begins to explain concentration of mind. "Concentration upon a single object may reach four stages: examination or questioning (*vitarka*), reflection or discrimination (*vichāra*), joyful peace (*ānanda*) and unqualified egoism" (Vivekananda, Vol. 1, 201). We can understand this by relating it to the process of research or learning. Examination or inquiry (*vitarka*) refers to isolating what is to be attended to. For instance, when we have many things to do, we are confused since we don't know where to begin. The only way to complete a task is to begin. The Chinese philosopher Lao-Tzu put it more poetically when he said, "The journey of a thousand miles begins with the first step." Thus the first step in concentrating the mind is to determine what to concentrate it on, to prioritize, to isolate the task before us and then, to begin.

The words "quest" and "question" are cognates. In our quest for knowledge of the external world or the internal world of our own mind, once we have determined what we must focus on, we begin by questioning. Through proper questioning, we slowly concentrate the mind. If we stop this questioning simply because a question is difficult, the process of questioning ends and the mind slips back into its distracted state. However, the mind can be gradually focussed by refinement of the questioning process, which leads to finer knowledge and as one reflects upon this finer knowledge, one experiences a "joyful peace," the "Eureka" moment or what has been labelled as a "peak experience" in modern psychology which is accompanied by a feeling "I know" or "I understand." Beyond this stage of the mind lies the stage of "unqualified egoism," where one experiences the sense of "I" without any object. This stage is reminiscent of the state Buddha experienced just before he attained *nirvāna.*

"The concentration is achieved through faith, energy, recollectedness, absorption and illumination" (Prabhavananda, 26). We have met the word *sraddhā* earlier and have given it the translation of "faith." Let us recall that this "faith" is two-fold, one in our own ability to achieve the goal and two, that the goal can be attained. If we examine our mind, we will find that there is always a powerful undercurrent of "background thought." The initial stages of concentration can be said to be of "house-cleaning type" where we remove gross distractions. Such external distractions are easily removed, but the internal ones, such as thinking that one is not capable or incompetent, are a little harder to eradicate. However, this feeling of inability is slowly removed through practice combined with an exercise of energizing the mind. This energy can be derived from the study of great lives and examples. By the recollection of their luminous example, concentration is sustained.

Now comes a remarkable idea that diverges from the Sāmkhya view, and which distinguishes the Yoga system from the other systems. The steady stream of knowledge has always been flowing. This mighty river of teaching[2] can be traced back to time immemorial. "Isvara is the Teacher of even the ancient teachers, being not limited by time. Its manifesting word is Om." Patanjali goes on to say that the mind can be gathered and focussed by awareness of the principle of Isvara.

Here then, we find the value of study. But this study must inspire, and as often the case, it is others' lives that can inspire our own. A study of great lives energizes the mind and gathers it for the purpose of concentration. We are reminded of the famous quotation of Sir Isaac Newton: "If I have seen further it is by standing on ye sholders of Giants." We also see why many

2 In Indian mythology, the great God Siva or Mahadeva symbolizes Isvara. The river Ganges is said to flow from his head and this represents the river of knowledge or the river of teaching. The goddess of learning is called Saraswati, and literally means "she of the stream, the flowing movement." Aurobindo writes, "It is a natural name both for a river and for the goddess of inspiration" (Vol. 10, 88).

of the Upanishads give us a listing of how the teaching has been handed down from generation to generation. From my own experience, I can certify that such an awareness is a powerful motivation sustaining purpose and keeping the mind focussed. This is what Patanjali means by "devotion to Isvara" (verse 23 of the Yoga Sutras, 458).

What is gained by this devotion? Patanjali says that all mental obstacles are destroyed. In modern psychotherapy, by contrast, mental obstacles are destroyed by direct confrontation; here rather by devotion to the "mighty river of teaching and example." This is corroborated by daily experience. When we give attention to something, it becomes magnified. Thus, the way to diminish the effect of mental obstacles is to keep focussed on the goal "through devotion to Isvara," according to Patanjali. What are the obstacles? "Disease, mental laziness, indecision, carelessness, sloth, sensuality, mistaken notion, missing the point, and instability cause distraction of the mind" (459).

Once the goal has been fixed to be concentration of mind, moral principles are deduced as corollaries to aid the mind in concentration. "Undisturbed calmness of mind is attained by cultivating friendliness towards the happy, compassion for the unhappy, delight in the virtuous, and indifference toward the wicked" (40). These moral attitudes are to be cultivated so that the mind can learn to be calm. The last part, "indifference toward the wicked," is especially worth noting. Strong hatred is often disabling mentally. We are advised not to get too worked up about things. Vivekananda explains:

> These attitudes of the mind towards the different subjects that come before it will make the mind peaceful. Most of our difficulties in our daily lives come from being unable to hold our minds in this way. For instance, if a man does evil to us, instantly we want to react [with] evil, and every reaction in the form of hatred or evil is so much loss to the mind. (Vol. 1, 222)

This does not mean that we are complacent when something wrong has been done, but rather we must learn to rectify it calmly, if we are able. Otherwise, we must adopt the attitude of indifference.

In all of this, we must keep in mind the targeted audience of the writing. What is being described is the path of exclusive meditation, or rāja yoga. It is not karma yoga as was encountered in the teaching of the Bhagavadgīta, where emphasis was laid on action without attachment. This yoga is also action, but action directed in the realm of the mind, and these instructions are preparations for the mind before meditation.

Patanjali offers another method for calming the mind, namely, rhythmic breathing. This leads to an entire subsection of the treatise called *prānayāma*, or the regulation of the breath. We can observe that when we are disturbed, our breathing becomes irregular. At such moments, it is best to sit alone and to calm oneself through rhythmic breathing. Once the mind has been calmed, one can go further by taking up a single idea for meditation, such as the "light within" or "an illumined soul." This gives rationale for religious iconography. Concentration of mind can also be achieved "by fixing the mind upon any divine form or symbol that appears to one as good" (47). As the mind learns to contemplate, it becomes subtle and wide in its vision.

Now comes a very important psychological principle that we had met earlier in the Maitrī Upanishad. "As one thinks, so one becomes." Patanjali writes:

> Becoming like a transparent crystal on the modifications disappearing, the mind acquires the power of thought transformation (*samāpatti*), the power of appearing in the shape of whatever object is presented to it, be it the knower, the knowable, or the act of knowing. (460)

The comparison is made to a piece of transparent crystal. Just as the crystal becomes coloured by the colour of the object placed before it, the mind becomes similarly coloured by the thought or idea it holds. It then comes into contact with the matrix of associations represented by the idea. This contact has three aspects: word (*sabda*), meaning (*artha*), and knowledge (*jnāna*) or deeper meaning. In the initial approach to meditation, these three are mingled together and the mind is not able to separate them. As one goes deeper, the mind can separate these and see the "meaning" alone or "the meaning of the meaning." Ultimately, the mind reaches the state of "seedless *samādhi*."

The method to enable the mind to reach this level of awareness is called *ashtanga yoga*, or the eight-limbed yoga. These are listed as restraints (*yama*), observances (*niyama*), posture (*āsana*), regulation of breath (*prānayāma*), drawing in the senses (*pratyahāra*), concentration (*dhārana*), meditation (*dhyāna*), and transcendence (*samādhi*). The restraints (*yama*) are five in number: non-injury (*ahimsa*), truthfulness (*satyam*), non-stealing (*āsteya*), austerity (*brahmachārya*), and non-possession (*aparigraha*). These five embody ethical principles derived for the explicit purpose of concentrating the mind. These are not just principles for action on external objects, but are importantly also directed internally, at one's own mind. Thus, *ahimsa* refers to non-injury in thought, word and deed, not just non-injury to others, but also to oneself. In the *Vivekachudamani*, we find "He who having obtained a human birth... does not exert himself to gain self-knowledge, verily commits suicide for he kills himself by clinging to things unreal" (Sankaracarya, 1.4). Thus all of these have both an outer component and inner component. Truthfulness is to be practised in thought, word, and deed and the same applies to the other restraints. Hence the practice of truth has both an outer component in our relation to others. But it also has an inner component in how we relate to ourselves. Are we true to ourselves? The last one, *aparigraha* or non-possession may require further elaboration. It refers to the tendency of the mind to be greedy, to be grasping or to extend the "tentacles of selfishness" outward. It also applies to our tenacious grip on our thoughts and feelings. Often we hold on to a dogma or a creed and seek comfort from it. *Aparigraha* implies non-attachment as an ideal amplified in the Gita. Thus we see that mastery even of the first step of this yoga will make one into a saint.

The observances (*niyama*) are also five in number: cleanliness (*sauca*), contentment (*santosha*), austerity (*tapas*), study (*svādhyāya*), and devotion to Isvara (*isvarapranidhāna*). Again, as these are preparations for meditation, they have two components, external and internal. We have explained in detail the notion of austerity (*tapas*) earlier. Let us understand the last two. By study is meant not only a study of writing that increases one's understanding of the external world, but more importantly, the study of one's own mind, which consists in reflection, giving one greater control over it. By "devotion to Isvara" is meant the awareness of the "river of Teaching," flowing since time immemorial, as a background thought.

In this part of the treatise, Patanjali provides a method for manipulating one's own mind. "To obstruct thoughts which are inimical to yoga, contrary thoughts should be brought" (Vivekananda, Vol. 1, 261). Vivekananda explains, "For instance, when a big wave of anger has come into the mind, how are we to control that? Just by raising an opposite wave. Think of love. Sometimes a mother is very angry with her husband, and while in that state, the baby comes in, and she kisses the baby; the old wave dies out and a new wave arises, love for the child" (Vol. 1, 261). We can see this in operation in daily life. Suppose you are disturbed and someone you like walks in and brings you some exciting news. Your mood changes immediately, not gradually. Patanjali writes that this method can be used with great effect in the control of thought and feeling.

Posture (*āsana*) and regulation of breathing (*prānayāma*) must also be practised as a means of achieving control of the mind. Over the millennia, these two have been expanded upon by the yogis into a series of stretching and breathing exercises. These were then encoded as *hatha yoga* and form part of the *rāja yoga* discipline. It is this system that, considerably modified, has gained prominence, especially in Europe and North America.

Unfortunately the popular current idea of "yoga" as primarily a system of physical exercise or alternative medicine for promotion of health is only rather distantly related to its ancestor in Patanjali's Yoga Sutras, which were designed as a means for the mind to reach higher levels of awareness.

It may be useful to make some remarks concerning posture and the control of mind. The essential idea for Patanjali is to keep the spinal column straight. This gives strength to the mind. One can see this every day. When we slouch, it is not only bad for the body, but also for the mind. Gradually, a tendency of laziness engulfs the mind. Thus, by controlling posture, we can manipulate the mind into a higher mood. When one is not feeling great, a brisk ten minute walk is often a great help in bringing cheerfulness to the mind. Such physical techniques are part of *rāja yoga* and come under the heading of *āsana* and *prānayāma*.

Restraint of sense organs (*pratyahāra*) is to be combined with concentration (*dhārana*). When we contemplate an abstract idea, we automatically withdraw the senses from the external world. The effort of concentration can cure restlessness of the mind; for example, when we sit to do some creative work and find we are unable to start, the best way to eliminate this restlessness is simply to begin the work at hand. Through effort, the restlessness disappears.

Vivekananda describes the restless mind as follows:

> Well has it been compared to the maddened monkey. There was a monkey, restless by his own nature, as all monkeys are. As if that were not enough someone made him drink freely of wine, so that he became still more restless. Then a scorpion stung him. When a man is stung by a scorpion, he jumps about for a whole day; so the poor monkey found his condition worse than ever. To complete his misery a demon entered into him. What language can describe the uncontrollable restlessness of that monkey? The human mind is like that monkey, incessantly active by its own nature; then it becomes drunk with the wine of desire, thus increasing its turbulence. After desire takes possession comes the sting of the scorpion of jealousy at the success of others, and last of all the demon of pride enters the mind, making it think itself of all importance. How hard to control such a mind! (Vol. 1, 174)

The best way to deal with this restlessness, according to Patanjali, is to put the mind on some creative work and to keep it engaged. Another way, more difficult, is simply to watch the bubbling of thoughts in a detached way and slowly, as one observes them, the oscillations decrease. Usually, we identify with the thought as it arises. The essence of *pratyahāra* is not to identity with the thought wave as soon as it rises, but to watch it.

The next two stages are *dhārana* and *dhyāna*. "Dhārana is holding the mind on to some particular object [or idea]. An unbroken flow of knowledge in that object [or idea] is *dhyāna*" (Vivekananda, Vol. 1, 270). Thus, *dhārana* is concentration, and *dhyāna* is continued concentration. The latter refers to the ability of maintaining concentration once attained. In *dhārana*, we must increase the stamina for sustained concentration.

The final stage is *samādhi* or total absorption. Patanjali writes that the three, *dhārana*, *dhyāna* and *samādhi*, comprise *samyama* and are to be taken together. This process has been compared to the trajectory of a three stage rocket, where the lower stages drop off at an appropriate time so that the rocket can be propelled into higher reaches of space. In a similar way, concentration merges into meditation, which finally culminates in *samādhi*.

According to the Yoga philosophy, all historical figures recognized for their spirituality have either attained this state of mind or have approximated it. Without a systematic scientific discipline, some have stumbled upon it. Others have approached it more scientifically. Vivekananda writes:

> There is a great danger in stumbling upon this state. In a good many cases there is the danger of the brain being deranged, and as a rule, you will find that all those men, however great they were, who had stumbled upon the superconscious state without understanding it, groped in the dark, and generally had, along with their knowledge, some quaint superstition.... To get any reason out of the mass of incongruity we call human life, we have to transcend reason, but we must do it scientifically, slowly, by regular practice, and we must cast off all superstition. We must take up the study of the superconscious state just as any other science. On reason we must have to lay our foundation, we must follow reason as far as it leads, and when reason fails, reason itself will show us the way to the highest plane. When you hear a man say, 'I am inspired,' and then talk irrationally, reject it. Why? Because these three states—instinct, reason and superconsciousness, or the unconscious, conscious and superconscious states—belong to one and the same mind. There are not three minds in one man, but one state of it develops into the others. Instinct develops into reason, and reason into transcendental consciousness.... Real inspiration never contradicts reason, but fulfils it. (Vol. 1, 185)

In conclusion, the Yoga philosophy is in essence a science of the human mind. Much of the treatise is directed towards describing methods of attaining higher states of awareness. Patanjali cautions that our approach must be scientific, guided by reason and experience. Its remarkable insights into the workings of the human mind, its practical techniques can be applied by everyone in their psychic journey for ultimate understanding. Later, this system is absorbed into the Vedānta philosophy as part of its four-fold yoga, already encountered briefly in the Bhagavadgīta.

11

PŪRVA MIMĀMSĀ AND VEDĀNTA

PŪRVA MIMĀMSĀ

Jaimini is said to be the author of the original Mimāmsā sutras dating back to around 400 BCE. Their central purpose was an inquiry into the nature of duty or *dharma.* In addition to this inquiry, we find elaborate discussions about sounds, words and meanings that are quite interesting in their own right. While the Nyāya system distinguishes four methods of knowledge, the Pūrva Mimāmsā system lists six. In addition to direct perception (*pratyaksa*), inference (*anumāna*), analogy (*upamāna*), and verbal testimony (*sabda*), it includes hypothesis (*arthāpatti*) and knowledge by negation (*abhāva*). The method of hypothesis is especially interesting to us because it is also an important feature in the modern analysis of the scientific method. A hypothesis is made on the basis that something already observed would have been impossible were that hypothesis not true—given what we already know. This is what is called the method of *arthāpatti.*

Concerning the nature of hypothesis and its role in the scientific method, the famous mathematician of the nineteenth century Henri Poincaré wrote,

> Science is built up of facts, as a house is built of stones; but an accumulation of facts is no more a science than a heap of stones is a house. Most important of all, the man of science must exhibit foresight.... It is that which enables us to predict, and to generalise. Without generalisation, prediction is impossible.... Detached facts cannot therefore satisfy us, and that is why our science must be ordered, or better still, generalised.... Thus, by generalisation, every fact observed enables us to predict a large number of others.... Every generalisation is a hypothesis. (141-50)

Let us note that the hypothesis cannot be arbitrary. It must be corroborated by experience. The relative certainty of the hypothesis is derived from the fact that the observed phenomenon cannot be explained otherwise. However, we cannot be sure that it cannot be explained otherwise, so we make only a relative hypothesis, or a "working hypothesis." All scientific theories are working hypotheses. Their virtue lies in their power of explanation and power of prediction. These are the two guiding principles we use in the scientific method. Concerning this point, Vivekananda writes:

> The first principle of reasoning is that the particular is explained by the general, the general by the more general, until we come to the universal. For instance, we have the idea of law. If something happens and we believe that it is the effect of such and such a law, we are satisfied; that is an explanation for us.... Knowledge is more or less classification. There is something more. A second explanation of knowledge is that the explanation of a thing must come from inside and not from outside. There had been the belief that, when a man threw up a stone and it fell, some demon dragged it down. Many occurrences which are really natural phenomena are attributed by people to unnatural beings. That a ghost dragged down the stone was an explanation that was not in the thing itself, it was an explanation from outside; but the second explanation of gravitation is something in the nature of the stone; the explanation is coming from inside. This tendency you will find throughout modern thought; in one word, what is meant by science is that the explanations of things are in their own nature, and that no external beings or existences are required to explain what is going on in the universe. (Vol. 1, 370-71)

The other method of knowledge indicated by *abhāva* or negation in the Pūrva Mimāmsā is equally interesting. Both what is seen and what is not seen must be taken together. If something is not seen, that too indicates knowledge:

> The non-operation [or non-application] of the (five) means of cognition (described above) is...what brings about the cognition that "it does not exist."...That is, in a case where sense perception and the other means of cognition are not found to be operative towards bringing about the notion of the *existence* of a certain thing, we have the notion of the *non-existence* of that thing; and the means by which this notion is brought about is called *abhāva*. (488)[1]

1 This and the other translations in this chapter, unless otherwise noted, are from Radhakrishnan and Moore.

This is best illustrated by an episode from Sherlock Holmes. In Conan Doyle's short story, *Silver Blaze*, there is an exchange between Holmes and a detective from Scotland Yard. Holmes begins by saying "I wish to draw your attention to a curious incident with the dog during the night." The detective retorts, "Why the dog did nothing in the night." Holmes replies, "That is the curious incident." The fact that the dog did not bark when the theft was committed also gives us knowledge.

The essential theme of the Pūrva Mimāmsā system is to define the notion of duty. To do so, it first investigates the relationship between the word and its meaning. Consequently, it is led to hypothesize that "words are eternal," similarly to Plato's theory of Forms or Ideas. The system distinguishes between revelation (*sruti*) and social custom (*smriti*). The former is very much like universal law and the latter, man-made law or convention. "*Sruti* is more authoritative than *smriti*. When there is a conflict between Veda and *smriti*, the *smriti* should be disregarded" (496). ("Veda," here, refers to the realm of pure idea or revelation.) "In plain words," Vivekananda writes, "we have first to learn the distinction between the essentials and the non-essentials in everything. The essentials are eternal, the non-essentials have value only for a certain time; and if after a time they are not replaced by something essential, they are positively dangerous" (Vol. 3, 174). The distinction in this system between universal and social laws is an important contribution; confusion of these realms is the root of many problems regarding social customs that hide behind the garb of religion.

VEDĀNTA

The Vedānta philosophy of Bādarāyana is also known as the Uttara Mimāmsā system and is said to have been written down sometime between 500 and 200 BCE. The Vedānta Sutras (also called Brahma Sutras) that form the foundation of the philosophy systematize the teachings of the Upanishads. The 555 sutras are often terse; consequently, over the centuries, many scholars and philosophers have written commentaries on this work, founding in the process new schools of philosophy. Most notable among these were Shankara (788-820 CE) and his school of non-dualism (*advaita*), Rāmānuja (eleventh century) and qualified non-dualism (*visista advaita*), and Madhva (1197-1276) with his school of dualism (*dvaita*). All three schools come under the heading of Vedānta.

The word *vedānta* can be split into two: *veda* and *anta* and literally means "end of the Vedas." This is taken to mean the distilling of the philosophy of the Vedas and the Upanishads into its essential components.

Shankara builds upon Gaudapāda's commentary (*kārikā*) of the Māndukya Upanishad, the shortest of the Upanishads dealing with the four states of consciousness. In his commentary of the Vedānta Sutras, Shankara begins by asking if there is anything in our experience that we can be certain of. This central philosophical question is, of course, familiar in later Western philosophy, for example, in its treatments by Descartes and Russell.

> Our senses may deceive us; our memory may be an illusion. The forms of the world may be pure fancy. The objects of knowledge may be open to doubt, but the doubter himself cannot be doubted.... It cannot be proved, because it is the basis of all proof. The self is self-established and is different from all else, physical and mental. As the subject it is not the object.... It is undifferentiated consciousness, which remains unaffected even when the body is reduced to ashes and the mind perishes. (506)

Reiterating the Upanishadic teaching, Shankara explains the eternal Self is the *ātman* and the universal Self is *Brahman*:

> The world is bound up by the categories of space, time and cause. These are not self-contained or self-consistent. They point to something unalterable and absolute.... *Brahman* is different from the space-time-cause world.... The empirical world cannot exist by itself. It is wholly dependent on *Brahman*... but *Brahman* depends on nothing. Ignorance affects our whole empirical being. It is another name for finitude. To remove ignorance is to realise the truth.... While absolute truth is *Brahman*, empirical truth is not false. (507)

Shankara concludes that the highest representation of *Brahman* through logical categories is *Isvarā* or *Saguna Brahman* (qualified *Brahman*) as described in Patanjali's Yoga Sutras. The *Nirguna Brahman* (or *Brahman* without qualities) transcends this and is the basis of the phenomenal world. Shankara's *advaita* has often been misunderstood and dismissed as the theory of *māya* or illusion. The statement "this world is an illusion" is an oversimplification of Shankara's view. Here is what he says precisely. Building on Gaudapāda's *Kārika* and his description of the four states of consciousness, namely, deep sleep, dreaming, waking, and transcendence (*turīya*), Shankara writes:

> As one dreaming person is not affected by the illusory visions of his dream because they do not accompany the waking state... so the one permanent witness of the three states... is not touched by the mutu-

> ally exclusive three states. For that the highest Self appears in those three states is a mere illusion, not more substantial than the snake for which the rope is mistaken in the twilight. (523)

The existence of the rope is not dependent on the appearance of the snake but the appearance of the snake is dependent upon the rope; so also, according to Shankara, the world is dependent upon *Brahman* but *Brahman* is not dependent upon the world.

A classic example given as the purpose of philosophic thought is that of a thorn. If a thorn is stuck in one's foot, we take another thorn and carefully remove it and then discard both thorns. We don't keep one as a souvenir. That is, philosophic thought and philosophical systems are used to expand our understanding. We should not become attached to a particular system of thought. Rather, we should ultimately transcend all systems of thought. Similarly:

> This doctrine of the individual self having its Self in *Brahman*... does away with the independent existence of the individual self, just as the idea of the rope does away with the idea of the snake (for which the rope has been mistaken). (526)

In a masterly stroke of impeccable logic, Shankara indicates that all that exists is *Brahman*. Vivekananda explains it as follows.

> Let us examine our perceptions. I see a blackboard. How does that knowledge come? What the German philosophers call "the thing-in-itself" of the blackboard is unknown. I can never know it. Let us call it *x*. The blackboard *x* acts on my mind, and the mind reacts. The mind is like a lake. Throw a stone in a lake and a reactionary wave comes toward the stone; this wave is not like the stone at all, it is a wave. The blackboard *x* is like a stone which strikes the mind and the mind throws up a wave towards it, and this wave is what we call the blackboard. I see you. You as reality are unknown and unknowable. You are *x* and you act upon my mind, and the mind throws a wave in the direction from which the impact comes, and that wave is what I call Mr. or Mrs. So-and-so. There are two elements in the perception, one coming from outside and the other from inside, and the combination of these two, *x* + mind, is our external universe. All knowledge is by reaction.... The real Self within me is also unknown and unknowable. Let us call it *y*. When I know myself as so-and-so, it is *y* + the mind. That *y* strikes a blow on the mind. So our whole world is *x* + mind (external), and *y* + mind (internal), *x* and *y* standing

> for the thing-in-itself behind the external and internal worlds respectively.... Now we will take up our *x* and *y* and show they are one.... *x* and *y* are both...unknown and unknowable. All difference is due to time, space and causation. These are the constituent elements of the mind. No mentality is possible without them. You can never think without time, you can never imagine anything without space, and you can never have anything without causation. These are the forms of the mind. Take them away, and the mind itself does not exist.... According to Vedānta, it is the mind, its forms, that have limited *x* and *y* apparently and made them appear as external and internal worlds. But *x* and *y*, being both beyond the mind, are without difference and hence one. We cannot attribute any quality to them, because qualities are born of the mind. That which is quality-less must be one; *x* is without qualities, it only takes qualities of the mind; so does *y*; therefore these *x* and *y* are one. (Vol. 2, 458-61)

What is involved in knowledge is mostly classification and arrangement. The mind is a network of associations; and we try to pigeonhole whatever we come across. Knowledge in any field arises from the arranging of facts, from the relationship between ideas. What we mean by a proof is a sequence of logical implications beginning with axioms that have been assumed without question. Explanation in science, like proof in arithmetic, involves relating what is already known to the current question. When it comes to existential questions raised by philosophy (or religion for that matter), we find the mind is baffled. In the sense we have outlined above, these questions are unanswerable. Vivekananda explains this state of affairs as follows:

> If knowledge means finding the associations, then it must be that to know anything we have to see the whole series of its similars.... Suppose you take a pebble; to find the association, you have to see the whole series of pebbles similar to it. But with our perception of the universe as a whole, we cannot do that, because in the pigeon-hole of our mind there is only one single record of the perception, we have no other perception of the same nature or class, we cannot compare it with any other. We cannot refer it to its associations. This bit of the universe, cut off by our consciousness, is a startling new thing, because we have not been able to find its associations.... It is only when we find its associations that the universe will stand explained. Until we can do that, all the knocking of our heads against a wall will never explain the universe, because knowledge is the finding of similars, and this conscious plane only gives us one single perception of it. (Vol. 2, 448-49)

This does not mean we abandon reason. We must take reason as far as it can go. When that is done, Vedānta says, reason is transcended. But until then, we must rely upon reason.

Shankara's *advaita* philosophy's insistence on rational thought and reason degenerated over the centuries into linguistic wrangling. Thus, in the eleventh century, Ramanuja derived a form of "qualified" *advaita* known as *visishtadvaita*. It can be thought of as a combination of Sāmkhyā, Yoga and *advaita*. Ramanuja correctly emphasizes that *saguna Brahman*, or *Brahman* with qualities, is the highest reading of *Brahman* we can aspire for. "A reality of oneness manifesting itself in a reality of numberless forms and powers of its being is what we confront everywhere," writes Aurobindo (Radhakrishnan and Moore, 595). Since plurality is what we experience, Ramanuja's objection to Shankara is that we should not posit anything we cannot experience. The mind perceives through images and symbols. To ascribe qualities and to make definitions is the very nature of the mental process. Thus, the way to realize *Brahman* is through symbology combined with devotion. Since *Brahman* manifests through numberless forms, this is not our own invention. Thus, he writes, "Joining the mind with devotion to that which is not *Brahman*, taking it to be *Brahman*" (Vivekananda, Vol. 3, 59), the mind reaches *Brahman*. In this connection, he stresses devotion as the means echoing Patanjali's devotion to Isvara. Hence, *bhakti* or devotion is a dominant theme in Ramanuja's philosophy.

At the time of Ramanuja, Shankara's *advaita* was viewed as a philosophy asserting *Brahman* as a "quality-less substance." Its subtle observations about "knowing" and "knowledge" were forgotten. The followers of Shankara's school may have claimed that they had proved the existence of *Brahman*, but Shankara never claimed that. Thus, from a historical perspective, Ramanuja's objection, which is quite valid, is that there is no proof of a non-differentiated substance. Shankara would not have argued with that. According to Ramanuja, differentiation is the only thing perceived. Consciousness and *Brahman* are not identical, but rather consciousness is an attribute of *Brahman*. Since the mind can only understand symbols and images, there is no point in discussing the abstract. Therefore, Ramanuja gave his "qualified" view of *Brahman* of the Upanishads. In Ramanuja's writings and life, we see that he felt for the poor and downtrodden. It is clear that by the time of Ramanuja, the Vedantic knowledge may have become the prerogative of the elite. Thus, Ramanuja appears as one who simplifies the teachings and gives the multitude concrete examples for a more transparent understanding. On this historical episode, Vivekananda writes:

> I do not know why Shankara should be represented as rather exclusive; I do not find anything in his writings which is exclusive.... This exclusiveness that has been attributed to Shankara's teachings is most possibly not due to his teachings, but to the incapacity of his disciples. (Vol. 3, 266)

For Ramanuja, *Brahman*, *ātman*, and *jagat* (world) are different and eternal and at the same time inseparable. "Inseparability is not identity. *Brahman* is related to the other two as soul to body.... The three together form an organic whole" (Radhakrishnan, *Principal*, 26). Sri Ramakrishna, the teacher of Vivekananda, offers us the following explanation of Ramanuja's theory:

> According to this theory, *Brahman* or the Absolute, is qualified by the universe and its living beings. These three—*Brahman*, the world, and living beings—together constitute One. Take the instance of a bel-fruit.[2] A man wanted to know the weight of the fruit. He separated the shell, the flesh and the seeds. But can a man get the weight by weighing only the flesh? He must weigh flesh, shell and seeds together. At first it appears that the real thing in the fruit is the flesh, and not its seeds or shell. Then by reasoning you find that the shell, seeds, and flesh all belong to the fruit; the shell and seeds belong to the same thing that the flesh belongs to. Likewise, in spiritual discrimination one must first reason, following the method of 'not this, not this': *Brahman* is not the universe; *Brahman* is not the living beings; *Brahman* alone is real and all else is unreal. Then one realizes, as with the bel-fruit, that the Reality from which we derive the notion of *Brahman* is the very Reality that evolves the idea of living beings and the universe. The Nitya (Absolute) and the Lila (Manifestation) are the two aspects of one and the same Reality; therefore, according to Ramanuja, *Brahman* is qualified by the universe and the living beings. This is the theory of qualified non-dualism. (Nikhilananda, 733-34)

The *dvaita* philosophy of Madhva of the thirteenth century builds upon Ramanuja. For Madhva, there is no interdependence between these three ideas: *Brahman*, *ātman*, and *jagat*. They are simply independent and eternal. Thus, it is quite natural that a dualistic philosophy of "God and the world" emerges from such a view. From such a dualistic view, Madhva derives his philosophy and develops an elaborate theory of devotion. Indulging in

2 This fruit, otherwise known as the wood-apple, is about the size of an orange. Inside its yellow or pale green, hard, woody shell is pale orange floury pulp around seeds, each encased in a clear, glutinous substance valued for its medicinal properties.

abstract speculations concerning the Infinite is not the way to reach the Infinite, according to Madhva. The whole emotional component of our psycho-physical being must become focussed on that one idea and this is the fundamental premise of *bhakti*. It can be said that many of the world's religious traditions have this *bhakti* structure and view. Commenting on *bhakti*, Vivekananda writes:

> The one great advantage of *bhakti* is that it is the easiest and the most natural way to reach the great divine end in view; its great disadvantage is that in its lower forms, it oftentimes degenerates into hideous fanaticism.... All the weak and undeveloped minds in every religion or country have only one way of loving their own ideal, that is by hating every other ideal. Herein is the explanation of why the same man who is so lovingly attached to his own ideal... becomes a howling fanatic as soon as he sees or hears anything of any other ideal. This kind of love is somewhat like the canine instinct of guarding the master's property from intrusion; only, the instinct of the dog is better than the reason of man, for the dog never mistakes its master for an enemy in whatever dress he may come before it.... The same man who is kind, good, honest and loving to people of his own opinion, will not hesitate to do the vilest deeds when they are directed against persons beyond the pale of his own religious brotherhood. (Vol. 3, 32-33)

However, this danger, Vivekananda says, is in the early stages of *bhakti*. "When *bhakti* has become ripe and has passed into that form which is called the *supreme* or *para-bhakti*, no more is there any fear of these hideous manifestations of fanaticism" (Vol. 3, 32-33). Thus, if one is aware of this danger, *bhakti yoga* can be used to take the mind to a higher level of awareness.

It is interesting to note that all of these schools of Vedānta are based on the original Vedānta Sutras of Bādarāyana. In all cases, the Upanishadic passages are cited to substantiate their view. In every culture, we find this phenomenon, the tyranny of the printed word. Whether it is the non-dualistic view, the qualified non-dualistic view, or the dualistic view, each commentator interpreted the original sutras to suit their view. So which one is right? Can this even be answered?

After surveying the centuries of Indian philosophical thought, the nineteenth-century philosopher Vivekananda writes:

> It is foolish to attempt to prove that the whole of the Vedas is dualistic. It is equally foolish to attempt to prove [it]... is non-dualistic. They

> are dualistic and non-dualistic both. We understand them better today in the light of newer ideas. These are but different conceptions leading to the final conclusion that both dualistic and monistic conceptions are necessary for the evolution of the mind. (Vol. 3, 281)

But there are times when the mind transcends its own limitations and perceives something that cannot be reasoned. Often this level is reached through the power of love by means of a secret and mysterious ritual, a "participation mystique." Aurobindo explains:

> In reality, all experience is in its secret nature knowledge by identity; but its true character is hidden from us because we have separated ourselves from the rest of the world by exclusion, by the distinction of ourself as subject and everything else as object, and we are compelled to develop processes and organs by which we may again enter into communion with all that we have excluded. We have to replace direct knowledge through conscious identity by an indirect knowledge which appears to be caused by physical contact and mental sympathy. This limitation is a fundamental creation of the ego. (Radhakrishnan and Moore, 580)

Sri Ramakrishna speaks of the "ripe ego" and the "unripe ego." Explaining this distinction, he says that one may keep the "ripe ego" even after enlightenment:

> Such a one feels either that he is a servant of God or that he is a lover of God. Shankara retained the "ego of Knowledge" to teach people about spiritual life. The "servant ego," the "Knowledge ego" or the "devotee ego" may be called the "ripe ego." It is different from the "unripe ego" which makes one feel: "I am the doer. I am the son of a wealthy man. I am learned. I am rich. How dare anyone slight me?" A man with an unripe ego cherishes such ideas. (Nikhilananda, 860)

The processes that Aurobindo refers to can be described as the four yogas, as expanded and amplified by many of the contemporary thinkers such as Vivekananda, Aurobindo, and Radhakrishnan. No single view can encompass the cosmos and the manifold experiences of the human psyche. It must be admitted that the mind is in evolution, and when its faculties of thinking, feeling, willing, and restraining are refined, higher levels of awareness are experienced. Aurobindo amplifies this idea as follows:

> None of them [these extensions of faculty], however, leads to the aim we have in view, the psychological experience of those truths that are "beyond perception by the sense but seizable by the perceptions of reason," *buddhigrāhyam atīndriyam* (Bhagavad Gita, 6.21). They give us only a larger field of phenomena and more effective means for the observation of phenomena. The truth of things always escapes beyond the sense. Yet it is a sound rule inherent in the very constitution of universal existence that where there are truths attainable by reason, there must be somewhere in the organism possessed of that reason a means of arriving at or verifying them by experience. The one means we have left in our mentality is an extension of that form of knowledge by identity which gives the awareness of our own existence. (Radhakrishnan and Moore, 581)

Thus, the Reality is both the One and the Many. It is both the noumenon and the phenomenon. *Brahman* expresses Itself in many ways and in many forms of consciousness. We may argue ad infinitum of whether it is One or the Many or neither. For the answers (if we can call them that) lie beyond the realm of reason, beyond the realm of sensory perception. Therefore, Vivekananda advises:

> Books are infinite in number and time is short, therefore, the secret of knowledge is to take what is essential.... Intellectual gymnastics are necessary at first. We must not go blindly into anything.... [But] there are much higher things.... The whole of life is not for schoolboy fights and debating societies.... Things of subtler planes have to be realised. (Vol. 1, 236 and 176)

The Vedānta philosophy begins with the premise that there is something deeper than what is perceived either by the senses or the mind. The way to discover this is through the mind. The "book" we must learn to read is our own mind. We must learn to manipulate its manifold abilities and faculties and refine them just as a scientist refines her deductive powers of reasoning or as an artist refines his intuitive feelings and gives them shape in his artistic creation. Life, according to Vedānta, is therefore a psychic journey and the means for this journey is our own mind. We must become aware of our own infinite dimension not in an egotistical sense, but in a universal sense, because when the mind soars beyond the intellect and the ego, it attains oneness with the Self, the *ātman*.

Radhakrishnan writes:

> Meditation is the way to self-discovery. By it we turn our mind homeward and establish contact with the creative centre. To know the truth we have to deepen ourselves and not merely widen the surface. Silence and quiet are necessary for the profound alteration of our being and they are not easy in our age. Discipline and restraint will help us to put our consciousness into relation with the Supreme. What is called *tapas* is a persistent endeavour to dwell in the divine and develop a transfigured life. It is the gathering up of all dispersed energies, the intellectual powers, the heart's emotions, the vital desires, nay the very physical being itself, and concentrating them all on the supreme goal. The rapidity of the process depends on the intensity of the aspiration, the zeal of the mind. (Radhakrishnan and Moore, 633)

Thus, aspiration, the zeal to know, slowly leads to inspiration. By higher levels of awareness, no mystical experiences are indicated. It is to see and experience what we experience in daily life with an expanded view. Out of this process emerges the required evolution of mind. This is the essence of the Vedānta philosophy. It is a masterly synthesis of the philosophical writings of earlier centuries reaching as far back as the Vedic period. Undoubtedly, the writing as it stands before us today is also facing the future and will inspire the sages of the future to ponder, reflect, and meditate on its profound observations.

But Vivekananda's view of Vedānta was not as a system of philosophy of Indian origin, but rather a way of looking at the world, both internal and external. Just as science does not belong to any particular nation, Vedānta does not belong to any nation. Science has many subdivisions like mathematics, physics, chemistry, biology and so on. These subdivisions are not contradictory. They are complementary. The diversity of disciplines is unified by the umbrella of science. It is from such a universal view that science and technology have advanced so far. In the same way, Vedānta has many subdivisions and these are the manifold ways of looking at the world represented by the world's religions. But Vedānta includes the subdivisions of science too, since it is a way of looking at both the external and the internal world. Thus, all approaches to knowledge are part of Vedānta. We need the diversity since no one system will enable us to understand this world. At the same time, we need to embrace the underlying unity. Vivekananda wrote:

> The whole universe is one existence. There cannot be anything else. Out of the diversities we are all going towards this universal existence. Families into tribes, tribes into races, races into nations, nations into

> humanity... It is all knowledge, all science—the realisation of this unity.... This Vedānta is everywhere, only you must become conscious of it. (Vol. 8, 138-39)

This message of Vedānta is echoed in the writings of the great savants of all nations and of all times. They seem to speak with an eternal voice and the refrain is the same, namely that we must learn to live together, to work together because the survival of the human race depends upon it. The twentieth-century poet Aimé Césaire wrote:

> But the work of man is only just beginning and it remains to conquer all the violence entrenched in the recesses of his passion and no race possesses the monopoly of beauty, of intelligence, of force, and there is a place for all at the rendezvous of victory. (85)

12

MODERN THOUGHT

In this chapter, we will give a brief survey of some of the nineteenth- and twentieth-century Indian philosophers and their contributions to contemporary thought. We will look at six: Vivekananda, Aurobindo, Tagore, Gandhi, Krishnamurti, and Radhakrishnan. This study will give us a wide spectrum of philosophical thought, ranging from the metaphysical and mystical philosophy of Sri Aurobindo to the social and political philosophy of Mahatma Gandhi. All of these people were born when India was still under British colonial rule. Consequently, some of their writings are tinged with nationalism. Still, we can extract from their writings a universal philosophy that might apply to all people in all times. Three—Vivekananda, Aurobindo, and Radhakrishnan—came from the Indian scholastic tradition, having the express goal of interpreting and reinterpreting the ancient philosophies of India in the modern context. By explaining the Sanskrit texts in the English language, they fulfilled their academic role, reinterpreted their ideas in the modern context, and gave them a wider circulation. With Gandhi, we see the development of a political philosophy based on the Upanishads and the Bhagavadgīta. In Rabindranath Tagore and Sri Aurobindo, the same philosophy finds new expressions in art, poetry, literature, and even music. Krishnamurti, by contrast, urges that we break totally from the past and think for ourselves. In Vivekananda and Radhakrishnan, we find a combination of all these viewpoints.

VIVEKANANDA

Vivekananda's lectures and writings were clearly influenced by the traditional Vedānta philosophy but reinterpreted in the modern context; thus his contribution is often called "neo-Vedānta." However, upon a closer examination of his writings, we see that he had a larger view of things. At the centre of his philosophy is the perfection of the individual, or more precisely, the science of human potential and betterment. First and foremost, he saw this science in the milieu of the scientific revolution, with its insistence on reason as the prime tool in its investigations. He recognized the universal appeal and acceptance of the sciences. They had tremendous power to unite the human race. His view of Vedānta was similar. Just as science studies external nature and has given rise to a manifold subdisciplines of mathematics, physics, chemistry, biology and so on, Vedānta, which studies the internal nature of man, has given rise to a multitude of religious and philosophical traditions on this planet. In his view, there was nothing "Indian" about Vedānta, in the sense that Vedānta is a method of understanding the internal world, just as science is a method to understand the external world, and we don't ascribe the scientific tradition to any particular race or culture. Indeed, modern historical researches have revealed that the scientific tradition in some form can be traced back to many ancient civilizations.

Swami[1] Vivekananda was born as Narendranath Dutta on January 12, 1863, in Kolkata (Calcutta), India. He had a traditional upbringing and a good education, including a law degree and considerable work in Western philosophy. However, he had shown signs of a spiritual quest from the time of his youth. He was dubious about orthodox religions and advocated reason as the foundation for life. In nineteenth-century India, British colonial rule had undermined the educated elite's faith regarding their own history and traditions, particularly the religious traditions. Young Narendranath was not immune to this and so he joined the Brahmo Samaj, an organization aimed at reforming Indian traditions both in religion and customs. It was in this context that he came to meet Sri Ramakrishna, then living in the nearby town of Dakshineswar. Narendranath was 18 years old at the time.

Sri Ramakrishna came from a rustic background, but since childhood had a mystical temperament. Imbued with a fiery zeal for spiritual enlightenment, he practised yoga and meditation, with visits from teachers of various spiritual traditions who came to teach him. For instance, following the tradition of Patanjali's yoga, he attained what was taken to be the highest level of consciousness, *samādhi*. After practising various Indian religious traditions, he came to the realization that each tradition is valid in that if it is faithfully practised, it leads one to the highest realization. He then explored the traditions of Islam and Christianity and again, reached the

1 "Swami" is an Indian term of respect for a religious teacher.

same realization, not as an intellectual understanding, but as a matter of experience. Thus, Sri Ramakrishna, who had no formal academic training but much practical experience, as insisted on by ancient traditions, was in many ways the antithesis of Vivekananda.

At first, meeting Sri Ramakrishna was very puzzling for Vivekananda. Yet, he was convinced that whatever Sri Ramakrishna could teach him would be not an academic opinion, but rather a matter of experience. Here was a master that matched the Upanishadic ideal of a spiritual teacher. From Sri Ramakrishna, he learned that all spiritual traditions, if faithfully followed, lead one to higher realizations. This resonated with the teachings of the Vedānta philosophy.

After the passing away of his spiritual teacher in 1886, Vivekananda took up the monk's garb and wandered through India, teaching what he had learned and intensifying his meditation to increase his own understanding about spirituality. As he wandered along the dusty rustic paths of rural India, he saw the plight of the multitude steeped in poverty. The problem at the forefront of his mind was how to regenerate the nation, how to revive its people. Meeting wealthy landlords and maharajahs, he tried to convince them that they were only custodians of power and wealth, and that their power and wealth were to be used for the welfare of the masses.

One such maharaja that became his disciple was the Maharaja of Khetri. Vivekananda heard from the Maharaja about a conference of world religions being organized for the World's Fair in Chicago, scheduled for September 1893. The Maharaja suggested that Vivekananda, with his vast erudition and spiritual knowledge, would be an excellent representative of the Indian spiritual traditions. Thus encouraged and supported by the Maharaja, Swami Vivekananda sailed to America. There, he presented the universal view of Vedānta, not as a particular system of Indian philosophy, but rather as an all-encompassing outlook on all of the religious and spiritual traditions of the world. He stayed on in America for four more years to teach the numerous students who were interested in Indian thought. At that time, he wrote his celebrated books on the four yogas. In this way, Vivekananda gave wider circulation to Indian philosophical thought, mainly in the Vedānta tradition. But at the same time, he was giving a new expression and new formulations for its practice.

He returned to India in 1897, and by this time, had enough support for his idea to establish the Ramakrishna Mission for social service. His idea was that all of the four yogas can be combined for the betterment of oneself and the betterment of society. His message was to combine meditation with action, knowledge with devotion. Today, this Mission has become international in its scope with an exemplary reputation for social work and education.

Swami Vivekananda passed away in 1902, at the young age of 39. However, he left a great legacy in his writings encompassing nine printed volumes. His grand synthesis of the four yogas must be considered his masterpiece of philosophical work.

Through his extensive travels, Vivekananda was keenly aware of the division between spiritual and secular pursuits in nineteenth-century India, its degeneration and consequent vulnerability to foreign rule. Vivekananda traced this to the loss of *purusārtha*, the four goals of life, spoken of in the ancient epics and philosophical treatises. A concise translation of the word is "that which is the purpose of human life" and this purpose has four pillars: *dharma* (social justice), *artha* (wealth), *kāma* (pleasure), and *moksha* (liberation). These four are not mutually exclusive but rather interdependent and must be sought together. Social justice in the form of a peaceable society is the foundation. The pursuit of wealth must be in the context of *dharma*, and the same with *kāma* and *moksha*. Wealth does not mean only monetary wealth, but also the wealth of knowledge and wisdom. Pleasure does not mean only sensual pleasure but also artistic, intellectual, and spiritual pleasure. This four-fold purpose of life is shared by all individuals and all nations. By creating the Ramakrishna Mission of service, he was able to attract strong individuals who would dedicate their life for the welfare of the many and thereby fulfill their four-fold aim of life. Through this mission, and by the revival of the four-fold yoga, he wanted to create a new type of human being, one who combines the heart of the Buddha with the intellect of Shankara.

Since his writings are in English, his ideas are now widely accessible. In his own words, he said that his mission was to bring out the abstruse teachings of the Vedas and the Vedānta and explain them so that a child could understand them. Many times in his lectures, he said that "it is an insult to a starving man to teach him metaphysics" (Vol. 1, 20). Indeed, he had an incisive way of explaining abstract ideas that made them seem obvious. For instance, in his *Karma Yoga*, he writes:

> In every religion there are three parts: philosophy, mythology and ritual. Philosophy of course is the essence of every religion; mythology explains and illustrates it by means of the more or less legendary lives of great people, stories and fables of wonderful things... ritual gives to that philosophy a still more concrete form. (Vol. 1, 72)

Thus to understand any religion, one must understand the underlying philosophy. Often we confuse and conflate rituals and mythology as being the essence of religion. Having simplified the understanding of religion into these three categories, he summarized the whole of Indian philosophy thus:

> Each soul is potentially divine. The goal is to manifest this divinity within, by controlling nature, external and internal. Do this either by work, or worship, or psychic control, or philosophy—by one, or more, or all of these—and be free. This is the whole of religion. Doctrines, or dogmas, or rituals, or books, or temples, or forms, are but secondary details. (Vol. 1, 124)

AUROBINDO

At the heart of Aurobindo's philosophy is the idea that the human being is still in a process of evolution. We are on the cusp of a transition, very much like the transition from the fish to the amphibian. He wrote that man is a "transitional being" (Vol. 17, 7-12). The human race must rise from its present level of consciousness to a higher level if it is to survive, and hence the need for philosophy and religion. Sri Aurobindo explains:

> Philosophy is the intellectual search for the fundamental truth of things; religion is the attempt to make the truth dynamic in the soul of man. They are essential to each other; a religion that is not the expression of philosophic truth degenerates into superstition and obscurantism, and a philosophy which does not dynamise itself with the religious spirit is a barren light, for it cannot get itself practiced. (Radhakrishnan and Moore, 578)

To this end, he wrote "The Synthesis of Yoga" and formulated the basic principles of an integral yoga. In essence, this is the four-fold yoga expanded and amplified. At the same time, the new yoga found a place for artistic creativity as a means for *sadhana* and self-knowledge.

The synthesis of art and yoga finds full expression in the life and teachings of Sri Aurobindo. In his book, *Future Poetry*, he writes:

> The voice of poetry comes from a region above us, a plane of our being above and beyond our personal intelligence, a supermind which sees things in their innermost and largest truth by a spiritual identity. It is the possession of the mind by the supramental touch and the communicated impulse to seize this sight and word that creates the psychological phenomenon of poetic inspiration. (Vol. 9, 298)

In his conversations with Dilip Kumar Roy, he said, "It is and must be the purpose of all true creation to lift man from his lower planes of vision to the higher. It must mean some sort of release of consciousness, the same as in Yoga" (Roy, 233).

The large size of Aurobindo's literary output—including 30 books—is largely due to the fact that he saw writing as a *sadhana*; he advocated it as a means of self-realization for his disciples as well. Poetry and literary writing was a means for meditation, for reflection, for grasping ideas from the supermind. In his essay, "Poetic Vision and the Mantra," Sri Aurobindo writes "Vision is the characteristic power of the poet, as is discriminative thought the essential gift of the philosopher and analytic observation the natural genius of the scientist" (Vol. 9, 29).

Sri Aurobindo's life story is puzzling to say the least. He was born in Kolkata on August 15, 1872. His father, Dr. Krishnadhan Ghose, had studied medicine in England and had returned to India completely Westernized in his views and outlook. Aurobindo was the youngest of his three sons and Krishnadhan wanted all of them to be educated in England free of what he thought was the foggy mysticism that was infecting India at the time. (Such was the influence of British colonialism in India on the educated elite.) One of Aurobindo's biographers, Satprem, writes:

> He did not even want them to know anything of India's traditions and languages. Sri Aurobindo was therefore provided not only with an English first name, Akroyd, but also with an English governess, Miss Pagett, and then sent off at the age of five to an Irish convent school in Darjeeling among the sons of British administrators. Two years later, the three Ghose boys left for England. Sri Aurobindo was seven. (20)

The three boys were put in the care of an Anglican clergyman in Manchester "with strict instructions that they should not be allowed to make the acquaintance of any Indian or undergo any Indian influence" (Satprem, 21. See also Aurobindo, Vol. 26, 1). Apparently, these instructions were carried out and Aurobindo was entirely ignorant of India and her culture. His life in England must have been very much like the abused orphans in Charles Dickens's novel. "During a whole year a slice or two of sandwich, bread and butter and a cup of tea in the morning and in the evening a penny saveloy [sausage] formed the only food" (Aurobindo, Vol. 26, 2). Why a father would do such a thing to his own sons is a mystery, but can only indicate the Indian educated class's conviction that India and her culture were something to be rejected totally. Satprem writes:

> Dr. Ghose was indeed a peculiar man. He also ordered Rev. Drewett [the guardian of his sons] not to give his sons any religious instruction,

> so they could choose a religion themselves, if they so wished, when they came of age. He then left them to their fate for thirteen years. Dr. Ghose may appear to be a hardhearted man, but he was nothing of the kind; he gave not only his services as a doctor but also his money to poor Bengali villagers (while his sons had hardly anything to eat or wear in London), and died of shock when he was—mistakenly—informed that his favorite son, Aurobindo, had been lost in a shipwreck. But he believed his children should have character. (21)

There was at least one positive outcome of Aurobindo's English education and that was his mastery of many European languages including Latin, Greek, and French as well as its literary and philosophical culture. (He did not learn his mother tongue Bengali until the age of twenty.)

Sri Aurobindo did well in school, often winning scholarships and prizes for his literary achievements. In his later years in England, he had some acquaintances with Indian students and some knowledge as to what was going on in India under British rule. At the age of twenty, he sailed back to India. When he reached her shores, he learned his father had died.

Satprem writes, "When he landed at the Apollo Bunder in Bombay, he was seized with a spontaneous spiritual experience, a vast calm descended upon him" (39). He quickly found a job as a lecturer in French and English at the State College in Baroda. He began to write articles exhorting his countrymen to get rid of British rule. He had a revolutionary bent of mind, which is not unusual for a 20 year old, something his father and guardians tried to prevent from happening for most of his life up to that point. In the context of the partition of Bengal, Aurobindo along with his younger brother Barin were arrested as part of the Alipore bomb conspiracy. The trial found Barin guilty and he was sentenced to life imprisonment in the Andaman Islands. Aurobindo spent a year in the Alipore jail and was then acquitted. After his release, he decided to go to Pondicherry in southern India, which was under French rule. There he decided to give up his revolutionary activities and turned to a study of yoga.

So it was time to catch up on the missed education concerning India. Thus began an intense period of study ranging from the Rāmāyana to the Upanishads. He also learned Sanskrit and tried to fathom the mystery of the Veda and dived deep into the system of yoga. He learned to silence the mind, the first step in yoga. He writes:

> But for the knowledge of the Self it is necessary to have the power of a complete intellectual passivity, the power of dismissing all thought, the power of the mind to think not at all which the Gita in one passage

> enjoins. This is a hard saying for the occidental mind to which thought is the highest thing and which will be apt to mistake the power of the mind not to think, its complete silence for the incapacity of thought. But this power of silence is a capacity and not an incapacity, a power and not a weakness. It is a profound and pregnant stillness. (Vol. 20, 302)

Regarding his beginnings of yoga, Sri Aurobindo writes:

> All developed mental men, those who get beyond the average, have in one way or other at least at certain times and for certain purposes to separate the two parts of the mind, the active part which is a factory of thoughts and the quiet masterful part which is at once a Witness and a Will, observing them, judging, rejecting, eliminating, accepting, ordering corrections and changes, the Master in the House of Mind, capable of self-empire, *sāmrājya*. The Yogi goes still farther.... It was my great debt to Lele [Aurobindo's spiritual teacher] that he showed me this. "Sit in meditation," he said, "but do not think, look only at your mind; you will see thoughts coming into it; before they can enter throw these away from your mind till your mind is capable of entire silence." I had never heard before of thoughts coming visibly into the mind from outside, but I did not think either of questioning the truth or the possibility, I simply sat down and did it. In a moment my mind became silent as a windless air on a high mountain summit and then I saw one thought and then another coming in a concrete way from outside; I flung them away before they could enter and take hold of the brain and in three days I was free. (Vol. 26, 84)

What we see here is the experience of "initial levels of supermind" of which Sri Aurobindo wrote about extensively later in life. From this higher vantage point, one can witness the thoughts and feelings and not be affected by them or identify with them.

Sri Aurobindo was a yogi of the highest order and since his writings are recent, we can gain much from looking at them. By his personal example and the sheer volume of his output, we can determine to what heights this faculty of writing can be taken. Just as we exercise the muscles to strengthen them, we can exercise our creative faculty by deliberate effort. In his biography of Sri Aurobindo, Satprem writes, "Sri Aurobindo spent twelve hours a day writing, from six in the evening till six in the morning, then eight hours walking up and down 'for the yoga'" (Vol. 26, 95).

At the heart of Aurobindo's philosophy is the idea that the human race is still in evolution. Aurobindo envisions a further development of mind, first into reason and intellectual development, but later into intuitive and supra-mental levels of development.

For Aurobindo, there are several gradations of mind. First is the ordinary mind, then there is the higher mind, followed by the illumined mind, and then the intuitive mind and finally the overmind. All of these represent increasing levels of awareness and understanding. The ordinary mind is the common experience of all humanity. The higher mind is manifest in the writings of thinkers and philosophers. But beyond this lies the illumined mind, gaining its insights through silent reflection, learning to accept silence, and expanding into a silent awareness. Access to this level of awareness is often accompanied by an outburst of creative activity, particularly of a poetic nature. Indeed, if we practice even several hours of silent reflection, it is easily seen that this poetic realm is awakened. It is from this level that the sages of the Rg Veda and the Upanishads wrote of their revelations.

Aurobindo, in his essay on rhythm and movement writes, "The mantra, poetic expression of the deepest spiritual reality is only possible when three highest intensities of poetic speech meet and become indissolubly one, a highest intensity of rhythmic movement, a highest intensity of verbal form and thought-substance, of style, and a highest intensity of the soul's vision of truth" (Vol. 9, 17).

The practice of stillness or silence is absolutely essential if we want the mind to evolve into the illumined mind, according to Sri Aurobindo. That is the primary reason that meditation is practised so that the mind develops the habit of silence and silent reflection. This importance of silence has been emphasized by great philosophers and sages since the dawn of civilization. In the Psalms, we find, "Be still and know that I am God." Lao-Tzu taught that "To the mind that is still, the whole universe surrenders." The sixteenth-century mathematician and philosopher Blaise Pascal is often quoted as saying that "all human evil comes from this, man's being unable to sit still in a room." Silence is seen as a prerequisite to attain a higher level of mind.

But beyond the illumined mind is the intuitive mind, which cognizes superconscious truths, not by cogitation but by perception of a higher kind. Finally, the overmind is the abode of cosmic consciousness or universal awareness. Great sages and saints have experienced this, and we can too, if, according to Aurobindo, we discipline the mind first into the habit of silence, and then train it to expand that silent awareness into intuition and then even beyond to cosmic consciousness.

Explaining the idea of overmind, Satprem writes, "The Mantra, or higher poetry, higher music, the sacred Word, all issue from the overmind. It is the source of all creative and spiritual activities" (215). In Sri Aurobindo's integral yoga, he advocates the fostering of the creative spirit especially in poetry and music. With regard to poetic fluency, he writes, "It is precisely the people who are careful, self-critical, anxious for perfection who have interrupted visits from the Muse. Those who don't mind what they write, trusting to their genius, vigor, or fluency to carry it off are usually abundant writers" (Vol. 9, 295). Commenting on the idea of inspiration versus effort in the field of creative poetry, he writes,

> Inspiration is always a very uncertain thing; it comes when it chooses, stops suddenly before it has finished its work, refuses to descend when it is called. This is a well-known affliction, perhaps of all artists, but certainly of poets. There are some who can command it at will; those who, I think, are more full of an abundant poetic energy than careful for perfection; others who oblige it to come whenever they put pen to paper.... Again there are some who try to give it a habit of coming by always writing at the same time; Virgil with his nine lines first written, then perfected every morning, Milton with his fifty epic lines a day, are said to have succeeded in regularizing their inspiration. It is, I suppose, the same principle which makes Gurus in India prescribe for their disciples a meditation at the same fixed hour every day. (Vol. 9, 296)

This passage underscores the importance of regular effort in daily practice (*sadhana*). To habituate the mind to stillness and silence, to regulate the flow of creative inspiration and insight is the reason for the practice of meditation and study. It will be observed that the mind is not always at the same level of vibration. It has its high moments and low moments. However, one can regulate the visitations from the Muse to some extent by maintaining regularity in *sadhana*.

If we examine the people around us, we see two kinds. The first kind is the ordinary kind, not very exceptional in talent or speech, moving aimlessly and randomly, like a piece of driftwood, on the river of life. They are buffeted by events and their security lies in inertia. The other kind is the creative individual. But of this kind, there are two types, those that know the secret of creativity and those that do not. Those that know the secret of creative exertion can be called yogis, and this is one of the central ideas in Aurobindo's philosophy. Just as the Olympic athlete trains daily, the great musician practises daily, the great writer writes daily, similarly, the yogi must put in several hours of deliberate yogic discipline every day at a fixed time. According to Aurobindo, the creative fire should emerge spontaneously when the instrument has been properly prepared. The secret of life therefore is self-discipline, not for the act of creation itself, but to prepare the ground for it.

From Sri Aurobindo's explanation, we must not infer that the creative artist does nothing, but just waits for the inspiration. On the contrary, according to Aurobindo, the artist must silence the mind and this requires effort and practice. In that silent milieu, the necessary inspiration descends. In explaining the nature of thought to a disciple, Sri Aurobindo writes,

> These thought waves, thought-seeds, or thought forms or whatever they are, are of different values and come from different planes of consciousness. And the same thought-substance can take higher or lower vibrations according to the plane of consciousness through which the thoughts come in (e.g. the thinking mind, vital mind, physical mind, subconscient mind) or the power of consciousness which catches them and pushes them into one man or another. Moreover, there is a stuff of mind in each man and the incoming thought uses that for shaping itself or translating itself (transcribing we usually call it), but the stuff is finer or coarser, stronger or weaker, etc. etc. in one mind or another. Also there is mind energy actual or potential in each which differs and this mind energy in its recipience of the thought can be luminous or obscure, sattwic (serene), rajasic (impassioned) or tamasic (inert) with consequences that vary in each case. (Satprem, 281)

It is fair to say that the average individual operates from the habit mind. He is a bundle of habits acquired in childhood, youth, and adult life through schooling, hobbies, and interests. But behind that is the animal man, coming from his evolutionary past, and so at best, the average man is some combination of animal and human with some talents and abilities. If he can eke out an existence on these acquirements, he will. He will make no effort to reflect, or to improve or acquire new talents. For he has not given any thought to what we may call the creative mind. One often inhabits the habit mind and life is just a trolley ride along the rails of past habits, some good and some bad. It is no wonder that the modern man is plagued with depression, since the immense power lodged in the mind has not been suitably expressed.

The habit mind and its imprisonment of man has been recognized by many thinkers and writers. Gurdjieff, for instance, speaks of man as a robot or a machine. Colin Wilson writes about Gurdjieff's philosophy:

> At the core of his work lies this notion that we possess greater powers than we realize, and that our apparent limitations are due to a peculiar form of laziness—a laziness that has become so habitual that it has developed into a mechanism. (14)

This is nothing new, having been recognized since ancient times, most notably in the Rg Veda. In fact, the opening verse of the Rg Veda, studied in Chapter 2, begins by saying "*Agnimile purohitam yajnasya devamrtvijam hotāram ratnadhātamam.*" As Sri Aurobindo pointed out, this is a prayer to awaken the creative fire within. Indeed, the obvious translation is "Agni I adore, who stands before the Lord, the god who seeth Truth, the warrior, strong disposer of delight" (Vol. 11, 439). Sri Aurobindo asks several questions regarding this opening verse. First, why an invocation to Agni before all other gods?

> Because it is he that stands before Yajna, the Divine Master of things; because he is the god whose burning eyes can gaze straight at Truth, at the *satyam*, the *vijnānam*, which is the Seer's own aim and desire and on which all Veda is based; because he is the warrior who wars down and removes all the crooked attractions of ignorance and limitation that stand persistently in the way of the Yogin; because as the vehicle of Tapas, the pure divine superconscious energy which flows from the concealed higher hemisphere of existence, (*avyakta parārdha*), he more than any develops and arranges Ananda, the divine delight. (Vol. 11, 439)

The image of fire is the image of *tapasya* and this is the recurrent theme of the Upanishads: how to awaken the inner fire, the fire of enthusiasm.

Agni is not fire, but exists in the fire. How does Agni exist in the fire? Sri Aurobindo answers:

> As the man lives in his body and as thought lives in the look or the gesture. The body is not the man in himself and the gesture is not the thought in itself; it is only the man in manifestation or the thought in manifestation. So too the fire is not Agni in himself but Agni in manifestation and the world is not God in Himself but God in manifestation. The man is not manifested only by his body, but also and much more perfectly by his work and action. Thought is not manifested only by look and gesture, but also and much more perfectly by action and speech. So too, Agni is not manifested only by fire, but also and much more perfectly by all workings in the world,—subtle as well as gross material,—of the principle of heat and brilliance and force; God is not manifested only by this material world, but also and much more perfectly by all movements and harmonies of the action of consciousness supporting and informing material appearances. (Vol. 11, 440)

The fundamental human problem, considered here, is how to awaken the creative mind and ignite[2] oneself to a higher purpose. The whole purpose of yoga is to awaken this fire. Artists and writers in all cultures often recognized this problem, and resorted to various contrivances, some of them ridiculous and bordering on the bizarre, to combat this lazy tendency of the mind. For instance, the American writer Ernest Hemmingway took up big game hunting, bullfighting, and working as a war correspondent. These people deliberately sought out dangers in order to avoid boredom or a life of laziness. Sadly, some people even turn to crime. The central premise of yoga is that our energies can be given a creative and purposeful direction.

The ancient sages realized that the human being becomes an automaton, a lazy individual, through inertia, through habitual thinking and action. We perform our daily tasks with our mind elsewhere and this is the source of automatic action. If we can perform our work with full attention and awareness, we can mitigate the habit-forming mechanism. This is one idea. The other idea is to deliberately challenge the mind through creative exertion and this is the essence of the idea of *tapas*.

In Aurobindo's view, writing can be used as a basis of a spiritual practice. One can rise from the morass of the habit mind to the level of the creative or inspired mind. This can be done through reflection and reading of inspired material. Ideas have power and when great ideas are meditated upon, they have power to rejuvenate and energize the mind and fill one with enthusiasm. The Bhagavadgīta was one result of this energizing. Arjuna was in a state of despondency and Sri Krishna's message on the battlefield was the message of the Atman. These words lifted up his spirit that by the end of the discourse he was inspired for action. This is what we want. We need a technique to lift the mind from depression or despair. The technique may differ from individual to individual; this is the essential theme of Vedānta and its insistence on an appropriate combination of the four yogas. We must find the right stimulus, the right challenge to the mind that will awaken new energies. If we take up too many tasks or too many projects, we find ourselves in danger of spreading ourselves too thin. This again is a dissipation of energies. No activity, or inertia, is *tamoguna*, and too much activity, with too many thoughts is *rajoguna*, and both of these extremes must be avoided. The study of great ideas is often an antidote for such an impasse of the mind. The habit of stillness is again another. Music is a third. One must determine for oneself which

2 As was mentioned in an earlier chapter, the word "ignite" is derived from the Latin word "ignitus," which again is related to the Sanskrit word "agni."

one works and when. It may even be possible that physical activity can help in this context. Many have found that a simple brisk walk around the block invigorates their spirit. At a very basic level where *tamas* manifests itself, such activities may help in getting back to a less dense state.

Commenting on this tendency of the human mind to spread itself thinly by trying to take up many things, Swami Vivekananda writes:

> There is the danger of frittering away your energies by taking up an idea only for its novelty, and then giving it up for another that is newer. Take one thing up and do it, and see the end of it, and before you have seen the end, do not give it up. He who can become mad with an idea, he alone sees light. Those that only take a nibble here and a nibble there will never attain anything. They may titillate their nerves for a moment, but there it will end. They will be slaves in the hands of nature and will never get beyond the senses. (Vol. 1, 177)

The zeal to complete a creative work is sometimes strengthened when we have a purpose and meaning in the task. One needs meaning in what one does. Creativity, for its own sake, is meaningless. There has to be a purpose and if that purpose is driven by an ideal of collective welfare, then there is more power in the work we do. This is the worship of the *Daridra Narayana*, as Vivekananda and Mahatma Gandhi have described it. By contrast, Sri Aurobindo describes creative work that is *ahaituka*, arising spontaneously from a source of inspiration not with any explicit purpose but an implicit one to express joy or *ananda* (Vol. 11, 444).

Sri Aurobindo died in 1950, at the age of 78, at his ashram in Pondicherry. His legacy of writing signals the way for future humanity. The present stage of the human race is transitional. There are higher spiritual levels to attain. Once attained, life on this planet will be taken to a higher standard. The means to achieve this end is integral yoga.

Though we chose Sri Aurobindo as an example of a mystic philosopher of modern India, we find that there is much that is practical in his integral yoga. Especially in connection with mental vagaries and laziness, the *sadhana* of artistic expression in the form of creative writing will help much in confronting our defects and raising us into the higher levels of the mind. In this sense, the integral yoga of Sri Aurobindo is part of the "neo-Vedānta" of the twentieth century.

TAGORE

Tagore's philosophical position can be called aesthetic humanism. He believed in the creative self-expression of the individual and felt that artistic and cultural dialogue between nations would lead to a better world. To this end, he wrote extensively and even created a university.

Rabindranath Tagore was born in 1861 in Kolkata, into a wealthy, artistic family. He started to write poetry at the age of eight. His early education was through private tutors at home, but later, he went to England to study law, returning within one year, however, without earning a degree. Though his early writings were in Bengali, he also wrote in English and translated some of his Bengali poems into English. Most of his work is imbued with a mystical quality and often borders on the devotional. He was awarded the Nobel Prize in literature in 1913, when he was 52 years old, most notably for his work *Gitanjali*, or Song Offerings. In writing the introduction to the English edition, the celebrated poet William Butler Yeats said:

> I have carried the manuscript of these translations about with me for days, reading it in railway trains, or on the top of omnibuses and in restaurants, and I have often had to close it lest some stranger would see how much it moved me. These lyrics—which are in the original, my Indian friends tell me, full of subtlety of rhythm, of untranslatable delicacies of colour, or metrical invention—display in their thought a world I have dreamed of all my life long. The work of a supreme culture, they yet appear as much the growth of the common soil as the grass and the rushes. A tradition, where poetry and religion are the same thing, has passed through the centuries, gathering from learned and unlearned metaphor and emotion, and carried back again to the multitude the thought of the scholar and of the noble. (7)

From his early childhood, Tagore lived and breathed poetry. He learned the essence of poetic style from the great poets themselves. In his *Reminiscences*, he writes of one Bihari Lal Chakravarti and how his sister-in-law admired his poetry and memorized the lyrics of many of them.

> He was a great admirer of Valmiki and Kalidas. I remember how once after reciting a description of the Himalayas from Kalidas[3] with all the strength of his voice, he said: "The succession of long 'a' sound here

3 The reference here is to the famous Hymn to the Himalayas written by Kalidas and the opening lines of the poem. The poem was set to music and made famous by Pankaj Mallik.

> is not an accident. The poet has deliberately repeated this sound all the way from *Devatatma* down to *Nagādhirāja* as an aid to realizing the glorious expanse of the Himalayas." (*Omnibus 2*, 506)

Tagore would say that one writes poetry, not to explain something or to convey a moral, but rather to convey a feeling. This feeling tries to find expression in the shape of a poem. He writes:

> That words have meanings is just the difficulty.... That is why poets have to turn and twist them in meter and rhyme so that meaning may be held somewhat in check and feeling allowed to express itself. The utterance of feeling does not involve the statement of some fundamental truth or a scientific fact or a useful moral precept. Like a tear or a smile, a poem is only a picture of what is taking place within. (*Omnibus 2*, 568)

When Tagore led a contemplative life he was a recluse, spending countless hours in reflection and meditation. Creative endeavour may require that one be somewhat of a recluse. In his essay on Tagore, Radhakrishnan writes:

> The poetry of human experience, the realities of life as distinct from its mere frills, are achieved in solitude.... Only the man of serene mind can realize the spiritual meaning of life. Honesty with oneself is the condition of spiritual integrity. We must let in the light to illumine the secret places of the soul. Our pretensions and professions are the barriers that shut us away from truth. We are more familiar with the things we have than with what we are. We are afraid to be alone with ourselves, face to face with our naked loneliness. (*East and West*, 135-36)

We never discover who we are unless we retire into solitude and confront our thoughts and feelings. Even the creative artist or scientist must retreat into silence to sort out ideas or to make a discovery, to find the underlying patterns. When we are alone with ourselves, we can feel the canker of our thoughts and desires, their tumultuous rumble that creates a certain fear, a certain anxiety. We can feel it all too well. When the *sadhana* is thus confronted by his own mind, the immediate reaction is to seek noise, to seek company, to seek amusement, or distraction, or to slip into sleep. Few people can accept the challenge of solitude. Yet, we know for true understanding of ourselves, we must confront ourselves. It is not an easy task. But it must be done. And if it is done, we emerge stronger, and more illumined. This is the *sadhana* of the poet, the scholar, the scientist. To quote Radhakrishnan again:

> It is with an effort that we have to pull ourselves together, cultivate the inner life, and abstract from the outer sheaths of body, mind and intellect. We then see the soul within and attain to a stillness of spirit. The discovery of inwardness is the essential basis of spiritual life. (*East and West*, 136)

Tagore had the temperament of the Upanishadic sage and felt that education should be imparted in that spirit. To this end, he founded in 1901 a hermitage (*ashram*) in Shantiniketan (which literally means "the abode of peace"), about 200 kilometres from Kolkata. There he began an experimental school and created a veritable forest retreat. He also penned many of his literary classics including the Nobel-Prize winning *Gitanjali*. Here is a sample verse from *Gitanjali*:

> My poet's vanity dies in shame before thy sight.
> O Master Poet. I have sat down at thy feet.
> Only let me make my life simple and straight,
> Like a flute of reed for thee to fill with music. (*Omnibus 2*)

His creativity expanded into music and art, writing more than 2000 songs, and creating a new style of music now called Rabindra Sangeet. Today, every villager hums a tune of Rabindranath Tagore. Two of these songs became the national anthems of India and (present-day) Bangladesh. Tagore is perhaps the only person on the planet to have penned the national anthems of two countries.

Though he opposed British imperialism, he did not embrace any form of nationalism. He believed that global peace could only be achieved through intellectual and artistic co-operation between nations, and often expressed the view that the globe was being torn apart by the cult of nationalism. Believing that education was the most effective path to international co-operation, he conceived of a new type of university that would become a world centre for the study of all great ideas from all corners of the world. Using the money from his Nobel Prize, he created the Visva Bharati University in December 1921. Today, it is one of the central universities in India.

Many scholars from all parts of the world came to Visva Bharati and exchanged ideas. Even Mahatma Gandhi came to visit him. Though they did not agree on many things, still they had mutual respect for each other. Today,

Visva Bharati University has an illustrious list of distinguished alumni, the most notable being Indira Gandhi (former prime minister of India), Satyajit Ray (noted film director), and Amartya Sen (a Nobel laureate in economics).

Tagore died in 1941 at the age of 80, leaving a legacy of inspiring writings. In "The Nation," an essay first published in 1922, Tagore writes, "I do not put my faith in any new institution, but in individuals all over the world who think clearly, feel nobly and act rightly, thus becoming channels of moral truth" (632).

GANDHI

In an earlier section, we outlined the ancient ideal of *purusārtha*. This ideal finds a powerful expression in the life of Mahatma Gandhi. In his life and writings, we find a marvellous synthesis of the spiritual and the secular life. In his magazine, *Young India*, he wrote as early as 1922 that the "human mind or human society is not divided into watertight compartments called social, political and religious. All act and react upon one another" (*Young India*, 131). Later, he amplified this statement in the following way:

> Human life being an undivided whole, no line can ever be drawn between its different compartments, nor between ethics and politics. A trader who earns his wealth by deception only succeeds in deceiving himself when he thinks that his sins can be washed away by spending some amount of his ill-gotten gains on the so-called religious purposes. One's everyday life is never capable of being separated from one's spiritual being. Both act and react upon one another. (*Harijan*, 85)

Thus, in this way, the ideal of *moksha* was intimately wedded to the other three components of *purusārtha*. One can even say that for Gandhi, the other three components were subordinate to the ideal of *moksha*. Indeed, he wrote in his autobiography,

> To see the universal and all-pervading Spirit of Truth face to face, one must be able to love the meanest of creation as oneself. And a man who aspires after that cannot afford to keep out of any field of life. That is why my devotion to Truth has drawn me into the field of politics; and I can say without the slightest hesitation, and yet in all humility, that those who say that religion has nothing to do with politics do not know what religion means. (370-71)

These statements reveal a deep and personal understanding of religion and politics that transcends the common understanding. To probe the mind of Gandhi and uncover how he came to formulate his philosophy is a mammoth task. For in one sense, Gandhi was not an academic philosopher and was not the creator of any "ism" or system of political thought. In a famous letter to Sarvepalli Radhakrishnan, dated September 16, 1934, Gandhi writes, "The fact that I have affected the thought and practice of our times does not make me fit to give expression to the philosophy that may lie behind it. To give a philosophical interpretation of the phenomenon must be reserved for men like you" (Gopal, 138).

But this is not a simple task. Gandhi is one of the most voluminous writers in human history. His collected works comprise more than 150 volumes! Most of the volumes are collections of his letters written to various people, but even if we remove these letters, we find that Gandhi had a vast array of essays that span more than fifty volumes. Like Aurobindo, he edited weekly journals, several during his lifetime. The only major book Gandhi wrote is his autobiography, modestly titled, *A Story of My Experiments in Truth*, written in prison.

Gandhi's motivation for writing is important to understand. In his own words:

> What I want to achieve—what I have been striving and pining to achieve these thirty years—is self-realization, to see God face to face, to attain *moksha*. I live and move and have my being in pursuit of this goal. All that I do by way of speaking and writing, and all my ventures in the political field, are directed to this same end. But as I have all along believed that what is possible for one is possible for all, my experiments have not been conducted in the closet, but in the open; and I do not think that this fact detracts from their spiritual value. (*Autobiography*, x)

Gandhi thought of his writing as part of his *sadhana*. However, unlike Sri Aurobindo, Gandhi did not aim for any literary excellence or poetic style. Rather, he wanted to get his message out as clearly and as quickly as possible. There is perhaps something to be learned from this attitude, especially for some of us who tend to procrastinate and try to aim for excessive perfectionism in our creative work.

Mohandas Karamchand Gandhi[4] was born in 1869 in Porbandar, in the province of Gujarat, the youngest of three sons. He lived there until he was

4 The word *mahatma* is Sanskrit for "great soul." It is said that many, including Rabindranath Tagore, bestowed this title on Gandhi for his work in both South Africa and India, and ever since, he has been called Mahatma Gandhi.

seven years old at which time his family moved to Rajkot. While still in high school, at the age of 13, he was married to Kasturbai, who was also 13. His wife did not have schooling and was illiterate. In September 1887, after his matriculation, when he was only 18 years old, he went off to England to study law. He left behind a son who was barely a few months old. After four years of study in England, he returned to India and set up a legal practice in Rajkot with limited success. Then a Gujarati firm of merchants who had a branch in South Africa asked him to go there to work on a legal case. So, in April 1893, Gandhi sailed to South Africa with the intention of staying there one year and returning to India. It turned out that he stayed there for 20 years.

In South Africa, he came face to face with the ugly and grotesque face of racial discrimination in all its forms and shapes, and, as he relates in his *Autobiography*, this was a turning point in his life.

> The train reached Maritzburg, the capital of Natal, at about 9pm. Beddings used to be provided at this station. A railway servant came and asked me if I wanted one. "No," said I, "I have one with me." He went away. But a passenger came next and looked me up and down. He saw that I was a "coloured" man. This disturbed him. Out he went and came in again with one or two officials. They all kept quiet, when another official came to me and said, "Come along, you must go to the van compartment." "But I have a first class ticket," said I. "That doesn't matter," rejoined the other. "I tell you, you must go to the van compartment." "I tell you, I was permitted to travel in this compartment at Durban and I insist on going on in it." "No you won't," said the official. "You must leave this compartment, or else I shall have to call a police constable to push you out." "Yes you may. I refuse to go out voluntarily." The constable came. He took me by the hand and pushed me out. My luggage was also taken out. I refused to go to the other compartment and the train steamed away. I went and sat in the waiting room, keeping my hand baggage with me, leaving the other luggage where it was. The railway authorities had taken charge of it. It was winter and winter in the higher regions of South Africa is severely cold. Maritzburg being at a high altitude, the cold was extremely bitter. My overcoat was in my luggage, but I did not dare to ask for it lest I should be insulted again, so I sat and shivered. There was no light in the room.... I began to think of my duty. Should I fight for my rights or go back to India, or should I go on to Pretoria without minding the insults, and return to India after finishing the case? It would be cowardice to run back to India without fulfilling my obligation. The hardship to which I was subjected to was

> superficial—only a symptom of the deep disease of colour prejudice. I should try, if possible, to root out the disease and suffer hardships in the process. Redress for wrongs I should seek only to the extent that would be necessary for the removal of the colour prejudice. So I decided to take the next available train to Pretoria. (*Autobiography*, 93-94)

This was indeed a decisive moment in Gandhi's life and the history of the world. Gandhi's great movement was born that night, when he refused to succumb to the discriminatory laws and move to the third class compartment as he was told to do. This episode was the source of Gandhi's spiritual strength since he made the right decision. Often we accept injustice since we feel we are not sufficiently strong to take on the Goliath of race prejudice or any other form of social injustice. We can assume that Gandhi spent the night in the station at Maritzburg without sleep pondering over this issue. For he writes:

> The following morning I sent a long telegram to the General Manager of the Railway and also informed Abdulla Sheth, who immediately met the General Manager. The Manager justified the conduct of the railway authorities, but informed him that he had already instructed the Station Master to see that I reached my destination safely. Abdulla Sheth wired to the Indian merchants in Maritzburg and to friends in other places to meet me and look after me. The merchants came to see me at the station and tried to comfort me by narrating their own hardships and explaining that what had happened to me was nothing unusual. They also said that Indians traveling first or second class had to expect trouble from railway officials and white passengers. The day was thus spent in listening to these tales of woe. (*Autobiography*, 94)

That day, Gandhi took the evening train to his destination. He reached Charlestown by morning but now had to take a stage coach to go from Charlestown to Johannesburg since there was no train service between these two cities. Again, even though Gandhi had a valid ticket, the coachman refused him a seat since he would be sitting next to white passengers. After some argument, Gandhi had to sit outside next to the driver. Sadly, he writes:

> I knew it was sheer injustice and an insult, but I thought it better to pocket it. I could not have forced myself inside, and if I had raised a protest, the coach would have gone off without me. This would have meant the loss of another day, and heaven only knows what would have happened the next day. So, much as I fretted within myself, I prudently sat next to the coachman. (*Autobiography*, 94)

That day, around three o'clock in the afternoon, one of the white passengers wanted to smoke and have some fresh air.

> So he took a piece of dirty sack cloth from the driver, spread it on the footboard and addressing me said, "Sami, you sit on this, I want to sit near the driver." The insult was more than I could bear. In fear and trembling I said to him, "It was you who seated me here, though I should have been accommodated inside. I put up with the insult. Now that you want to sit outside and smoke, you would have me sit at your feet. I will not do so, but I am prepared to sit inside." As I was struggling through these sentences, the man came down upon me and began heavily to box my ears. He seized me by the arm and tried to drag me down. I clung to the brass rails of the coachbox and was determined to keep my hold even at the risk of breaking my wrist bones. The passengers were witnessing the scene—the man swearing at me, dragging and belaboring me, and I remaining still. He was strong and I was weak. Some of the passengers were moved to pity and exclaimed: "Man, let him alone. Don't beat him. He is not to blame. He is right. If he can't stay there, let him come and sit with us." "No fear," cried the man, but he seemed somewhat crestfallen and stopped beating me. He let go my arm, swore at me a little more, and asking the Hottentot servant who was sitting on the other side of the coachbox to sit on the footboard, took the seat so vacated.... The coach rattled away. My heart was beating fast within my breast, and I was wondering whether I should ever reach my destination alive. The man cast an angry look at me now and then, and pointing his finger at me, growled: "Take care, let me once get to Standerton and I shall show you what I do." I sat speechless and prayed to God to help me. After dark, we reached Standerton and I heaved a sigh of relief on seeing some Indian faces.... I told them all that I had gone through. They were very sorry to hear it and comforted me by relating to me their own bitter experiences. (*Autobiography*, 95-96)

Gandhi's sole aim was to correct injustice.

These painful episodes led Gandhi to evolve a viable political philosophy and gave birth to the idea of *satyagraha*. This word, coined by him, means zeal for, or insistence on, truth, and became the name of his movement of non-violent resistance to evil.[5]

He began to write about his ideas in weekly journals. The philosophy of *satyagraha* evolved over decades and became refined in thought and

5 Apparently, Gandhi ran a competition in his magazine, *Indian Opinion*, for the right word to denote non-violent resistance. His close relative Maganlal Gandhi came up with *sadagraha* and Gandhi changed it to *satyagraha* to make the meaning clearer (*Essential Writings*, 317).

practice through Gandhi's writings, mainly in his journals *Young India* and *Harijan*. When Gandhi undertook the fight of unjust laws, first in South Africa and then later in India, he had a cause to fight for, a matter of life and death. The writings, the meditations, and the experiments all had a singular purpose and the *Daridra Narayana* (the God in the Poor) was the sole object of his worship. If we read his autobiography and see that there was nothing extraordinary about his childhood, we are only amazed how a single idea such as non-violent resistance can catch fire and ignite a nation to achieve freedom from British imperialism. But it did. This is the power of spirit, the power of an idea and this power spread through the writings of Mahatma Gandhi.

Gandhi did not view writing, per se, as a *sadhana*. I don't think he ever thought, "Let me sit down and meditate. Let me sit down and write." His writings and meditations were inspired by the immediate need to solve a problem of life and death. From the scriptural lore, from the philosophical writings of learned scholars of all countries and all climes, he forged a plan, a philosophy to suit his particular needs and the particular people he was serving. This was his originality. We are often too timid to get our feet wet. But he managed to plunge in and find a way out. That was his genius.

If Gandhi had not written his words through his journals and magazines, the mobilization of the masses to work for a cause would have never taken place. Gandhi writes:

> Through these journals I now commenced to the best of my ability the work of educating the reading public in *Satyagraha*. [These journals] reached a very wide circulation, which at one time rose to the neighborhood of forty thousand.... These journals helped me also to some extent to remain at peace with myself, for whilst immediate resort to civil disobedience was out of the question, they enabled me to freely ventilate my views and to put heart into the people. Thus I feel that both the journals rendered good service to the people in this hour of trial and did their humble bit towards lightening the tyranny of martial law. (*Autobiography*, 395)

The mental energy that is expressed through the word is to a large extent tamed and channeled through writing. This the ancient sages knew. Karma yoga is the yoga of action, but it is sometimes not seen that writing is action. There is transformational power in the word. *Satyagraha* was such a word and in the hands of Mahatma Gandhi had the power of emancipation and transformed India. On August 15, 1947, India became free from colonial rule.

In speaking about this energy of the word, Swami Vivekananda writes:

> In one sense we cannot think but in symbols; words themselves are symbols of thought. In another sense everything in the universe may be looked upon as a symbol. The whole universe is a symbol and God is the essence behind. This kind of symbology is not simply the creation of man; it is not that certain people belonging to a religion sit down together and think out certain symbols, and bring them into existence out of their own minds. The symbols of religion have a natural growth.... Language is not the result of convention; it is not that people ever agreed to represent certain ideas by certain words; there never was an idea without a corresponding word or a word without a corresponding idea; ideas and words are in their nature inseparable. The symbols to represent ideas may be sound symbols or colour symbols.... The study and practice of these things form naturally a part of karma yoga. (Vol. 1, 72-74)

The essence of *satyagraha* is to hold on to truth at all costs. But this must be done through the principle of *ahimsa*, non-violence. In 1917, Gandhi writes:

> *Satyagraha* is not a physical force. A *satyagrahi* does not inflict pain on the adversary; he does not seek his destruction. A satygrahi never resorts to firearms. In the use of *satyagraha*, there is no ill-will whatever. *Satyagraha* is pure soul-force. Truth is the very substance of soul. That is why this force is called *satyagraha*. The soul is informed with knowledge. In it burns the flame of love. If someone gives us pain through ignorance, we shall win him through love.... Non-violence is a dormant state. In the waking state, it is love. Ruled by love, the world goes on.... We forget the principle of non-violence, which is the essence of all religions. The doctrine of arms stands for irreligion. (*Essential Writings*, 316)

Gandhi's writings delineate a powerful political philosophy that has been adopted by many other leaders since. Martin Luther King Jr., Nelson Mandela, Vaclav Havel, Lech Walesa, and more recently Aung San Suu Kyi, among many others, were able to fashion and modify the principles of *satyagraha* to suit their own freedom struggles in their respective countries. Gandhi became a voice of the conscience of all people.

In his autobiography, Martin Luther King Jr. writes in the spring of 1950,

> One Sunday afternoon, I traveled to Philadelphia to hear a sermon by Dr. Mordecai Johnson, president of Howard University.... Dr. Johnson had just returned from a trip to India, and to my great interest, spoke of the life and teachings of Mahatma Gandhi. His message was so profound and electrifying that I left the meeting and bought half a dozen books on Gandhi's life and works. Like most people, I had heard of Gandhi, but I had never studied him seriously. As I read, I became deeply fascinated by his campaigns of nonviolent resistance. I was particularly moved by his Salt March to the Sea and his numerous fasts. The whole concept of *satyagraha* was profoundly significant to me. As I delved deeper into the philosophy of Gandhi, my skepticism concerning the power of love gradually diminished, and I came to see for the first time its potency in the area of social reform.... Gandhi was probably the first person in history to lift the love ethic of Jesus above mere interaction between individuals to a powerful and effective social force on a large scale. Love for Gandhi was a potent instrument for social and collective transformation. It was in this Gandhian emphasis on love and nonviolence that I discovered the method of social reform that I had been seeking. (23-24)

Dr. King was so inspired by Gandhi's life and message that he made a visit to India in 1959. In his autobiography, in the chapter entitled "Pilgrimage to Nonviolence," Dr. King writes,

> Gandhi was able to mobilize and galvanize more people in his lifetime than any other person in the history of this world. And just with a little love and understanding goodwill and a refusal to cooperate with an evil law, he was able to break the backbone of the British Empire. This, I think, was one of the most significant things that ever happened in the history of the world. More than 390 million people achieved their freedom and they achieved it non-violently. (129)

The noted historian Arnold Toynbee writes:

> Today we are still living in this transitional chapter of the world's history, but it is already becoming clear that a chapter which had a Western beginning will have to have an Indian ending if it is not to end in the self-destruction of the human race. In the present age, the world has been united on the material plane by Western technology. But this Western skill has not only "annihilated distance"; it has armed the peoples of the world with weapons of devastating power

> at a time when they have been brought to point-blank range of each other without yet having learnt to know and love each other. At this supremely dangerous moment in human history, the only way of salvation for mankind is an Indian way. The Emperor Ashoka's and the Mahatma Gandhi's principle of non-violence and Sri Ramakrishna's testimony to the harmony of religions; here we have the attitude and the spirit that can make it possible for the human race to grow together into a single family—and, in the Atomic Age, this is the only alternative to destroying ourselves. (6)

Gandhi had to sacrifice his life for the sake of the ideal he believed in. On January 30, 1948, he was killed by an assassin's bullet. Yet Gandhi lives through his legacy, his message, and his writings. He has inspired and continues to inspire many who dare to dream of a better world free of conflict and strife.

KRISHNAMURTI

The fundamental message of Krishnamurti is that "Truth is a pathless land and you cannot approach it by any path whatsoever, by any religion, by any sect.... Truth, being limitless, unconditioned, unapproachable by any path whatsoever, cannot be organized; nor should any organization be formed to lead or coerce people along a particular path" (Luytens, 293). In this message, he is one with the Buddha, who also advocated his students to think for themselves and not to accept an idea because it was tradition, or that it was written in a book, or someone taught it to them. But rather, reason it out and if it is beneficial to one and all, accept it. How did Krishnamurti come to this realization? That is an amazing story.

Jiddu Krishnamurti was born in 1895 in Madanepalli, Andhra Pradesh. He was the eighth of eleven children, and being the eighth, was named Krishna (since according to Indian mythology, Sri Krishna was also the eighth child of Devaki and Vasudeva). Krishnamurti's mother passed away when he was only ten, and so his father moved to Chennai (Madras) for employment. He found work at the Theosophical Society.

Theosophy is a mystical religion and combines theology with philosophy. Its central tenet is that there is a mystical spiritual hierarchy and that humanity must evolve to a greater perfection through this hierarchy. It was founded in 1875 by Helena Blavatsky and theosophy, with its occult overtones, found a fertile home in Chennai, India. Soon, this had become an international religious cult with Annie Besant as leader. Theosophists had prophesied the emergence of a messiah-like "world teacher," and a member of the society, seeing young Krishnamurti and his brother Nitya playing on the seashore, noticed their "spiritual auras."

In 1909, Annie Besant took custody of both Krishnamurti and Nitya and began the training of the new "world teacher." It must have been a financial relief for the father to let go of the two sons, though there were some legal battles in this connection in later years. Krishnamurti was 14 and Nitya was 11 when Annie Besant took over as their guardian. She sent both of them off to England for studies in 1911. Nitya had difficulty adjusting to his new environments and had numerous health problems. They were moved around to various places to see if his health would improve. Finally, in 1922, they were moved to Ojai, California, where their guardians felt the weather would be more suitable for Nitya's recovery.

It was around this time that Krishnamurti would have his three-day life changing experience. First it began as an intense pain at the back of his neck, and then it swelled. He would then lapse into unconsciousness. He would relate later,

> I was supremely happy, for I had seen. Nothing could ever be the same. I have drunk at the clear and pure waters and my thirst was appeased... I have seen the Light. I have touched compassion which heals all sorrow and suffering; it is not for myself, but for the world.... Love in all its glory has intoxicated my heart; my heart can never be closed. I have drunk at the fountain of Joy and eternal Beauty. I am God-intoxicated. (Luytens, 171-72)

In November 1925, his younger brother Nitya passed away at the age of 27. Undoubtedly, this must have had an impact on Krishnamurti. After he had his spiritual experience and after his younger brother died, Krishnamurti started formulating his own ideas and thoughts without being coached by the theosophist guardians. This development reached its climax in 1929, when he was supposed to announce to the world that he was the new messiah of Besant's society. In August, 1929, in front of Annie Besant and an audience of thousands, and with a world-wide radio audience, he spoke thus:

> You may remember the story of how the devil and a friend of his were walking down the street, when they saw ahead of them a man stoop down and pick up something from the ground, look at it, and put it away in his pocket. The friend said to the devil, "What did that man pick up?" "He picked up a piece of the truth," said the devil. "That is a very bad business for you, then," said his friend. "Oh, not at all,"

> the devil replied, "I am going to help him organize it." I maintain that truth is a pathless land, and you cannot approach it by any path whatsoever, by any religion, by any sect. That is my point of view, and I adhere to that absolutely and unconditionally. Truth, being limitless, unconditioned, unapproachable by any path whatsoever, cannot be organized; nor should any organization be formed to lead or coerce people along a particular path. (Luytens, 293)

This was indeed a turning point and a defiant act of courage, Gandhian in proportion. It must have been a very difficult thing for him to do since he viewed Annie Besant as his foster mother. He continued:

> This is no magnificent deed, because I do not want followers, and I mean this. The moment you follow someone you cease to follow Truth. I am not concerned whether you pay attention to what I say or not. I want to do a certain thing in the world and I am going to do it with unwavering concentration. I am concerning myself with only one essential thing: to set man free. I desire to free him from all cages, from all fears, and not to found religions, new sects, nor to establish new theories and new philosophies. (Luytens, 294)

Krishnamurti saw that the problem of the human being lies in his sense of complacency, his inability to act, his inability to think for himself. In all of his lectures we see an exhortation to think through things clearly. According to him, it is pure laziness that one does not do so. We allow others to think for us. Undoubtedly, he saw his guardianship of the Theosophical Society as symbolic of the problem of man. His words seem to echo the famous words of Kant who writes:

> Laziness and cowardice are the reasons why so great a portion of mankind…remains under lifelong tutelage, and why it is so easy for others to set themselves up as their guardians.… If I have a book which understands for me, a pastor who has a conscience for me, a physician who decides my diet, etc., I need not trouble myself. I need not think, if I can only pay—others will undertake the work for me. That the step to competence is held to be very dangerous by the greater portion of mankind is seen to by those guardians who have so kindly assumed superintendence over them. After the guardians have made their domestic cattle dumb and have ensured that these placid creatures will not dare take a single step without the harness of the cart to which they are tethered, the guardians then show them the danger which threatens if they try to go alone. (83)

The core of Krishnamurti's message is that one must think for onself, not accepting any authority. One must break out of a conditioned mode of thought. From this perspective, it is the same essential message of the Buddha.

So from then on, he spent his years travelling around the world and teaching one must not live according to a formula, that meditation is really a form of awareness and not an attainment of a higher consciousness. He established numerous schools in many countries where knowledge would be taught in a holistic, non-traditional way so that the student discovers for himself or herself the truth of things. In this endeavour, he shared Tagore's philosophy of education.

He died in Ojai, California, in February 1986, at the age of 90.

RADHAKRISHNAN

Radhakrishnan's story represents a different approach to philosophy and spirituality. He rose from poverty to the presidency of India, simply by the power of his philosophy and intellect. We see a scholar, an academic, a philosopher, and a great thinker. When he became the president of India in 1962, Bertrand Russell remarked that "It is an honor to philosophy that Dr. Radhakrishnan should be the president of India and I, as a philosopher, take special pleasure in this. Plato aspired for philosophers to become kings and it is a tribute to India that she should make a philosopher, her president" (Murty and Vohra, 154). On this accolade bestowed upon him, Radhakrishnan said later:

> Generally, wherever addresses are presented to me, Plato is brought out as one who said that philosophers should rule the state. This is not a Platonic axiom. It is something common to all great cultures. In our own country, we said that thinkers must also act.... Even Sri Krishna and Janaka were men not only of philosophical wisdom but also of practical efficiency. We should also behave in the same way. So the Platonic axiom is something which is common to all great cultures.... We must have vision, we must have practical work.... Once you have the vision, you must try to transform the vision into reality, by efforts, dedicated work. This is what all great people are expected to do. All students of philosophy are called upon not merely to interpret but to change the world, not only to exert their vision but also to exert honest service, honest dedication. (Murty and Vohra, 155)

Sarvepalli Radhakrishnan was born in 1888 in the south Indian town of Tirutani and schooled in Tirupati. He was one of eight children and the family lived in extreme poverty. Despite their poverty, the parents made every effort to educate their children. In 1908, at the age of 20, he enrolled in the Madras Christian College for his higher education; reading philosophy books given him, he decided to take up philosophy as his main subject. This would also save him the considerable expense of buying new books. Thus his decision to study philosophy seems to have been a chance event. Commenting on this later in life, he writes:

> To all appearances this is a mere accident. But when I look at the series of accidents that have shaped my life, I am persuaded that there is more in this life than meets the eye. Life is not a mere chain of physical causes and effects. Chance seems to form the surface, but deep down other forces are at work. If the universe is a living one, if it is spiritually alive, nothing in it is merely accidental. "The moving finger writes and having writ moves on."[6] (Murty and Vohra, 3)

Of his early years, he writes: "From the time I knew myself I have had firm faith in the reality of an unseen world behind the flux of phenomenon, a world which we apprehend not with the senses but with the mind, and even when I was faced with grave difficulties, this faith has remained unshaken" (Parthasarathi and Chattopadhyaya, 3). But he said of his college philosophy teachers that they were "apologists for the Christian way of thought and life, but were not, in the strict sense of the term, seekers of truth. By their criticism of Indian thought, they disturbed my faith and shook the traditional props on which I leaned" (Schilpp, 9).

All of his education was done in India. He started his professional life as a philosopher in April 1909, when he was appointed as a lecturer at the Madras Presidency College. At that time, he dived into a detailed and intense study of both Eastern and Western philosophies. Even though he studied many of the great thinkers of the world, he remained an independent spirit, never becoming a follower of any system. These comparative studies enabled him to synthesize and explain many of the systems of philosophy, both Eastern and Western. He writes, "The comparative method is relevant in the present context, when the stage is set, if not for the development of a world philosophy, at least for that of a world outlook" (Schilpp, 13).

Thus began a period of prolific writing. His magnum opus was under-

6 The last sentence of the quotation is a famous line from the Rubaiyat of Omar Khayyam. "The Moving Finger writes; and having writ, moves on: nor all the piety nor wit shall lure it back to cancel half a line, nor all thy tears wash out a word of it."

taken in 1923 when he wrote a two-volume treatise on Indian philosophy. Later works included *An Idealist's View of Life* (1932), which summarized his philosophical outlook; *Eastern Religions and Western Thought* (1939); a scholarly survey of the principal Upanishads (1953); *Sourcebook of Indian Philosophy* (1957); and a commentary on the Brahma Sutras (1960). It is inspiring that he could find time to write these scholarly volumes in the middle of his exceedingly busy schedule, first as an ambassador, then as the vice-president and finally as the president of India.

For Radhakrishnan, philosophy was not a mere profession but rather the very reason for living. In his autobiography, he admits,

> Though I have not had a sense of vocation, a sense that I was born to do what I am now carrying out, my travels and engagements in different parts of the world for over a generation gave me a purpose in life. My one supreme interest has been to try to restore a sense of spiritual values to the millions of religiously displaced persons, who have been struggling to find precarious refuges in the emergency camps of Art and Science, of Fascism and Nazism, of Humanism and Communism. The first step to recovery is to understand the nature of the confusion of thought which absorbs the allegiance of millions of men. Among the major influences which foster a spirit of skepticism in regard to religious truth are the growth of the scientific spirit, the development of a technological civilization, a formal or artificial religion which finds itself in conflict with an awakened social conscience and a comparative study of religions. (Schilpp, 14)

Radhakrishnan's philosophy is absolute idealism, but not of an abstract kind. It recognizes the value of everyday experiences, their richness and variety to educate and fortify the human being. At the same time, he emphasized that one must experience life through the prism of a transcendental absolute. Highlighting this point, Charles Moore writes:

> In all phases of his philosophy, he reveals a synthesizing ability which enables him, in conformity with the essence of the great Indian tradition, to avoid all extremes. In this spirit, Radhakrishnan resolves the traditional oppositions between the Absolute and the non-absolute, God and the world, appearance and reality, intuition and reason, philosophy and religion, and philosophy and life, as well as contradictions and oppositions among the various religious and philosophical systems. (Radhakrishnan and Moore, 610)

Radhakrishnan had phenomenal powers of concentration. The ancient sages referred to the faculty of focussing the mind on one idea as the essence of *tapas*. In his Hibbert lectures, delivered at Oxford University, Radhakrishnan writes, "*Tapas*, the energizing of conscious force, austere thinking, the inward travail of the spirit is the brooding which is responsible for creative work. *Tapas* is the force by which some mighty force possibility is actualized" (*East and West*, 75). In the Taittirīya Upanishad, we find this idea in bold relief:

> *Sa tapa tapyata sa tapas taptva*
> *Idam sarvam asrjata*
>
> He performed *tapas*; having performed *tapas*, he produced all this whatsoever. (2.6)

So what exactly is *tapas*? For Radhakrishnan, it is thinking with one's whole being, one's whole mind, one's whole body. It is integral yoga. And writing is the method by which we grasp an idea and make it part of our being. Every word and every sentence is a step in the ascent towards heaven. He elaborated, "We must concentrate or hold on to an idea... we can write it down, visualize it, paint or draw it, until it sinks into the unconscious and recreates us.... Brooding is creative energy" (*East and West*, 97-98).

Radhakrishnan had a long and exemplary academic career. He was the Spalding Professor of Philosophy at Oxford University from 1936 to 1952. He was India's ambassador to the Soviet Union in the 1950s. Then from 1952 to 1962, he was India's vice-president and from 1962 to 1967, president. During all of his appointments, he promoted world unity and intellectual dialogue, building a bridge of understanding between the east and the west, between the north and the south. In 1954, he was awarded the Bharat Ratna, India's highest civilian honour, and in 1975, the Templeton Prize. In 1967, he retired from public life and spent his last years in his home in Mylapore, a suburb of Chennai (Madras). He passed away on April 17, 1975.

In many ways, Radhakrishnan was a cultural, intellectual, and spiritual ambassador of India. Through his life, he demonstrated the power of ideas to transform society. Through his writings, he explained the ancient philosophy and explained it in a modern context. He wrote extensively on how these ideas can be applied in today's world. His legacy is an East-West synthesis of philosophical thought.

APPENDIX 1

POSSIBLE TOPICS FOR ESSAY 1

1. In his introduction to the *Sourcebook*, Radhakrishnan writes, "The study of Indian philosophy is important historically, philosophically, and even politically." Expanding on this theme, compare Radhakrishnan's main points with Russell's "The value of philosophy" in Chapter 15 of his book entitled *Problems of Philosophy*. Does the study of the Upanishads support either of the men's main arguments? Discuss.

2. In his introduction to the *Sourcebook*, Radhakrishnan writes, "Indian philosophy is characterized by the introspective attitude and the introspective approach to reality." What is the introspective attitude and approach? How do the Upanishads approach these questions? Do they confirm or contradict Radhakrishnan's statement? Discuss.

3. In his Yoga Sutras, Patanjali writes that there are four faculties of the mind that need to be strengthened and focussed: thinking, feeling, willing, and restraining. Does the Isa Upanishad address this thesis in any way? Substantiate your statements with detailed discussion.

4. Mahatma Gandhi writes that the Isa Upanishad influenced his philosophy of non-violence. What is the basis of this claim? Discuss in detail.

5. The Maitrī Upanishad introduces the notion of "elemental self" (*bhutātman*) to distinguish it from the Self (*ātman*). How are these notions different? How does this support the main thesis of the Upanishad?

6. In the Katha Upanishad, the imagery of the chariot appears. In Plato's *Phaedrus*, chariot imagery is also used. What are the similarities and differences of this imagery in these different contexts? Discuss.

7. In both the Prasna and Kausitaki Upanishads, the concept of *prāna* is introduced. Is this concept used in the same way in both of the Upanishads or is it different? Compare and contrast.

8. Several Upanishads attempt to discuss "levels of awareness." This theme appears in the Māndukya Upanishad and the Taittirīya Upanishad in its formulation of a "calculus of bliss." Discuss how these Upanishads delineate levels of awareness and compare how effective this delineation is with respect to an understanding of the nature of awareness.

9. Visual symbols are used in the Upanishads to support a philosophical idea. Discuss what symbols are used and if these symbols are effective.

10. Choose one of the following Upanishads: Prasna, Mundaka, Māndukya, Taittirīya, Aitareya, Chāndogya, Brhadāranyaka, Svetāsvatara, Kausitaki, and Maitrī. After reading the summary description in the *Sourcebook*, consult two to three translations of the Upanishad and discuss its main thesis. Some of the Upanishads, like Brhadāranyaka and Chāndogya, are quite long. You may have to select a chapter in these instead of taking the entire Upanishad for study.

APPENDIX 2

POSSIBLE TOPICS FOR ESSAY 2

1. Chapter 3 of the Bhagavadgīta outlines the basic principles of karma yoga. What are action, non-action, and inaction according to the Gita? Discuss these principles and explain how non-attachment and work are to be combined in this yoga.

2. In karma yoga, Krishna emphasizes that we should work without being attached to the fruits (or rewards) of our work. What does attachment mean? What is non-attachment? Discuss in detail from all perspectives.

3. Chapter 6 of the Bhagavadgīta highlights the fundamentals of raja yoga, or the yoga of psychic control. Compare and contrast the principles outlined in this chapter with Patanjali's Yoga Sutras.

4. Chapter 12 of the Gita emphasizes the role of devotion in the spiritual journey. Is this essential? What are the positive and negative aspects of bhakti yoga in this context? Discuss.

5. Several scholars have viewed each of the 18 chapters of the Gita as defining a different yoga. Is this viewpoint accurate? Why or why not?

6. What role do concentration and creative work play in the four yogas? Are they an integral part of yoga? Discuss in detail.

7. The Dhammapada plays an essential role in Buddhistic thought. What are the main principles outlined in the Dhammapada. Compare this with the Bhagavadgīta. What are the similarities and differences.

8. The Nyāya system is a philosophy of logic. What are the central ideas in this system. Is there any intersection with Upanishadic thought? Discuss.

9. What distinguishes a dualistic philosophical system from ones that are not? The Sāmkhya system is described as a dualistic philosophical system. Is this view correct? Discuss in detail.

10. The Vedānta system of philosophy claims to include all of the systems preceding it and all of the systems yet to be. Is this claim valid? What is the meaning of Vedānta? How does this meaning support or refute this claim?

APPENDIX 3

HOW TO WRITE AN ESSAY

There are three rules for writing a novel.
Unfortunately, no one knows what they are.
—Somerset Maugham

There is no algorithm for great writing. If there were, we could program computers to churn out literature. However, all of us recognize bad writing when we read it and so there are probably a few rules or guidelines for good writing. I will delineate some below.

First and foremost, we must decide on a topic and having decided that, we should collect ideas on that topic. This is the research phase of writing. This research is a combination of two methods. The first method is to gather ideas from external sources, mainly from the writings of others. The other method, which is a bit more difficult, is to bring out ideas from oneself, by the process of reflection. Many find it easier to first gather ideas from external sources and then to reflect on these ideas to distill from them newer ideas. The gathering of ideas can be a time-consuming process and one must determine, at the outset, how much time should be devoted to this task. Usually, there is a temptation to collect too much information. Thus, one must be ruthless in putting an end to this phase of information gathering since too much information is often the cause of the disease known as "writer's block." Part of this problem is reduced by determining the audience we are writing for. There is no such thing as the general public. A certain amount of facility emerges when we can visualize our reader since that determines the style, tone, and choice of words in our writing.

The second step is to begin with the main thesis. This is largely impelled by meditation upon the ideas gathered in the first step and organized in a coherent way. Indeed, reflection can be defined as the conscious, coherent correlation of ideas. Hence writing is a method of meditation and one can argue that it is a very powerful method utilized from time immemorial by the greatest minds of human civilization. Writing can be viewed as a "participation mystique." It acts as an intermediary through which we understand the external world and commune with the internal.

The thesis should be clear and crisp. In the subordinate paragraphs, it should be substantiated by examples and discussion. Very likely, the examples have been garnered from the preliminary research and the discussion should blossom forth through reflection on these examples.

Sometimes it is useful just to begin writing without worrying about coherence or organization. One can edit and re-arrange later.

The final paragraph should summarize the essential ideas and draw some conclusions based on the discussion in the essay. The length of the essay defines the number of examples to be included. Sometimes, it is useful to adopt the Hegelian dialectic method. Hegel's approach was to examine a thesis, and then its opposite which he called the antithesis. After investigating the antipodal viewpoints, one formulates a synthesis that reconciles both their essential aspects. In this approach, the essay writes itself and so one can adopt this method, depending upon the circumstance.

In the exercise of gathering facts, arranging and correlating them, the technique of speed writing is effective. Setting aside half an hour and writing non-stop on the topic at hand seems to act as a stimulant for the creative juices. Usually, a cup of coffee adds further fuel to the exercise. One can average three pages to the cup.

Writing takes effort. In fact, the word "essay" is derived from the French word "essayer," which means "to try, to attempt, to make an effort." The usage of this word in this context can be traced back to the writings of the French philosopher Montaigne, who published in 1580 a collection of compositions entitled "Essais." He wrote that the collection is a series of "attempts" to express his personal thoughts and experiences. This usage of the word was again taken up in the same way by Francis Bacon, who in 1597 published his reflections in the form of "Essayes." Later writers followed this lead and the word came into general circulation.

Writing is a solitary art. It gives us an opportunity to reflect, to understand, to give expression to our thoughts and feelings. It is such a powerful and effective tool that one writer has been quoted as saying, "I don't know what I am thinking until I write it down." It is therefore not an exaggeration to say that writing is the royal road to self-knowledge.

After the first draft is complete, it is best to put it aside and return to it again after a day or two and work on it some more to produce a second draft. Only a few gifted individuals like Bertrand Russell have the ability to write a single draft and be done with it. But for the rest of us mortals, re-writing is an important aspect of essay writing. Often, putting the work aside for a while and doing something different is helpful. The subconscious takes over. This can be done not just after the first draft, but at any time. So, it is important not to wait till the last minute to begin the essay.

Once the composition is complete, it is good to proofread the piece. This is easier if there is a substantial time gap between the completion and the proofreading. In this way, we can bring greater objectivity to analyze our writing. At the same time, we must remember that too much revision is probably a bad thing. One has to decide, depending on the time factor, how much revision and review are needed.

In summary, it is true that there are no rules for great writing. However, there are some guidelines that, if followed, can simplify the process. These guidelines are choosing a topic (and choosing an audience), gathering facts, and correlating these facts into a coherent form. Good writing is both a science and an art. It is a science since we gather ideas and organize them using deductive and inductive reasoning. It is an art because we bring our reflective consciousness to give these facts shape, coherence, and interpretation. Invariably, such an arrangement of thought leads to new knowledge, both of the world outside, and the world within our mind.

WORKS CITED

Artin. Emil. *Collected Papers*. Reading, MA: Addison-Wesley, 1965.

Aurobindo, Sri. *The Collected Works of Sri Aurobindo*. Vols. 1-30. Pondicherry, India: Aurobindo Ashram, 1972.

Blake, William. "Auguries of Innocence." Written in his Pickering Manuscript (1803), first published in 1863.

Bronowski, Jacob. *The Ascent of Man*. London: Futura Publications, 1981.

Bukkyo Dendo Kyokai (Society for the Teaching of Buddha), ed. *The Teaching of Buddha*. Tokyo: Kosaido Printing Co., 1966.

Cannon, Garland. *The Life and Mind of Oriental Jones: Sir William Jones, the Father of Modern Linguistics*. Cambridge: Cambridge University Press, 1990.

Césaire, Aimé. *Return to My Native Land*. Baltimore: Penguin, 1969.

Dasgupta, Surendranath N. *A History of Indian Philosophy*. Vols. 1-5. Delhi: Motilal Banarsidass, 1997.

Durant, Will. *The Story of Philosophy*. New York: Washington Square Press, 1961.

Einstein, Albert. "Physics and Reality." Jean Piccard, tr. *The Journal of the Franklin Institute* 221 (March 1936): 349-82.

Emerson, Ralph Waldo. "Brahma." *Atlantic Monthly* (1 November 1857): 48.

Frost, Robert. "Stopping by Woods on a Snowy Evening." *New Hampshire*. New York: Henry Holt and Company, 1923.

Gandhi, Mohandas K. *An Autobiography: The Story of My Experiments with Truth*. Ahmedabad, India: Navajivan Trust, 2000.

———. *Collected Works of Mahatma Gandhi*. Ahmedabad, India: Navajivan Trust, 1976.

———. *Harijan*, March 30, 1947.

———. *The Essential Writings: Mahatma Gandhi*. Oxford: Oxford University Press, 2008.

———. *Young India*, March 2, 1922.

Glashow, Sheldon L. *From Alchemy to Quarks: The Study of Physics as a Liberal Art*. Pacific Grove, CA: Brooks/Cole Publishing, 1994.

Gopal, Sarvepalli. *Radhakrishnan: A Biography*. Oxford: Oxford University Press, 1989.

Hamilton, Sue. *Indian Philosophy: A Very Short Introduction*. Oxford: Oxford University Press, 2001.

Hastings, J., ed. *Encyclopedia of Religion and Ethics*. New York: Charles Scribners and Sons, 1915.

Hawking, Stephen W. *A Brief History of Time: From the Big Bang to Black Holes*. Toronto: Bantam Books, 1988.

James, William. *The Energies of Men*. New York: Moffat Yard and Company, 1914.

Kant, Immanuel. "What is Enlightenment?" (1784) in *Foundations of the Metaphysics of Morals and What is Enlightenment?* Upper Saddle River, NJ: Prentice Hall, 1959.

Keller, Helen. *Optimism: An Essay*. Boston: The Merrymount Press, 1903.

———. *The World I Live In*. New York: Century, 1909.

King, Martin Luther, Jr. *The Autobiography of Martin Luther King Jr.*, Clayborne Carson, ed. New York: Warner Books, 1998.

Lienhard, John H. "Engines of our Ingenuity No. 1576: The Wind." http://www.uh.edu/engines/epi1576.htm.

Luytens, Mary. *Krishnamurti, The Years of Awakening*. New York: Avon Books, 1975.

McFetridge, Paul. *A Linguistic Introduction to the History and Structure of the English Lexicon*. Burnaby, BC: Simon Fraser University Publications, 2008.

Merton, Thomas. *New Seeds of Contemplation*. New York: New Directions, 1961.

Mohanty, J.N. *Classical Indian Philosophy*. Lanham, MD: Rowman and Littlefield, 1999.

Murty, K. Satchidananda, and Ashok Vohra. *Radhakrishnan: His Life and Ideas*. Albany, NY: SUNY Press, 1990.

Newton, Isaac. Letter to Robert Hooke. February 15, 1676.

Nhat Hanh, Thich. *The Diamond That Cuts through Illusion*. Berkeley, CA: Parallax Press, 1992.

Nikhilananda, Swami. *The Gospel of Sri Ramakrishna*. New York: Ramakrishna-Vivekananda Center, 1984.

Parthasarathi, G., and D.P. Chattopadhyaya, eds. *Radhakrishnan, Centenary Volume*. Delhi: Oxford University Press, 1989.

Planck, Max. *Das Wesen der Materie* [The Nature of Matter]. Speech at Florence, Italy (1944), from *Archiv zur Geschichte der Max-Planck-Gesellschaft*, Abt. Va, Rep. 11 Planck, Nr. 1797.

Poincaré, Henri. *Science and Hypothesis*. New York: Dover, 1952.

Pope, Alexander. "A Little Learning" in *An Essay on Criticism*, 1711.

Prabhavananda, Swami. *Patanjali Yoga Sutras*. Madras, India: Sri Ramakrishna Math, 1953.

———, and Frederick Manchester. *The Upanishads: Breath of the Eternal*. Hollywood, CA: Vedānta Press, 1947.

Radhakrishnan, Sarvepalli. *East and West in Religion*. London: George Allen and Unwin, 1958.

———. *The Bhagavadgita*. New York: Harper Colophon Books, 1973.

———. *The Dhammapada*. Oxford: Oxford University Press, 1950.

———. *Indian Philosophy*, Vols. 1-2. London: Allen and Unwin, 1923 and 1927.

———. *The Principal Upanishads*. Oxford: Oxford University Press, 1989.

———, and Charles A. Moore, eds. *A Sourcebook in Indian Philosophy*. Princeton: Princeton University Press, 1989.

Ranganathananda, Swami. *The Message of the Upanishads*. 2nd ed. Bombay: Bharatiya Vidya Bhavan, 1971.

Roy, Dilip Kumar. *Among the Great*. Bombay: Jaico Publishing House, 1950.

Russell, Bertrand. *The Problems of Philosophy*. Oxford: Oxford University Press, 1997.

Sankaracarya. *Vivekachudamani of Sri Sankaracarya*. Swami Turiyananda, tr. Madras, India: Sri Ramakrishna Math, 1987.

Sarvagatananda, Swami. *God is Everything*. Toronto: Vedānta Society of Toronto, 2001.

Satprem. *Sri Aurobindo or the Adventure of Consciousness*. Mysore, India: Techprints, 1970.

Schilpp, Paul Arthur, ed. *The Philosophy of Sarvepalli Radhakrishnan*. La Salle, IL: Open Court, 1952.

Tagore, Rabindranath. *Omnibus*, Vols. 1-2. New Delhi: Rupa and Co., 2006.

———. "The Nation" in *The English Writings of Rabindranath Tagore*, vol. 4. New Delhi: Atlantic Publishers, 2007.

Teilhard de Chardin, Paul. *Toward the Future*. London: Collins, 1975.

Toynbee, Arnold. Introduction to *World Thinkers on Ramakrishna and Vivekananda*, Swami Lokeswarananda, ed. Calcutta: Sri Ramakrisha Mission Institute of Culture, 1983.

Vivekananda, Swami. *The Complete Works of Swami Vivekananda*. Vols. 1-8, 16th ed. Calcutta: Advaita Ashram, 1984.

Wells, H.G. *The Outline of History.* Garden City, NY: Garden City Publishing, 1920.

Weyl, Hermann. *The Classical Groups: Their Invariants and Representations.* Princeton: Princeton University Press, 1997.

Wilson, Colin. *Poetry and Mysticism.* San Francisco: City Lights Books, 1970.

Yatiswarananda, Swami. *Universal Prayers.* Mylapore, India: Sri Ramakrishna Math, 1977.

Yeats, William Butler. Introduction to *Gitanjali* by Rabindranath Tagore. Boston: International Pocket Library, 2000.

INDEX

Page numbers in bold indicate that the corresponding topic is treated at some length on that page. Sanskrit terms appear in italics for ease of reference.

About the Publisher

The word "broadview" expresses a good deal of the philosophy behind our company. Our focus is very much on the humanities and social sciences—especially literature, writing, and philosophy—but within these fields we are open to a broad range of academic approaches and political viewpoints. We strive in particular to produce high-quality, pedagogically useful books for higher education classrooms—anthologies, editions, sourcebooks, surveys of particular academic fields and sub-fields, and also course texts for subjects such as composition, business communication, and critical thinking. We welcome the perspectives of authors from marginalized and underrepresented groups, and we have a strong commitment to the environment. We publish English-language works and translations from many parts of the world, and our books are available world-wide; we also publish a select list of titles with a specifically Canadian emphasis.

broadview press